Reflections

on Automotive History

VOLUME III

Bill Vance

Eramosa Valley Publishing

Canadian Cataloguing in Publication Data

Vance, Bill, 1935-
   Reflections on automotive history, volume III

Includes index.

ISBN   0-9698922-4-1 (case bound)
         0-9698922-5-x (soft bound)

1. Automobiles — History. I. Title.

TL15.V35 1994   629.222'09
C94-932460-4 rev.

Published by
Eramosa Valley Publishing
Box 370
Rockwood, Ontario, Canada
N0B 2K0
Telephone: (519) 856-1065
Facsimile: (519) 856-2991

Printed in Canada by
Ampersand Printing
123 Woolwich Street
Guelph, Ontario N1H 3V1
Telephone (519) 836-8800
Fax (519) 836-7204

Additional copies can be obtained from the publisher

Photo Credits
Cover: 1911 Ford Model T owned by Henry "Hank" Theaker of
Guelph, Ontario (see *Car of the Century* chapter, page 146)

All photos by the author, except the following pages:
    Berrys, John 130
    British Motor Corporation 181
    British Motor Industry Heritage Trust 185
    Citizen Works 196
    DaimlerChrysler AG 95 (left),124,154,159,168,194
    Ford Motor Company 95 (right),162
    General Motors Corporation 98,157,160,164,171,173,174
    General Motors of Canada 166
    Goodyear Tire and Rubber Company 155
    Honda Motor Company 183
    ISC Publication Archives 190
    Mason, Beth 63
    The MIT Press 179
    Road & Track (Rolofson) 192
    Spiegelman, Richard 14
    Strachan-Johnson, Susan (portrait) 187
    Toyota Motor Company 102,176
    United Auto Workers union 188
    Volkswagen AG 169,177

I would like to dedicate this book to:

Andrew, Dianne and Susan
for their continuing interest and encouragement
&
To the many readers of my syndicated auto history column
who inspired me to write the Reflections series

TABLE OF CONTENTS

Twenty-Five Who Made A Difference

FOREWORD

In this, the third volume in the *Reflections* series, I have attempted to bring together the various streams of automotive history in a logical and easy-to-read way. *Through the Decades, 1900 - 2000* traces the evolution of automotive progress decade by decade through the twentieth century. In addition to such technical advances as the self starter and catalytic converter, I have also included social changes that the car has created or influenced.

Such developments as installment buying, war production by the industry, labour unionism, highway expansion, women in the workforce, travellers' accommodation, suburbia, environmental concern, and the fast-food industry, have resulted from the proliferation of the car or been impacted by it. All are touched on here.

Engineering and Evolution is an eclectic mix of subjects, from aerodynamics to turbocharging. This led nicely into the *Ten Most Significant Automotive Developments* as chosen by the Fellows of the Society of Automotive Engineers.

Because the car has so dramatically impacted twentieth century life, it seemed fitting to outline the process by which an international jury, including the author, elected the Ford Model T as the *Car of the Century*.

Finally, *Twenty-Five Who Made A Difference* is my selection of 25 men who, in one way or another, affected the auto industry. This group varies from engineers to labour leaders, from entrepreneurs to writers. While not intended to be a definitive list, those chosen made their special contributions.

The aim of this volume is to provide readers with an authoritative yet not burdensome overview of automotive history. For those seeking more in-depth knowledge, the number of automotive books available is rich and varied. I have noted several of them throughout.

The *Reflections* books were inspired by my weekly automotive history column that is syndicated to newspapers in Canada and the U.S. Volume I was, in fact, a compilation of expanded columns prepared at the request of readers. Its success encouraged me to write Volumes II and III, which are not column based, but original material.

As a long time student of the automobile and its history, I have found writing about it to be enjoyable and rewarding. One of the reasons is that I am always learning. Since history is subject to the interpretation and prejudices of the historian, this book represents the "take" of an automotive enthusiast, not an academic. I have done my best to make it authentic.

I would again like to express my appreciation to Richard Carroll, my diligent and accurate proof reader. Not only is Richard a keen grammarian, he is also, by a happy coincidence, a knowledgeable "car guy." Any errors will be my own. Carolyn Klymko and Mike McDonald of Ampersand Printing were a continuing source of expertise and guidance, for which I am very grateful.

I also wish to express my gratitude to the automobile manufacturers and others for generously providing photos.

Bill Vance
Rockwood, Ontario
November, 2002

Automotive History
Through the Decades
1900-2000

1900 – 1910
LAYING THE FOUNDATION

Although the internal combustion engine powered automobile was invented by Germans Carl Benz and Gottlieb Daimler in 1885, it took a while to gain acceptance. Until the turn of the century cars were largely experimental, and were produced in small numbers. While invented in Europe, it remained there for many years a hobby for the privileged few.

When America adopted the car a decade after the Europeans had invented it, it was soon seen in the New World as an instrument of mass mobility, one that was welcomed into a more egalitarian social environment than that of Europe. Even though North America hadn't invented the car, it immediately embraced it, and its great contribution would be the organization of the resources for its manufacture in huge numbers at an affordable price. The car was quickly accepted by an eager public.

The groundwork for this mass production was laid by the standardization of parts, which was dramatically demonstrated by Cadillac in England in 1908, of which more later. Mass production would be brought to full flower by the

moving automobile assembly line invented by the Ford Motor Company and implemented in 1913.

By the turn of the century the automobile was gaining popularity and credibility. The recognized birth date of the North American industry was 1896 when brothers Frank and Charles Duryea built a run of 13 identical Motor Wagons in Springfield, Massachusetts. The Duryea Motor Wagon Company was the first North American firm formed expressly for the purpose of producing road-going motor vehicles.

The Duryea brothers would later become estranged after a bitter dispute over which one had really invented their car. Their contribution to the advancement of the automobile would be minimal, but they deserve the credit for establishing the industry in America.

When the automobile was in its infancy, it was relatively easy to enter the business. With some technical ability and a shop, often a carriage facility or bicycle business, an entrepreneur could set up as an automobile manufacturer. Although the banks would rarely extend loans for what was then considered a very precarious venture, this was surmounted by buying the components on credit from suppliers, and selling the cars to eager customers for cash. Sometimes this was even paid in advance. If the budding automobile magnate was lucky, or shrewd enough, to exploit this strategy successfully and stay afloat financially, success could be had in the car business. Most, however, couldn't manage this cash flow juggling act, and the result was a very high attrition rate in the early days. Often only one car was made.

As the automobile was evolving, three types of powerplants were vying for supremacy: steam, electricity and gasoline. Steam, having been under development for some 150 years, had a big lead on the internal combustion engine. Steam engines were quiet and powerful, but were also heavy, required a skilled operator, and took time to generate steam. There was also the fear, although unfounded, of boiler explosions. In spite of these disadvantages, steam enjoyed some brief popularity when the American car was in its infancy.

The electric car's appeal was its cleanliness and ease of operation. Its big disadvantage was a short driving range, which relegated it to urban areas. There was also the heavy and expensive battery pack required. In spite of these drawbacks, which still burden the electric car to this day, it's an indication of where the industry was

that in 1899 America's largest auto producer was the Columbia Automobile Company that manufactured electric cars in Hartford, Connecticut. Columbia produced 440 cars that year, but would soon change to gasoline engines.

Electric cars also held the world's first official land speed record from December 1898 to April 1902. The best speed attained was 105.9 km/h (65.79 mph), the first machine to exceed 96 km/h (60 mph). This was accomplished in April 1899 by a Belgian named Camille Janetzy in a cigar-shaped car which he called La Jamais Contente (French for "Never Satisfied").

This record lasted for three years, before being broken on April 13, 1902, by a steam powered Serpollet driven by Leon Serpollet, holder of French driver's licence number 1. He achieved a speed of 120.8 km/h (75.06 mph).

A mere four months later, Serpollet's record was broken by a gasoline engined French Mors at 122.5 km/h (76.08 mph), driven by American W.K. Vanderbilt, Jr. Gasoline cars would dominate from then on, until the advent of the 1960s jet powered "rockets on wheels," which aren't really cars, but more like airplanes of the earth.

While automobile pioneers would use steam, electricity and gasoline engines to power their fledgling cars, another type of powerplant had been patented in 1892 by a German engineer named Rudolf Diesel. Rather than igniting the fuel in the cylinder with an electric spark as was done in a gasoline engine, Diesel used the heat generated by a very high compression ratio to ignite the fuel.

Although it would take over 40 years of development to make the diesel suitable for powering automobiles, it would ultimately prove more efficient than a gasoline engine. It became widely adopted in cars in Europe due to high fuel costs, but was to be only marginally successful in North America, except in periods of perceived fuel shortages. It would become universal in large, line-haul trucks.

The gasoline engine was still in a smelly, noisy, and often unreliable state, but its inherent advantages encouraged rapid development. It was easier to operate than a steamer, and could travel much farther on a tank of gasoline than an electric could on a full battery charge, or a steamer could on a load of water.

One of the earliest demonstrations of the gasoline engine's potential came in 1900 when a Cleveland-built Winton was driven 1304 km (810 miles) from Detroit, Michigan, to the first New York automobile show. It averaged 34 km/h (21 mph).

Development came quickly. The architecture of the car evolved and stabilized, thanks in large part to the seminal 1901 Mercedes, with the engine in front, the passenger compartment behind it, and drive going to the rear wheels. High buggy wheels, direct descendants of the carriage heritage, gave way to smaller, bicycle type wheels. Shaft drive gradually displaced chain drive. Steering wheels replaced tillers. Powerplants became better fitted and more reliable, thanks to the precision and fine tolerances pursued by pioneers like Henry Leland whose Leland & Faulconer Company of Detroit supplied engines to Oldsmobile and Cadillac. Leland & Faulconer was considered the finest American engine builder of the period.

David Dunbar Buick, a wealthy Detroit plumbing contractor, decided to go into the automobile business. Although he would ultimately fail, and sell out to General Motors founder Billy Durant, he and his associates Walter Marr and Eugene Richard made a significant advance in engine technology with their valve-in-head Buick engine, patented in 1904.

Also significant was the propitious emergence of an abundant supply of fuel, this happy coincidence occurring when the Spindletop oil well near Beaumont, Texas, blew in on January 10, 1901. Fortune seekers flooded into Beaumont and it became a boom town overnight. The price of crude oil plunged to five cents per barrel, and Texas was the new oil capital of the world, surpassing the fields in the eastern states like Pennsylvania and Ohio, and even Russia, then the world's leading oil producer.

It had been just over 40 years earlier when the world's first commercial oil well was constructed and put into production. In 1858 James Miller Williams began pumping 50 gallons of oil per day from his 4.3 m (14 ft) deep oil well in Oil Springs, Lambton County, in south-western Ontario. He also built a refinery that year in Oil Springs, and was soon drilling more and deeper wells. The oil boom was on. Just a year later, in 1859, oil was discovered in Titusville, Pennsylvania.

Chemists and engineers knew how to distil the crude oil into its various fractions, including gasoline. Gasoline had at first been considered mostly a waste product, but its volatility and high energy content made it an ideal fuel for the internal combustion engine. The rising popularity of gasoline powered cars quickly made gasoline one of the most important constituents derived from crude oil. The symbiotic relationship between the automobile and the petroleum industry was a boon for the oil segment too because the demand for kerosene was declining as the kerosene lamp was gradually giving way to gas and electric lighting. The 20th century would become known as the Oil Century, a time in which oil supplanted coal as the predominant energy source.

In spite of a rather wobbly start, the first decade of the 20th century saw the foundations laid for the North American industry. Henry Ford, a mechanical genius who would make a name for himself during a brief racing career, built his first car, called the "Quadricycle," in 1896.

1903 Ford – Henry Ford is successful on his third attempt

Ford's racing success attracted financial backing. But his first venture, the Detroit Automobile Company, failed after a few months. The second, the Henry Ford Company, had showed some promise but lacked the organization to fill its orders. The result was that engine builder Henry Leland was brought in to sort this out. Ford, not surprisingly, departed. Leland re-organized the Henry Ford Company and got it functioning efficiently. Its name was changed to the Cadillac Automobile Company, with Leland as its president.

On his third attempt, in 1903, Henry Ford was finally successful with the Ford Motor Company. The Ford Motor Company of Canada was established in 1904 by Gordon McGregor, president of the Walkerville Wagon Works in Walkerville, Ontario, now part of Windsor.

The Thomas B. Jeffery Company, a successful bicycle manufacturer in Kenosha, Wisconsin, began building Rambler cars, named after its bicycles, in 1902. The New York & Ohio Company, later the Ohio Automobile Company, and still later the Packard Motor Car Company, was established in Warren, Ohio, in 1899. It moved to Detroit in 1903, and established a well deserved reputation for soundly engineered luxury cars.

By 1900, the Stanley brothers, Francis and Freelan, of Newton, Massachusetts, who had grown wealthy manufacturing dry-plate photography equipment, had been building steam cars for three years. Although steamers would ultimately fail in the automobile business, the Stanley name became the one most associated with the steam car.

In 1902 the first air cooled Franklin cars were built in Syracuse, New York. Franklin would stay loyal to air cooling until the company went out of the car business in 1934. It then became Air-Cooled Motors Corporation, builders of aircraft engines. An interesting sidelight is that it was a horizontally-opposed Air-Cooled Motors helicopter engine, converted to water cooling, that Preston Tucker used in the unorthodox rear engined Tucker car he attempted to launch in the 1940s.

1906 Stanley Steamer – steam tried, but ultimately failed

The South Bend, Indiana, wagon maker, Studebaker, had been established in 1852, and had prospered selling wagons to the army during the American Civil War. It decided to go into the automobile business at the turn of the century, and produced its first car, an electric, in 1902; it would soon switch to gasoline power.

Canada's auto industry was largely, but not totally, involved in building American designs with some Canadian trim. Examples of American-based cars were Gray-Dort (Chatham, Ontario) and Tudhope-McIntyre (Orillia, Ontario). An exception was the Russell car, originally manufactured by Canada Cycle and Motor Company (CCM) of Toronto, a company better known for bicycles and ice skates.

Under the capable presidency of Thomas Russell, the Russell became so successful that it out-

1904 Oldsmobile Curved Dash – the first mass produced car

grew its CCM parent. The Russell Motor Car Company became a entity in its own right in 1910.

The Russell prospered for a decade as an indigenous Canadian car. It held exclusive Canadian rights to the ultra-quiet, Knight sleeve-valve engine invented by Charles Yale Knight of Chicago in 1903, installing it in many of its models. Alas, a concentration on upscale cars, and the First World War, brought an end to Russell's automobile manufacturing in 1915. Willys-Overland of Cleveland, Ohio, would take over the plant and build W-O cars there until 1933.

One of the biggest accomplishments of the decade was made by Oldsmobile of Lansing, Michigan, America's oldest continuous automobile manufacturer. Established in 1897 by Ransom E. Olds, it introduced a small, light, reliable car called the Curved Dash in 1901. An instant success, it made Oldsmobile into America's first mass produced car. Oldsmobile production was 2500 in 1902, 4000 in '03, and over 5500 in '04, making it the top producer. It even inspired its own popular song, "In My Merry Oldsmobile," written by Gus Edwards and Vincent Bryan.

Two Curved Dashes, "Old Scout" and "Old Steady," made coast-to-coast drives in 1904, further demonstrating the reliability of the gasoline powered car. Although Ransom Olds left the company in 1904 and formed the Reo Car Company (from his initials), the Curved Dash was made until 1907. Olds moved into more expensive cars, before being embraced by General Motors.

William Crapo (Billy) Durant, a dynamic millionaire carriage magnate, was co-owner of the Durant-Dort Carriage Works of Flint, Michigan, America's largest builder of horse-drawn vehicles. He became interested in the evolving motor car in 1904, and after test driving a local doctor's Buick for an afternoon, brought the failing Buick Motor Car Company under the control of Durant-Dort.

Buick's founder, David Buick, would soon leave the company, but Durant's marketing wizardry, the sound Buick overhead valve engine, and Durant-Dort's well established dealer network, quickly made Buick profitable. By 1907 it was America's second largest automobile manufacturer, after Ford, a position it would hold until 1910.

Just as Durant had sensed that the carriage business would go into decline after the turn of the century, another carriage entrepreneur in Oshawa, Ontario, was noting the same thing. Samuel McLaughlin of the McLaughlin Carriage Company also wanted to get into the emerging automobile business. His quest led him to several American automobile manufacturers seeking a suitable car to build. Among these was the Buick, which he liked, but couldn't come to an agreement with Billy Durant.

McLaughlin returned home and decided to have his own car designed. This venture came to an unfortunate end when McLaughlin's American engineer, Arthur Milbrath, became ill and was unable to continue the project. McLaughlin again approached his old friend Billy Durant, this time with a request for engineering assistance.

Durant had an even better idea; he immediately boarded the train for Oshawa where he met Sam. They made another attempt to reach an agreement, this time with success. A 15-year contract was signed under which McLaughlin would buy Buick engines and chassis and fit them with Oshawa-built bodies. McLaughlin began Canadian production of these McLaughlin-Buicks late in 1907 as 1908 models.

Billy Durant had larger dreams than just Buick; he had a vision of a huge automobile empire. In September 1908 he incorporated a holding company called the General Motors Company (later changed to the General Motors Corporation) in New Jersey. He soon brought in Buick, and by 1910 had added Oldsmobile, Cadillac and Oakland (later Pontiac), plus others. Alas, Durant's acquisitions overloaded the company with debt, and he lost control of GM to the bankers in 1910. Billy was soon back in the car business with Chevrolet.

At about the same time, a seasoned manager at the Durant-Dort company, Charles Nash, became the general manager of Buick. As works manager he hired a man named Walter P. Chrysler who had learned his trade as a journeyman machinist in the railroad industry. Thus was introduced into one of the tributaries of the auto industry another person who would go on to become very much a part of its mainstream.

The other significant event of 1908 besides the formation of General Motors was the introduction of the Model T Ford. Henry Ford, now in control of the Ford Motor Company, was free to pursue the kind of car he preferred, a simple, sturdy vehicle that was easy to drive and maintain, and had plenty of ground clearance. Its durable 20 horsepower engine was adequate for the car's light weight, and the three-pedal transmission system, comprised of pedals for high-low, reverse and braking, was easy to learn and operate. The use of vanadium steel made the less than robust looking Model T deceptively strong.

By late 1908 Henry's dream was realized when he introduced his beloved Model T to the public. It was exactly what the market needed and wanted. It would be built in many countries, and by the time production ceased in 1927 over 15 million had been produced.

Henry Ford was well on his way to becoming an American folk hero. His cheap and sturdy Model T was right for the times. And Ford's fight against, and ultimate defeat of the burdensome Selden patent, was seen as the triumph of the little man over the greedy establishment. The Selden patent is covered in the next chapter.

A third important 1908 event was Cadillac's demonstration of interchangeable parts, a process well known in the firearms industry where its implementation was credited to Eli Whitney. Frederick Bennett, the Cadillac distributor in England, was aware of Henry Leland's fetish for precision. In response to a Royal Automobile Club "Standardization Test," cleverly conceived and promoted by Bennett himself, he brought three new Cadillacs to the huge Brooklands race track southwest of London.

Under RAC supervision the Cadillacs were completely disassembled, the parts scrambled, and many original parts replaced with new ones. The three cars were then re-assembled and driven trouble-free 805 km (500 mi.) around the

1908 Cadillac – demonstrated interchangeable parts

Brooklands track at an average of 55 km/h (34 mph).

It was an astounding demonstration of the interchangeability of parts, the basic principle on which automobile mass production would be based. For this feat Cadillac was awarded the prestigious Dewar Trophy.

Standardization was also being strongly advocated and facilitated by the Society of Automobile Engineers, later the Society of Automotive Engineers, founded in 1905. The SAE established standards for items such as screw-threads, spark plugs, tires, oil and steel. Standardization was particularly important to smaller automobile companies who built "assembled" cars which depended heavily on components from outside suppliers. The SAE also acted as an engineering forum and disseminator of technical information, a function that it continues to this day. Its establishment would prove to be a critically important factor in the development of the automobile.

John Willys, a New York Overland dealer rescued the Overland Company of Indianapolis in 1908, turned it into the Willys-Overland Company, and relocated it to Toledo, Ohio. Packard, now moved from Warren, Ohio, to Detroit, was well established as a manufacturer of quality cars.

In 1909, Joseph L. Hudson of Detroit department store fame underwrote the establishment of a new automobile company that bore his name. The Studebaker brothers, Henry and Clem, in South Bend, Indiana, were becoming more serious about the car business.

As the first decade of the 20th century drew to a close the foundation of the automobile industry in North America had been laid. General Motors and Ford had been founded, as had Maxwell-Briscoe, which would become Maxwell, and ultimately the Chrysler Corporation. Many of the pioneers such as Charles Nash and Sam McLaughlin were beginning to make their marks. The gasoline engine was becoming more and more established as the power of choice, but events of the following decade would make it unassailable.

1910 – 1920
MASS PRODUCTION AND STANDARDIZATION

With the foundation of the North American automobile industry having been laid in the first decade, the second would see significant engineering advancements, and the advent of mass production on a scale never before imagined.

By 1910 Billy Durant's General Motors was in debt and disorganized as a result of his haphazard management. Billy was forced out by the Eastern bankers who took control and would nurse the sick giant back to health. Within weeks of his ouster the irrepressible Durant was planning his return to the automobile business.

He formed the Chevrolet Motor Company, bought the Whiting Motor Car Company of Flint, Michigan, and turned the Whiting into a car called the Little. The Little didn't last long, but by combining some of its qualities into a car designed for Durant by former Buick racing driver/mechanic Louis Chevrolet, it became a good seller. The Chevrolet proved successful enough to enable Durant, with the assistance of the duPont Corporation's Pierre S. duPont, to amass sufficient General Motors stock to recover control of GM in 1915.

Another entrepreneur, Benjamin Briscoe, had the same vision as Durant. He organized the United States Motor Corporation in 1909 in an attempt to rival Durant's General Motors. It was based on the successful Maxwell-Briscoe car, and although it collected several marques, Durant had beat him to many of the best ones. USMC failed in 1912, the same fate that would have befallen General Motors if the bankers had not stepped in.

Maxwell Motor Corporation was resurrected after USMC collapsed, and prospered for a while, but fell into financial difficulties in the early 1920s. Walter Chrysler, who had retired from the general managership of Buick in 1919, was brought in by the bankers to salvage Maxwell. He was successful in saving the company.

The Selden patent, taken out by a Rochester, New York patent attorney named George Selden, had been plaguing the industry for many years. In 1879 Selden had applied for a patent on plans for a car with a "liquid hydrocarbon engine." No car was constructed at that time, although two would be built later in an attempt to defend the patent. They would prove to be pretty pathetic efforts as cars. Through delays and updating of the patent, which was then allowed, Selden was able to defer its granting until 1895. It was valid for 17 years.

Apparently not wanting to pursue the patent himself, Selden sold it to a New York City consortium, and it ended up under the control of an organization called the Association of Licensed Automobile Manufacturers. The ALAM set out to enforce the patent by requiring all auto manufacturers to take out ALAM membership, and pay a royalty on each car produced.

Most automakers joined and paid the ALAM Selden Patent royalty. One who refused was Henry Ford, no doubt in part because his fledgling Ford Motor Company had been rebuffed as a mere "assembler," not an auto manufacturer, when it had enquired earlier about ALAM membership. Henry steadfastly fought the patent in the courts, and in the press, losing in 1909, but finally winning on appeal in 1911. The patent was found to be "valid but not infringed" by the industry because it referred to a Brayton type, two-stroke engine which compressed its air/fuel mixture outside the cylinder.

Beating the Selden patent, even though it was about to expire the following year, and the wildly successful Model T, raised Henry Ford to American folk hero status. He was hailed as the little man who had defeated what the public perceived as a pernicious Wall Street monopoly. Ford was already the world's largest automobile manufacturer, and this further consolidated his position.

At the dawn of the second decade the car still had to be started with a difficult and dangerous hand crank. This was part of the reason that electric cars were still very much on the scene, particularly favoured by women. The quest for a self-starter gained new impetus when Cadillac president Henry Leland's friend and business associate Byron Carter died as a result of a cranking accident. Carter was the builder of the Cartercar which had an infinitely variable friction-drive mechanism, an early but unsuccessful attempt at a fully automatic transmission. Leland was so depressed at the loss of his friend that he became obsessed with replacing the dangerous crank.

He engaged the services of a gifted young engineer named Charles Kettering of Dayton, Ohio. Kettering had recently left the National Cash Register Company where he had motorized the company's cash register. Kettering, along with Edward Deeds, organized the Dayton Engineering Laboratories Company (Delco) to design and manufacture automobile ignition systems. This brought him into contact with Cadillac's Henry Leland.

A variety of automobile starters had been tried using such methods as compressed air and steel springs, but none had proved satisfactory. The electric motors that had been tried as starters were too big and heavy to be practical, their designs having been based on the assumption of continuous operation. Kettering would bring greater insight, and apply the same principle to the starter as he had to electrifying the cash register.

He knew that a starter motor, like a cash register, was subject to only short-term use. He reasoned that he could use a smaller electric motor because it would be subject to only a temporary overload, a condition that electric motors could tolerate. He tried it on a gasoline engine starter and it was successful.

Kettering made the starter and generator one unit that was permanently connected to the crankshaft. After it started the car, the starter was converted to a generator. Then in 1913 Vincent Bendix invented the "Bendix Drive," a small gear mounted on a screw shaft extending from the end of the starter. When the starter was activated the gear spun along the shaft and meshed with the flywheel to turn the crankshaft. It disengaged as soon as the engine started. This invention allowed the starter and generator to be separated.

Cadillac introduced the electric self-starter on its 1912 models, and it was a watershed development in automotive history. It gave Cadillac an unprecedented second Royal Automobile Club Dewar Trophy; its first had been for the demonstration of interchangeable parts in 1908. The self-starter spread through the industry like wildfire, enabling the gasoline engine to thoroughly

1912 Cadillac – electric starter was watershed development

vanquish electric and steam powered cars.

Horace and John Dodge, suppliers of mechanical components to the industry, including the Ford Motor Company, in which they also held shares, decided to launch out on their own to manufacturer cars. They introduced their first Dodge Brothers car in 1914. It was a pioneering effort, being fitted with an all-steel body, developed in cooperation with the Edward G. Budd Company of Philadelphia. Dodge became the first high production user of an all-steel body, and Budd would lead the motor industry into adopting the all-steel automobile body.

Henry Ford's Model T had been an immediate success when he introduced it late in 1908. With high demand for its cars Ford soon outgrew the Piquette Avenue plant in Detroit, and moved to larger premises in Highland Park in 1910. When Model T production surpassed 200,000 in 1913 it was putting excessive strain on Ford's recently expanded assembly capacity.

A more efficient method was required. Ford's production chief, and later chief executive, Charles Sorensen, known as "Cast Iron Charlie" for his pattern-making skills, set about to explore a more streamlined production method. It would result in the moving automobile assembly line.

According to Sorensen, the assembly line concept had really been born at the Piquette Avenue plant several years before. In his book, *My Forty Years With Ford*, he wrote that he and a few assistants spent several Sundays in the summer of 1908 doing some assembly line experimenting. They began by pulling a car frame, first on skids, and then on its wheels, past piles of parts. As the chassis moved slowly along, Sorensen and some helpers bolted the parts on as the car passed each group of components. It was, he said "...the first car, I'm sure, that was ever built on a moving line." Henry Ford was skeptical, but didn't discourage the moving assembly line idea.

Such pressures as launching the Model T, getting it into production, and meeting the burgeoning demand, shelved the assembly line idea for five years. As exploratory steps, various components, such as the flywheel and magneto unit, were gradually organized for continuous moving assembly. Finally, by August 1913 the building of the entire car on a moving assembly line was implemented at the Highland Park plant. Within a year these "rivers of steel" had decreased assembly time for a Model T from 12-1/2 hours to 1-1/2. The assembly line and the electric starter would be the major technical achievements of the decade.

Ford's annual production jumped to over 300,000 in 1914, and would rise to over half a million in 1915. Henry Ford knew that rising production meant falling cost per unit. After reviewing the figures, he dropped a bombshell early in 1914: Ford was raising its daily wage to five dollars.

The $5 day was a bold, innovative move, causing the rest of the industry to predict dire consequences, which didn't materialize. If Henry Ford was a hero to the masses before, he was almost legendary now, assuring his place in the all-star pantheon of American industrial giants. It made the workers who assembled the cars able to afford them, and - not coincidentally - solved Ford's severe labour turnover problem. By 1919 Ford's annual production would rise to over 800,000, and to more than a million in the early 1920s.

While Henry Ford had relieved farmers from their rural isolation with his ubiquitous Model T, he also sought to improve their lives through agricultural mechanization. Ford introduced its small, low priced Fordson farm tractor in 1917, and it would enable Ford to dominate the tractor market for a decade. No other American automobile manufacturer successfully entered the farm implement business.

As car production climbed, the need for better roads followed. Governments were hard pressed to keep up with the demand. In the U.S. the Lincoln Highway Association was formed in 1913 to promote the construction of a coast-to-coast highway. In the Province of Ontario the Toronto-to-Hamilton highway, the first concrete road in Canada, was officially opened in 1917.

Increased automobile population also brought a rapidly escalating demand for fuel. The process of extracting gasoline from crude oil was quite inefficient until William Burton of the Standard Oil Company of Indiana invented a method called the Burton process. It used high temperature and pressure to "crack" the crude oil's molecules, a technique that doubled the gasoline yield to 50 percent of a barrel of crude.

As cars became more popular, sportier models were offered, such as the Stutz Bearcat and the Mercer Raceabout. These were little more than a chassis with a "doghouse" covering the engine, a basic monocle windshield, two bucket seats, and a cylindrical, barrel-shaped fuel tank. There were usually two spare ties strapped on the back because tires were woefully prone to punctures in those days.

Racing was also increasing in importance and

1914 Stutz Bearcat – early American sports car

popularity. It had been a part of the automotive scene almost since the beginning, and was seen as a route to favourable publicity for carmakers, as well as a sort of vehicle proving ground. Much early racing was held on public roads, an activity that proved both dangerous and disruptive. It was soon decided, particularly in North America, that racing should be relegated to closed tracks.

Among the early dedicated motor racing circuits was a 2-1/2 mile "square oval" track built in Indianapolis, Indiana. It was completed in 1909 and the Indianapolis Motor Speedway's first 500-mile race was held in 1911. The Indy 500 would soon become an American institution, and in spite of Ray Harroun, the first winner, pioneering the rearview mirror, the sporting and entertainment aspects soon overshadowed any automotive development that may have resulted.

In 1915 Cadillac, now free of the difficult

crank-starting method, startled the automotive world by going straight from four cylinder engines to V-8s exclusively. It elevated Cadillac even higher on the prestige ladder, and vee-type engines would be Cadillac's hallmark; besides its standard V-8, it introduced V-12s and V-16s in 1930. Cadillac stayed exclusively with vee-type engines until 1982 when energy concerns motivated it to produce the Cimarron with an inline four.

Not to be outdone by luxury car rival Cadillac, Packard announced its V-12 "Twin Six" engine in 1915. Besides providing Packard with a measure of exclusivity, it gave Packard's engineers invaluable V-12 experience which would stand them in good stead to take the lead in developing America's 1917-18 First World War V-12 Liberty aircraft engine. The Liberty, an overhead camshaft design that was engineered in a few weeks in 1917, became a very successful aero engine. It was built in the thousands by several auto companies.

The automobile industry made an important contribution to the First World War, particularly in its ability to supply trucks, including those with four-wheel drive, that quickly replaced horses. Although the industry would not shut down car-building as it did during the Second World War, material shortages would curtail production.

After recovering control of General Motors in 1915, Billy Durant went on another of his customary buying sprees. Two of the companies he acquired would have a major impact on the

1917 Liberty aircraft engine – auto industry contributes to war effort

future of GM because of two men it brought into the organization.

With the Hyatt Roller Bearing Company of New Jersey came its president, Alfred P. Sloan Jr., a Massachusetts Institute of Technology engineering graduate. He would prove to be an administrative wizard. Sloan already had gained many contacts in the automotive industry through his role as Hyatt's sales engineer, so the transition to GM was a natural one. He became GM's president in 1923, and chairman in 1937, and his administrative and organizational skill would guide and mould General Motors into the world's largest enterprise.

The other significant acquisition, Dayton Engineering Laboratories Company, or Delco, brought to GM the engineering brilliance of Charles Kettering of electric starter fame. Kettering became

GM's research chief, and contributed to the development of many significant engineering advances, including knock-resistant ethyl gasoline, the high compression engine, Freon refrigerant, and the two-stroke diesel engine.

Ford had outgrown its Highland Park factory, and was now in a vast new vertically integrated River Rouge plant that had been completed in the late teens. In addition to its car assembly facilities, it boasted a steel mill, a glass plant, and its own internal railroad. Raw materials such as coal, iron ore and wood came in at one end of the Rouge, and finished Model Ts went out the other. The Ford Motor Company bestrode the industry like the colossus it truly was.

Walter Chrysler, who had resigned from the general managership of GM's Buick Division in 1919 because he couldn't take any more of Billy Durant's meddlesome and arbitrary management, would rise to prominence in the 1920s.

Billy Durant would be forced out of GM for the second and last time, but would be back in the car business in the 1920s. Charles Nash, who had started as an upholsterer in the Durant-Dort carriage company, and rose to be president of General Motors, resigned from GM in 1916. He acquired the Thomas B. Jeffery Company of Kenosha, Wisconsin, which he turned into the Nash Motor Car Company.

The Hudson Motor Car Company, which had been formed in 1909, was well established with a reputation for cars of good quality and performance.

By 1919 John N. Willys's Willys-Overland Company, a pioneer in the use of the ultra quiet Knight sleeve-valve engine, was fourth in industry sales behind only Ford, Chevrolet and Buick.

As the decade drew to a close the stage was set, and the cast of characters assembled who would guide the rapid automotive development and sales battles that would take place in the "Roaring Twenties."

1920 – 1930
PROSPERITY IN THE "ROARING TWENTIES"

The "Roaring Twenties" brought a period of general prosperity, and some consolidation in the automobile industry. The decade started with a post-First World War financial "Panic," and ended with the stock market crash and the beginning of the "Great Depression." In between, there would be good times, with automobile building growing into North America's largest industry.

Since the automobile industry did not discontinue car production during the First World War, as it did during the Second, there was no wrenching adjustment to return to building cars after the war. There was, however, a post-war financial Panic to deal with. It was a sharp recession, and although of brief duration, it nevertheless had a strong impact on the auto industry because for a short period the market for new cars all but evaporated.

Recovery came, and some new car companies arrived, such as Rickenbacker and Wills Sainte Claire. The Rickenbacker company was headed by First World War American air hero Eddie Rickenbacker, but his famous name wasn't enough to ensure prosperity.

1925 Chrysler – Walter Chrysler launches his own company

Wills Sainte Claire was formed by ex-Ford engineer Childe Harold Wills. The Wills Sainte Claire was a handsome, well engineered car, perhaps too well engineered and expensive for its own good. Both the Rickenbacker and the Wills Sainte Claire would depart before the decade ended, along with several others.

In January 1920, Walter Chrysler, recently resigned from the general managership of Buick, was hired by the bankers to turn around the ailing Willys-Overland Company. He accomplished this in less than two years, and was then engaged to perform the same corporation-saving feat for the Maxwell Motor Corporation. He wisely opted to take his remuneration in the form of a modest salary and generous stock options.

Chrysler succeeded in reinvigorating Maxwell, and through some loans and stock acquisition was soon in control of the company. The first Chrysler badged car was produced by Maxwell in 1924, and the Maxwell Motor Corporation became the Chrysler Corporation the following year.

Once the hard driving Walter Chrysler had his own company there was no stopping him. Just three years later, in 1928, he was able to bring out the Plymouth to compete in the low priced field, acquire car and truck manufacturer Dodge Brothers, and introduce a new mid-priced model called the DeSoto. It was a momentous year for the fledgling company.

The Plymouth would soon make Chrysler, along with Ford and General Motors, one of the American Big Three. The Dodge purchase added a respected marque to the corporation, and what was equally important, added valuable production capacity and an established dealer network. The DeSoto, originally priced between Plymouth and Dodge, would soon be moved above Dodge where it became a lower priced alternative to the Chrysler.

1929 Plymouth – brought the Chrysler Corporation into the Big Three

General Motors was a wounded giant as it entered the new decade. The high flying promoter and stock market plunger William "Billy" Durant hadn't changed, and under his second reign from 1915 to 1920 GM again lacked effective central control. The result was haphazard expansion, over-production, and crippling debt. The situation became so serious that the company faced bankruptcy in the post-First World War Panic. Durant was deposed by the bankers in 1920 for the second, and last, time, and the corporation was rescued by the chemical giant duPont to protect its large investment in General Motors.

Pierre S. duPont became the reluctant president of General Motors, holding that position from 1920 to 1923. At that time his executive vice-president, Alfred P. Sloan, Jr., who had in

1923 Duesenberg Model A – pioneered hydraulic brakes

effect been running the company, assumed the presidency. It would prove to be one of the most significant appointments in automotive history.

Billy Durant couldn't be kept down, and within six weeks was back in the automobile business with the formation of Durant Motors Incorporated. His boast was that he would build "just a real good car," and his charisma and reputation easily attracted financial backers. The Durant company built a variety of makes, including the Durant, Eagle and Flint. The Star was Durant's low priced car, launched as a competitor to the Ford Model T and the Chevrolet. Durant had factories in several cities, including Toronto, but succumbed to bankruptcy in 1932.

Engineering advancements continued. In 1921 the Duesenberg Corporation, famous for its racing engines and cars, expanded its activities into the passenger car field. Their initial offering, the Model A Duesenberg, was the first American production car to be fitted with a straight-eight engine. But even more significant was the fact that it had four-wheel hydraulic brakes. Duesenberg had used them to excellent advantage in the 1921 French Grand Prix where they were a decisive factor in Duesenberg's victory. They decided to transfer the idea to production cars. It was the first to have them, and it would prove to be the major automotive engineering development of the decade.

Ford came into the 1920s with a debt load left over from the construction of the mammoth Rouge plant. Henry Ford was deeply suspicious of the "Eastern Establishment," and was paranoid about bankers, whom he tried to avoid at all costs. He survived the economic Panic by loading up his dealers with cars which they were required to pay for or lose their franchises. Ford then closed the factory for six weeks. His ploy, in effect, made his dealers into his banker. It was a mean spirited way to treat dealers, but since a Ford agency was too valuable an asset to relinquish, they had little choice but to make whatever arrangements they could to pay for the cars. It was a revealing insight into Ford's darker side.

The Model T Ford was so successful that Henry Ford had seen no reason to expand to other models. It suited his narrow gauge thinking, but unfortunately for him, the automotive world was changing. Rival General Motors offered a wide line of vehicles from the entry level Chevrolet to the luxurious Cadillac. Henry's son Edsel, who had become Ford president in 1919, although Henry still had *de facto* control, began to move the Ford Motor Company away from its one-model policy. A start was the purchase of the failing Lincoln Motor Company in 1922 founded by the father and son team of Henry and Wilfred Leland.

Henry and Wilfred Leland had left the Cadillac Motor Car Company in 1917 after a dispute with Billy Durant over the production of Liberty aircraft engines; the Lelands wanted GM to build them, and Billy didn't. They formed their own company, Lincoln (Henry Leland was a great admirer of Abraham Lincoln), to build Liberty engines. When the demand for these ended following the war, they developed a large V-8 powered luxury car which came to market in the poor economic conditions of 1921. Lincoln was soon in financial difficulties, which paved the way for Ford's purchase. Edsel Ford, who had championed the idea of Ford diversification, was made president of Lincoln, while the Lelands were to stay on and run the company. This arrangement proved unworkable and the Lelands soon departed.

As cars became more mechanically reliable, motorists began looking for increased comfort and weather protection. The Hudson Motor Car Company had introduced its low priced Essex car early in 1919. In 1922 Hudson brought out the closed Essex two-door coach at the very reasonable price of $1495. This was $300 more than a closed Essex, but still a bargain compared with what others were charging for closed cars. The price was soon reduced to $1245, making it the lowest cost closed car available. The Essex coach would ultimately fall to $895 in 1925, $5 less than a comparable touring car.

Hudson had judged the market correctly, and although dismissed by the competition as "a packing crate on wheels," the snug Essex coach was a rousing success, leading the way to a rapid transition from traditional open roadsters and phaetons, to closed coaches, coupes and sedans. As GM president Alfred P. Sloan, Jr., commented in his book, *My Years With General Motors*, "Nothing like that had ever been seen before in the automobile industry, and the Essex coach had a considerable vogue." He added that it would "profoundly influence the Pontiac, the Chevrolet, and the Model T."

By 1925 sales of new closed cars would exceed those of open ones, and roadsters and convertibles shrank permanently to a small percentage of the market. The situation would reverse itself within a decade; whereas in 1919 new open cars outnumbered closed ones by nine to one, by 1929 it was just the opposite. Station wagons, pioneered by the Durant Motor Company's Star in 1923, would also slowly gain their place in company lineups.

In addition to comfort, motorists were becoming more discerning about the styling of their cars. General Motors president Alfred P. Sloan, Jr., was observing this. It complemented his evolving concept of constantly upgrading GM's cars, and of incorporating this into an annual model change, a process that GM's future chief stylist Harley Earl would call "dynamic obsolescence."

Sloan's approach was two-pronged: to make consumers dissatisfied with their current cars by bringing out annual improvements in engineering and styling; and to lure them up the hierarchy of General Motors marques, which he had rationalized from 10 to five. Sloan sought a progression from the popular priced Chevrolet to the luxurious, and not coincidently, more profitable, Cadillac. He called it "a car for every purse and purpose."

Sloan's philosophy led to the formation of the industry's first formalized styling studio. It evolved from the discovery in California of a young man named Harley Earl who had started out working as a stylist for his family's firm, the Earl Automobile Works in Hollywood. He designed custom one-off cars for movie stars and other wealthy patrons, and established a considerable following in the burgeoning motion picture industry. One of the company's best customers was Don Lee, Cadillac's California distributor. The association became so close that Lee purchased the Earl Automobile Works in 1919.

Earl's work came to the attention of General Motors when Lawrence Fisher, the Cadillac Division's general manager, was visiting Lee in California. He was very impressed with the work that Earl was doing, and upon returning to Detroit, told GM president Sloan about the talented young man who was styling cars out in California.

GM was in the process of developing a lower priced Cadillac "companion" car, the LaSalle, and Sloan agreed to offer Earl a contract to come east and style this new model. In designing the LaSalle Earl gave it deeply drawn fenders, rounded corners, a lower silhouette, and imaginative colours. Although its appearance was heavily influenced by the French Hispano-Suiza luxury car, no one seemed to care.

The LaSalle was such a styling sensation that Sloan invited Earl to join General Motors permanently, and set up what was called the Art and Colour Section reporting to Sloan. Its mandate was to apply Earl's styling talent to all of GM's cars. Art and Colour would later become the Styling Department, and an indication of the growing importance of styling was demonstrated when Earl became GM's, and the industry's, first vice-president of styling in 1940.

The 1927 LaSalle's success, and the formation

1927 LaSalle – formalized automobile styling

of the Art and Colour Section, formalized automobile styling. It also exemplified an emerging interest in greater luxury and convenience, and those who didn't adapt would suffer in the marketplace.

Styling was aided by the fact that cars were gradually getting lower. One significant development was the introduction of the hypoid rear axle gear by Packard in 1927. This lowered the driveshaft up to two inches, which in turn allowed the car's floor to be lowered. Another contributor to lower cars was the use of smaller wheels, facilitated by improvements in roads, particularly the increase in hard surface highways.

As the market was changing, Henry Ford's venerable Model T was an example of staying with an austere model for too long. While Sloan had sensed where the market was going, and even influenced its direction, stubborn Henry

Ford was still locked into his one-model philosophy. Although changes were made to the Model T over the years, such as balloon tires and an electric starter, it remained basically the same car. Ford continued to stay with a foot-shifted planetary transmission, primitive brakes, "buggy spring" transverse leaf suspension, basic steering, and angular styling, while the rest of the industry standardized on lever-shifted transmissions, more effective suspensions and brakes, and other improvements.

Ford's rapid decline began in the mid-1920s. Its 1913 implementation of the moving assembly line, and its move to the giant River Rouge plant in the late teens, had dramatically increased its production capacity. Sales had continued surprisingly strong; the peak year was 1924 when more than 1.4 million Model Ts were built. But when sales slid to 393,000 in 1927 it was apparent that the days of the Model T were rapidly drawing to a close.

Ford finally shut down Model T assembly in 1927 to prepare for the Model A, which was not ready for production. Old Henry was so reluctant to abandon the Model T that he had not authorized the development of its successor. When Model T production finally ceased on May 26, 1927, more than 15 million of the legendary "Tin Lizzies" had been built.

It would be nine months before production of the new Model A would begin, and in the mean-

1929 Chevrolet – six cylinder power began assault on Ford's sales leadership

time, workers were laid off and Ford dealers had to survive on servicing cars. Charles Sorensen, Ford's chief executive and Henry's most loyal employee, said in his book, *My Forty Years With Ford*, that most of the delay was because of a dispute between old Henry and his progressive son Edsel.

Edsel, president of Ford, if mostly in name, wanted a modern, Lincoln-inspired car, while Henry wanted to continue with his old Model T ways. He wanted, for example, to keep the planetary transmission, rather than the sliding gear type, which he called a "crunch gear." Ironically, history would vindicate him to an extent; the planetary gearset would form the heart of the fully automatic transmission which Oldsmobile would pioneer in 1940, and which would go on to become almost universal.

The hiatus in Ford production allowed Chevrolet to surge ahead in sales, much to the delight of Chevrolet's general manager, ex-Ford production chief William Knudsen, who had left Ford in 1921. Although the popular Model A Ford would recover the leadership for 1929 and '30, it would be temporary supremacy.

The "mass" market as exemplified by Henry Ford's model T had come to an end. The industry was moving into what GM's Sloan called the "mass-class" market of a wider variety of cars with more luxury features. An example was Chevrolet's introduction of its new overhead valve six cylinder engine in 1929. Its smoothness and power immediately put Ford's four cylinder Model A at a disadvantage, and Henry Ford vowed to get more than even, which he would in 1932 with a V-8.

As motorists became more attuned to comfort and style, advertisers began to recognize the importance of also selling image and adventure, what we would now call lifestyle advertising. Edward "Ned" Jordan's Jordan Motor Car Company of Cleveland, Ohio, launched this theme in the 1920s. His "Somewhere West of Laramie" advertisement for the cleverly named Jordan Playboy was a classic of the genre.

The advertisement featured an attractive young woman driving a Playboy, and passing a fast riding cowboy on a spirited horse. "Somewhere west of Laramie," said the copy, "there's a broncho-busting [sic], steer-roping girl that knows what I'm talking about..." Jordan launched many more of those imaginative commercial messages, including the suggestive one showing a Jordan parked outside a brothel. It was entitled "The Port of Missing Men." Alas, creative advertising couldn't save Jordan; it disappeared under the weight of the Depression in 1931.

Style, comfort and inventive advertising were not all that was taking place of course. Technical advancements were continuing apace. A significant development in motor fuel was the addition of tetraethyl lead to gasoline in the mid-1920s to increase its resistance to knocking. General Motors research chief Charles Kettering and researcher Thomas Midgley, Jr., discovered that engine knock, or "ping," was not the fault of the engine, as was then believed, but was caused by the fuel it was burning.

After much experimentation Kettering and Midgley found that adding tetraethyl lead to gasoline eliminated the knock and allowed higher compression ratios, which improved both the power and fuel economy of the engine. In 1927 Graham Edgar discovered a way to rank the octane, or resistance to knock, of gasoline on a scale from one to 100. Heptane, which had a very low resistance to knock, was given a value of zero, and iso-octane (high resistance) a value of 100. The octane rating of a gasoline reflected the percentage of heptane and iso-octane, e.g. 87 octane fuel would have 13 percent heptane and 87 percent iso-octane. Leaded gasoline was a major breakthrough that would have a long term impact on engine development. Many years after this discovery, lead was found to have a negative influence on health, and to be destructive to emission reducing catalytic converters, but viewed in the context of its time, the addition of tetraethyl lead to gasoline was an important advancement.

Kettering and the duPont company, working together in the early 1920s, made another major improvement in the form of fast drying "Duco" paint. This speeded up the automobile production process significantly.

While engineering and styling progress was taking place, there was also an important marketing change occurring. This was the financing of car purchases by time payments. The General Motors Acceptance Corporation was formed in 1919, and time payments, plus the rapidly increasing practice of trading in used cars, often Model T Fords, for new ones, more often not Model Ts, were an important marketing development of the twenties. Most cars would soon be bought on the time payment plan.

With the increasing number of cars travelling the highways the inevitable roadside commerce emerged. Whereas motorists formerly had to buy gasoline at the general store, there were now dedicated service stations and garages that offered not only fuel, but repairs and service. Eating establishments and lodging were also developed to cater to motorists. And with roads that were both improved and better marked came reliable road maps, readily available from oil companies and others.

Roadside signs to advertise businesses were a natural evolution. One of the most effective highway advertising programs was initiated by the Burma-Vita Company of Minneapolis, Minnesota, manufacturers of a brushless shaving cream called Burma-Shave. Burma-Vita was owned by the Odell family, father Clinton and sons Allan and Leonard. The company enjoyed only modest sales, and they were becoming discouraged. But as Allan travelled the road trying to sell Burma-Shave he began to notice the magnetic affect that road signs had, particularly if there was a series of them. He had to read every one. Why not, he thought, try advertising Burma-Shave that way.

The company erected a few series of signs in 1925, and sales picked up; unsolicited orders even started to come in. The idea evolved into catchy five-line jingles on six road-side signs spaced approximately 30 metres (100 feet) apart. The last sign always said Burma-Shave. They were located just inside the property line, with the farmer receiving a small fee for the privilege of erecting the signs and allowing access for maintenance.

Soon travellers, particularly children, were watching for messages like: "She kissed/the hairbrush/by mistake/she thought it was/her husband Jake/Burma-Shave," or "Beneath this stone/lies Elmer Gush/tickled to death/by his shaving brush/Burma Shave." Sometimes the signs were purely commercial: "Half a pound/for half a dollar/spread on thin/ above the collar/Burma-Shave." Others were fractured paeans of patriotism: "Let's make Hitler/and Hirohito/look as sick/as old Benito/Burma-Shave," or tales of lost love "His tenor voice/she thought divine/till whiskers/scratched/sweet Adeline/Burma-Shave." There were also social messages: "Drinking drivers/nothing worse/they put/the quart/before the hearse/Burma-Shave."

The number of signs, carrying 600 jingles, gradually grew to some 40,000 in 45 states, and Burma-Vita became a $3 million a year business. Clinton Odell died in 1958, and the company was sold to Philip Morris, Incorporated, in 1963. The signs were seen as anachronistic, and were all uprooted in the 1960s. They were, however, a genuine piece of folksy Americana, and a set has been preserved in the Smithsonian Institution in Washington.

As the decade drew to a close, North America dominated global automobile production. The United States, for example, manufactured 85 percent of the world's cars. But it is ironic, in view of the looming Depression, that some of the most extravagant cars in history began to make their appearance – models like the mighty Model J Duesenberg and the front-wheel drive Cord L-29. Events late in 1929 would demonstrate just how out of sync they were with the times. The industry would have to cope with dramatically falling demand, and further attrition as the difficult 1930s unfolded.

Burma Shave signs became a piece of American folklore

1930 – 1940
THE DEPRESSION'S RAVAGES, MORE CONSOLIDATION

The world suffered though the Great Depression of the 1930s, the worst economic downturn in modern history. It was a watershed in both the automotive industry and society at large. Cars like the American Duesenberg J and SJ and Cadillac V-12 and V-16, the French Bugatti Royale, the English Rolls-Royce Phantom III, and the German Mercedes-Benz SSK are now considered classics. But when these giants were built, hardly anyone could afford them, or if they could, they were often reluctant to display such opulence in the face of poverty.

Like everyone else, the automobile manufacturers were caught in the sudden economic collapse brought on by the stock market crash of October 1929. Those mighty cars that arrived in the thirties had been conceived in the better economic times of the "Roaring Twenties" when enthusiasm and optimism ran high - too high as it would turn out.

The Depression's impact was felt by the auto industry almost immediately; American car production would fall from 3.8 million in 1929 to 2.6 million in 1930, and 1.9 in 1931. In 1932 it reached 1.1 million, a 75 percent drop from the late twenties.

General Motors and Ford had been predominant in sales through the 1920s, but when the Chrysler Corporation, formed out of Maxwell in 1925, introduced the low priced Plymouth in 1928, it was such a sales success that by 1932 it had risen to third place behind Chevrolet and Ford. It propelled Chrysler into real contention with GM and Ford, enabling it to become one of the Big Three manufacturers.

Henry Ford had been stung by Chevrolet's 1929 model, which had a six cylinder engine while his Model A had only a four. He would counter with his V-8 in 1932, making eight cylinder power and smoothness affordable to buyers of popular priced cars.

It was a compact engine, and unlike other V-8s, had a one-piece cylinder block, thanks to the pattern-making skill of Ford's "Cast Iron Charlie" Sorensen. Due to its good power potential, the V-8 soon became a favourite among racers and hot rodders. The Ford V-8 and Hudson's new 1933 eight cylinder Terraplane

1932 Ford V-8 – eight cylinder smoothness for low price field

were two of the fastest cars on the road. The V-8 engine would be Henry Ford's last major technical achievement.

Cadillac, which had gone exclusively from four cylinders to a V-8 in its 1915 model, stunned the world in 1930 with its huge, powerful and beautiful overhead valve V-16. It was really two straight-eights on a common crankcase and crankshaft, and was a magnificent engine both mechanically and stylistically. Cadillac wisely continued the V-8.

The V-16 consolidated Cadillac as the American prestige marque. Marmon, a company know for its fine engineering, would also offer a V-16, and Peerless would attempt it, although the firm was in its death throes and only one was built. Of the three marques, only Cadillac would survive

the Depression. A Cadillac V-12 joined the V-16 late in 1930, and Cadillac continued to offer V-12s until 1937, and V-16s right through to 1940, although it changed to a wide-angle side valve V-16 in 1938. It was a mark of the times that only 4403 Cadillac V-16s were built during its 11-year run.

The Duesenberg Model J, called America's mightiest motorcar, arrived late in 1928, the dream of Errett Lobban Cord whose Auburn Automobile Company of Auburn, Indiana, had taken over Duesenberg in 1926. Cord wanted to build a world-class super car, and asked the German-born American brothers, noted race car designers and builders Fred and August Duesenberg, to design it. With the J they brought the technology of the race track to cars of the highway.

The Duesenberg J was powered by a 265 horsepower 6.8 litre (420 cu in.) double overhead camshaft Lycoming straight-eight engine with four valves per cylinder. It was joined in 1932 by the even more powerful 320 horsepower supercharged SJ version. Duesenberg production was never high, and it would cease in 1937 with the collapse of the Cord empire.

E.L. Cord was responsible for another unusual car beginning in the late twenties. In 1929 he launched the front-wheel drive Cord L-29, powered by a side-valve, straight-eight engine. The long engine and transaxle unit gave

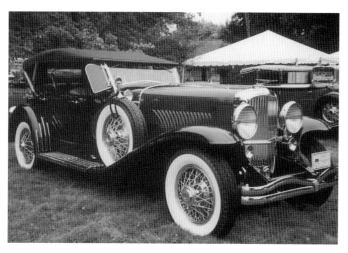

1929 Duesenberg J – mighty cars that were wrong for the times

1931 American Austin – too small to be taken seriously

the L-29 a very extended hood, and this, combined with the low silhouette made possible with front-wheel drive, made the L-29 a favourite among coachbuilders. The L-29 would by built only from 1929 to 1931.

The Cord name then languished for a few years, but was revived in 1936 with the stunningly styled front-wheel drive "coffin nose" 810, and supercharged 1937 812 models. They had the distinction of bringing hidden headlamps to automobiles. But the Cord was an expensive car, and sales didn't meet expectations. It also died with the demise of the Cord holdings.

At the other end of the automotive spectrum, the American Austin Car Company was established in Butler, Pennsylvania, to manufacturer an economical little car which should have been

right in step with the times. American Austin built an Americanized version of the tiny English Austin Seven which Herbert Austin's Austin Motor Company had launched in 1922. The Austin Seven, a kind of everyman's car, had been very successful in Britain, and in Germany, France and Japan where it was built under license.

In spite of its success abroad, and even when the parlous economic times of the Depression should have favoured economical cars, the American Austin was seen as just too small for the North American market. It was never taken seriously, being considered more as a novelty than as real transportation.

American Austin went into receivership in 1934, and was revived in 1936 as the American

Bantam Car Company by an Atlanta, Georgia, American Austin dealer named Ray Evans. Although it survived until 1940, the company never flourished.

The American Bantam company has, however, one significant achievement to its name: it produced the first American military Jeep in 1940. It manufactured a prototype in the amazingly short time of 49 days, the only company that was able to meet the Army's extremely stringent deadline. Although testing proved that the American Bantam Jeep was acceptable, American Bantam's production facilities were unfortunately too limited to produce anything like the quantity required by the Army. Although the company built 1500 Jeeps, and many Jeep trailers, Willys-Overland got the big contract, and along with Ford, built almost 600,000 Jeeps during the Second World War. The Jeep would then make a successful transition into a peacetime vehicle.

Another proponent of tiny cars was Powel Crosley, Jr., a Cincinnati entrepreneur who had made his fortune selling low cost radios, and his pioneering "Shelvador" refrigerators with shelves in the doors. Always an advocate of small, economical vehicles, Crosley launched a tiny car in 1939 powered by a two-cylinder, air cooled engine. It was stark and marginally engineered, and sold in modest numbers until the auto industry shut down for the Second World War in February 1942. Crosley would return to car production in 1946.

Automotive technology continued to improve in the 1930s with such advancements as the proliferation of all-steel bodies, independent front suspensions, and the synchromesh transmission that had been pioneered by Cadillac in its 1929 models. Column shifted transmissions arrived, and were welcomed because they made it more convenient to carry three passengers in the front seat. There was almost universal acceptance of hydraulic brakes, although Henry Ford didn't fit them to his cars until 1939.

There were also developments of dubious value. In 1931 Studebaker introduced a free-wheeling transmission which had a roller-bearing type over-running clutch that disconnected the engine from the driveline when the driver released the accelerator pedal. It was intended to save fuel, but the heavy brake wear, and the danger of having no engine compression braking, soon relegated it to automotive history.

In a quest for shiftless driving, Reo introduced its "Self-Shifter" transmission in 1933. This required the driver to use the clutch to start off, and would then shift automatically to high gear. Unfortunately it was prone to slippage and grabbing, depending on throttle opening, and was soon discontinued. Another transmission development was Hudson's 1935 vacuum shifted "Electric Hand," a kind of early semi-automatic gearbox. It proved slow to shift, and was often troublesome. It also saw an early demise.

General Motors was also actively pursuing a fully automatic transmission through its Oldsmobile Division. Oldsmobile anticipated the shiftless future with its 1937 "Safety Automatic Transmission." Although it still required some shifting and the use of a clutch, it was the clear forerunner to the fully automatic "Hydra-Matic" transmission that Oldsmobile would introduce in 1940. The Hydra-Matic used the same basic planetary gear-set that Henry Ford had used in his Model T, although now hydraulically controlled, not foot shifted as in the Model T.

The Depression drastically depleted the ranks of automakers. By 1940 such marques as Auburn, Cord, Duesenberg, Detroit Electric, Durant, Graham, Hupmoble, Jordan, LaSalle, Marmon, Peerless, Pierce-Arrow, Stutz, Willys-Knight, and more, had disappeared. Reo stopped building cars in 1936, wisely converting to the production of commercial vehicles, which it did successfully for many years.

Some that remained, such as Studebaker and Packard, went through difficult times. Packard survived by bringing out its less expensive 120 model in 1935, which brought the cachet of the Packard name into a more affordable price range, but marked the beginning of the decline in Packard's once grand reputation for prestige.

Studebaker, after recovering from receiver-

1940 Oldsmobile – the magic of shiftless driving

ship in 1933, boosted sales in 1939 with its all new, smaller and more economical Champion model. The Champion would be resumed after the Second World War, and would become a mainstay of Studebaker, and its longest running nameplate.

Willys, which had risen to third place in sales in the industry in 1928 on the strength of its successful small Whippet, struggled during the 1930s, but remained alive. It would flourish during the Second World War building military Jeeps.

The Nash Motor Company of Kenosha, Wisconsin, formed by ex-General Motors president Charles Nash out of the Thomas B. Jeffery Company in 1916, suffered declining sales in the 1930s. It managed to stay in business, but decided to diversify in 1936 by joining with refrigerator maker Kelvinator Corporation, becoming the

1939 Studebaker Champion – revived Studebaker, became its most enduring nameplate

1937 Chrysler Airflow – failed attempt at aerodynamics

Nash-Kelvinator Corporation. Thus it was in competition with General Motors in both motor vehicles and refrigerators. It seemed unusual for an automobile maker to be in the refrigerator business, but when Billy Durant had been questioned by fellow General Motors board members about why he had purchased a refrigerator company for GM – it became Frigidaire – he replied that they were just like cars; both were boxes with motors in them.

Streamlining, more correctly called aerodynamics, was gaining in importance. Chrysler Corporation tried to steal a march on the industry with the aerodynamic 1934 Chrysler and DeSoto Airflow models. Despite such engineering advances as between-the-axles seating, and semi-unit construction, the swoopy, Art Deco styling overwhelmed everything else. It was not a success in the marketplace. Chrysler Corporation would abandon the Airflow in 1937, and remain conservative in styling until its "Forward Look" cars arrived for 1955.

Lincoln's large V-12s, like other ostentatious models, were selling poorly. To improve its position Lincoln followed Packard's lead and introduced the less expensive 1936 Zephyr. Although cheaper, it still boasted a V-12 engine like the big Lincoln. The Zephyr was aerodynamic and nicely styled, and since its streamlined shape was more conservative than Chrysler's, it was better accepted. The Lincoln Zephyr set the tone for

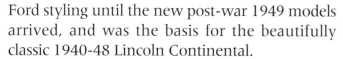

1938 Buick Y-Job – set the tone for American car styling

1940 Volkswagen Kubelwagen – Germany's "Jeep"

Ford styling until the new post-war 1949 models arrived, and was the basis for the beautifully classic 1940-48 Lincoln Continental.

A more prescient styling development was the pioneering 1938 Buick Y-Job concept car designed by GM's chief stylist Harley Earl. With its prominent hood, stretched fenders and horizontal grille, it was the first of the so-called "dream cars." It predicted American car styling into the 1950s. Unlike today's concept cars, some of which are simply "pushmobiles," the Y-Job served as Harley Earl's personal transportation for many years.

In other parts of the world developments were taking place that would have long-term implications for the industry. In 1934 Germany's Chancellor Adolf Hitler commissioned the Porsche Design Office to design an economical, affordable car, which was soon dubbed the "People's Car," or Volkswagen.

Porsche completed the first prototype in 1935, followed by two more in 1936. Independent testing proved that it was a practical and sturdy design. After established German automakers proved reluctant to produce this new low price model, a state-owned Volkswagen factory was constructed near the Wolfsburg castle in the State of Lower Saxony. It was completed in 1938, but due to the advent of the Second World War, almost no Volkswagen cars were produced

1954 Citroen Traction Avant – legitimized front-wheel drive

before or during the war. The plant was used for military purposes, including the production of a Volkswagen based German "Jeep" called the Kubelwagen, and an amphibious version, the Schwimmwagen. The plant was bomb-damaged during the war, but under the direction of Major Ivan Hirst of the British forces, who had control of that section of Germany following the war, Volkswagen production got under way at Wolfsburg in 1945.

In France the Citroen company introduced its Traction Avant model in 1934. It was a very advanced car for its time with its front-wheel drive, unit construction, and a low centre of gravity. Its tenacious road holding and superior traction demonstrated the advantages of front-wheel drive, and it was instrumental in popularizing and legitimizing the front-drive layout.

In Japan the auto industry was beginning to stir. Datsun (now Nissan) produced its first car in 1931, while Toyota's came along in 1935. Out of necessity the Japanese industry concentrated on trucks, however, and would have to wait until after the Second World War to get into significant car production.

Another pivotal development for the industry was the rise of the United Auto Workers union in the 1930s under the leadership of such labour pioneers as the Reuther brothers, Walter, Roy and Victor. The automobile manufacturers, and even many government officials, were bitterly opposed to unionization. Union organizers and those bold enough to stage strikes were usually summarily fired.

Then the union adopted a European tactic called the sit-down strike in which workers simply stayed at their work stations but refused to work, thus preventing the use of replacement labour. It proved successful, first against General Motors, and then Chrysler. General Motors recognized the UAW as the bargaining agent for its workers in February 1937, and all American automobile companies were ultimately unionized. But unionization didn't come without a struggle, the most dramatic of which was the "Battle of the Overpass" on May 26, 1937, when Walter Reuther and other union leaders were badly beaten by Ford's "Service Department" headed by Harry Bennett. It would take until 1941 to unionize Ford, and only then under strong court pressure.

The 1930s were a tumultuous time, marked by huge, multi-cylinder classics, a severe downturn in auto production due to the Depression, the rise of unionism, and steady technical improvement in automobiles. The scene would change dramatically in the next decade as the world was plunged into the Second World War. The automobile industry would play a critically important role in that conflict.

1940 – 1950
DETROIT IS "ARSENAL OF DEMOCRACY," RESUMES PEACETIME PRODUCTION

The 1940s started on an up-beat note for the American auto industry. Although the Second World War had been raging in Europe since late in 1939, and Canada was at war, the U.S. had not yet joined so its impact was not being felt in America. The Depression had finally waned, and 1940 new car sales reached 3.4 million, their third highest in history. They rose even higher to 3.7 million in 1941 as buyers became alarmed over the war, and decided to get a new car while they could. Their assessment was correct; conditions were due to change very quickly.

Before auto production was shut down, the opening of the decade saw the introduction of two automotive technical milestones: the fully automatic transmission, and air conditioning.

The automatic transmission had been an elusive goal which several manufacturers had attempted. In the early part of the century the Carter friction drive and the Owen magnetic drive tried to eliminate gear shifting, but success eluded them for several reasons, including excessive weight and wear. In 1933 Reo's "Self Shifter" used a planetary gearset and multi-plate clutch, but it still required use of the clutch pedal for getting under way.

General Motors introduced the first fully automatic "Hydra-Matic" transmission in the 1940 Oldsmobile. The automatic transmission proved to be one of the most significant, complicated, and yet unappreciated advancements in automotive engineering.

The other major development, Packard's "Weather Conditioner" refrigerated air conditioning, came along as an option in 1940. Its underhood- and trunk-mounted units were heavy and cumbersome, and it was only partially effective, but it did begin the process which eventually led to the fully automatic climate control systems that motorists enjoy today.

In the meantime the Nazi blitzkrieg was sweeping over Europe. Then on December 7, 1941, in what must be one of the most ill-advised military strategies in history, Germany's ally Japan attacked the U.S. military base at Pearl Harbor, Hawaii, waking the sleeping American giant.

America entered the war, and General Motors president William Knudsen was called to

Washington to chair the advisory committee of the Council of National Defense. The increasing advancement of Germany in Europe, followed by the Pearl Harbor attack, soon spurred the U.S. into a more dedicated effort on production planning for wartime materiel. In February 1942, the car companies ceased building automobiles to begin converting to military work.

Because there had been little incentive to do so, the automobile industry had made almost no preparation for military production. In spite of this it was able to quickly convert to the war effort, and turn its highly developed mass production techniques to supplying the needs of the military. When the industry heeded the call to arms, companies that were fiercely competitive in peacetime became co-operative in the face of the external threat.

The industry's contribution to the war effort was massive, the decisive factor in the Allied victory. In addition to approximately 600,000 four-wheel drive Jeeps produced by Willys-Overland and Ford, plus 1500 by American Bantam, all manufacturers pitched in to build everything from steel helmets to anti-aircraft guns to bombers. Many of the products were completely new to the industry. For example, over 60 percent of the $12 billion worth of war-time production from General Motors constituted items they had never made before.

Trucks, many fitted with four-wheel drive,

1944 Jeep – wartime hero pioneered Sport Utility Vehicle

were a particularly essential contribution to the cause. The transition to military trucks was relatively easy because they could be based on civilian truck designs.

Packard built Rolls-Royce aircraft engines, after Henry Ford, then in a pacifist mood, refused to have the Ford Motor Company do so. Henry, now in his dotage, was unfortunately back in control of the Ford Motor Company following the premature death of his son Edsel in 1943. Henry Ford eventually realized the seriousness of the military situation, and relented a few months later, allowing Ford to begin building Pratt and Whitney aircraft engines. Chrysler would become the main supplier of army tanks, although General Motors also produced them.

A major contribution, and one that was new to the auto industry, was the production of airplanes and aircraft engines. An auto industry that had made thousands of V-12 Liberty aircraft engines during the First World War was expected to easily convert to aircraft production during the Second. There was a massive difference, however, between a Packard-based V-12 Liberty, and a Second World War air cooled, 18-cylinder radial. The changeover to aircraft production, therefore, took longer than the public, and the politicians, thought it should, and the industry came in for considerable criticism.

Through co-operation between the auto and aircraft companies, airplane production finally got under way in the automobile industry. The most significant contribution in this area was by the Ford Motor Company. In 1941 under the leadership of Ford's production chief Charles Sorensen a huge new plant was constructed in Willow Run, Michigan. After some initial start-up problems, during which wags referred to it as "Will It Run," it was turning out four to five hundred B-24 Liberator bombers per month by 1944. The path to mass production of aircraft had not been smooth, but when it was achieved it was a major demonstration of the effectiveness of the auto industry's manufacturing expertise.

Unfortunately for Sorensen, in the process of pushing aircraft production forward the hard nosed production wizard had lost the political fight going on inside the Ford Motor Company. Ford's shady Harry Bennett, head of Ford's Service Department (company police force), who aspired to become Ford's president, had gained the favour of a Henry Ford now descended into senility. With aircraft production humming along, Sorensen was let go by Ford; he left unceremoniously in 1944.

Although Sorensen was certainly not a graduate of charm school, it was still a sad end for the only man who had been able to stomach Henry Ford's mercurial ways through 40 years of unwavering service. He resurfaced briefly as president of Willys-Overland, and then retired from the industry.

There were many far ranging implications associated with the war. One was the rationing of food, such as meat and butter. And in addition to being unable to buy new cars, motorists had to endure gasoline rationing caused by the wartime disruption of crude oil shipments. There were also tire shortages due to the scarcity of natural rubber brought about by the Japanese invasion of rubber producing countries in the Far East. But one benefit was that in complying with gasoline rationing, motorists at least conserved their precious tires.

Another social implication that would have far reaching consequences was the wartime entry of women into the workforce. With so many men away in the service, women went to the factories and kept the production machinery going in the auto industry and others. For many of them it was their first experience at working outside the home. And although the work was difficult and often dirty, it gave them a paycheque, and a sense of freedom, camaraderie and independence they had never known. While most women returned to being homemakers after the war, many did not, and the workplace would never be the same. Women had learned that they could do the same work as men, and they expected to be paid and treated as equals.

When peace came in 1945 there was tremendous pressure on manufacturers to get back into car building. Low auto production during the Depression, and a three-and-a-half year wartime hiatus, resulted in a sellers' market in which any kind of operable motor vehicle could be sold. The conversion to civilian auto production was delayed by material shortages, and a United Auto Workers strike against General Motors that lasted more than 100 days, from November 1945 to March 1946.

Militant workers were expecting the same high incomes during peacetime as they had come to enjoy during the war. Although wage rates had been frozen during the war, extensive overtime work had inflated workers' pay. Needless to say the automobile manufacturers didn't agree with a continuation of these high incomes. They regarded wartime production as extraordinary circumstances, and fully anticipated a return to pre-war conditions.

The long GM strike was finally settled at an 18-1/2 percent increase, rather than the 30 percent the UAW had demanded. Other manufacturers generally followed this pattern in their settlements. When the union contract came up for negotiation again in 1948 it was realized by both the manufacturers and the union that prolonged strikes were bad for everybody. The target was again General Motors, but the mood of the negotiations was considerably softer. In effect the parties had arrived at a tacit understanding that labour and management were in this together, that they were partners whether they liked it or not. It was further realized that any settlement reached could be passed on to the customers who bought the cars. The industry was, after all, an oligopoly dominated by a few large companies with little competition. And they were operating in an environment of high demand for their products.

The 1948 agreement was a historic one. In addition to other adjustments, GM and the UAW agreed to include periodic wage increases tied to inflation, the rising cost of living. The result was the so-called cost-of-living agreement, or COLA. Since the auto industry was so large and pervasive in society, it was looked to as the pattern setter in dealing with labour. Other industries soon adopted the COLA.

As production resumed in the now depleted auto industry, all of the established manufacturers except tiny Crosley, and Willys-Overland, returned to building their pre-war designed cars while they developed new post-war models.

Willys-Overland concluded that its pre-war cars would not be competitive in the post-war environment. It decided instead to launch a civilian version of the famous military four-wheel drive Jeep. This proved successful, and additional models such as Jeep station wagons, pickup trucks and panel trucks were added. The civilian Jeep established the very popular sport utility segment of the market, and spawned many imitators such as the English Land Rover and the Japanese Toyota Land Cruiser.

Powel Crosley, Jr., of radio and home appliance fame, and an automobile manufacturer who had produced a few tiny, two-cylinder air cooled cars before the war, also felt that this design would not be suitable for the post-war market. He had a new model developed, and returned to production with his new little car in 1946. It had a lightweight sheet metal four cylinder engine that Crosley had discovered powering military generator sets.

Unfortunately the sheet metal engine soon corroded in automotive service and developed disastrous leaks, badly damaging Crosley's reputation. A cast iron block solved the problem in 1948, but the stigma lingered on. In spite of this,

1949 Crosley – tiny cars from the man who popularized radio

Crosley prospered for a few years, even becoming the world's largest producer of station wagons, albeit tiny ones, in 1948.

In spite of its relatively short life, Crosley boasted several advanced technical features. Its engine was oversquare, meaning that its 63.5 mm (2.5 in.) cylinder bore was larger than its 57.1 mm (2.25 in.) piston stroke. This was definitely futuristic in an era of long stroke engines. The Crosley was also fitted with an overhead camshaft which no modern American car had at that time, and had a compression ratio of up to 10.0:1, anticipating the rest of the industry by several years.

Crosley cars were also years ahead in braking, being fitted in mid-1949 with calliper type four-wheel disc brakes. Chrysler also had disc brakes, but they were not the calliper type that would later be universally adopted. Crosley's disc brakes proved troublesome, however, and since the company lacked the funds to properly develop them they were discontinued in 1950. Not all of Crosley's features were so advanced, however. It still had a solid front axle suspended on leaf springs, and a non-synchromesh transmission. In spite of the addition of its spirited little Hotshot/Supersport sports car and tiny "Jeep type" dual purpose Farm-O-Road model, Crosley's automobile business ended in 1952.

Studebaker built pre-war designs briefly after the war, but was able to beat the rest of the industry with an all-new "three box" style in 1947. This was the sensational "coming-or-going" model styled under the direction of Raymond Loewy, and it led the industry in a new styling direction.

The Hudson Motor Car Company also returned with pre-war offerings until it was able to launch its new 1948 models. This was their famous low, wide, "Step Down" design, achieved by lowering the floorpan in the chassis. Hudson was also one of the early American users of unit construction.

General Motors, Ford, Chrysler and Nash introduced their full lines of new models in 1949 (GM had launched a few in mid-1948). Packard, which never really recovered its pre-eminent pre-war position, wasn't able to get its all-new style out until 1951.

While most of the industry was returning to a firm peacetime foundation, there was trouble in the Ford Motor Company. When Edsel Ford, Henry Ford's only son, and president of Ford, died in 1943, old Henry resumed control of the company. But due to age and mental deterioration he was unable to operate it effectively. The result was that Ford's management was in shambles.

The United States government became so concerned about the Ford Motor Company's health, and its ability to continue its war work, that it released Edsel's 26 year old son, Henry Ford II, from the Navy in 1943 to nurse it back to health. He was appointed vice-president of Ford, and soon elevated to president.

Young Henry Ford II had courage and foresight; one of his first acts was to fire the ambitious and ruthless Harry Bennett. Fortunately he realized that he needed help in running this huge enterprise, and was not too proud to seek it.

In 1946 Henry Ford II hired Ernest Breech away from the presidency of the Bendix Aviation Corporation, a subsidiary of General Motors. Breech was a gifted accountant who had risen quickly through the GM hierarchy. He loved the challenge of analyzing a situation and turning an organization around, and the Ford Motor Company presented ample scope to exercise these talents; it was losing almost $10 million a month. He was given the title of executive vice-president, second in command to Henry II.

Breech's sound, modern, management systems and procedures would rescue the company, and put it on a strong businesslike foundation. Ford was also successful in attracting many other seasoned executives from General Motors. The all-new 1949 Ford model, which Breech had insisted must be developed, would save the company.

Ford also hired a demobilized group of bright young military logistics experts, the so-called "Whiz Kids," which included Robert McNamara, President Kennedy's future secretary of defence, and Charles "Tex" Thornton who would later found Litton Industries. They and Breech, plus the GM executives that Breech recruited, were able to turn Ford around.

Also in 1946, on August 1st, a brash young engineering graduate named Lido "Lee" Iacocca began working for the Ford Motor Company. He started in engineering, but quickly realized that it was too stifling for him, so managed to get himself switched to sales. While his arrival didn't have an immediate impact, he would make important future contributions not only to Ford, but to the American automobile industry.

The favourable post-war market conditions attracted several entrepreneurs who attempted to enter the car-starved North American automobile market. The most successful of these companies was Kaiser-Frazer.

Henry Kaiser, a successful California con-

1949 Ford – the car that saved Ford

struction and shipbuilding magnate, teamed up with Joseph Frazer, president of Graham-Paige Motors, to form the Kaiser-Frazer Corporation in 1945. They acquired the huge Willow Run plant where Ford had built the B-24 bombers. It was available from the War Assets Administration, and Kaiser-Fraser was able to get it at very reasonable rates.

After experimenting with ideas like torsion bar suspension and front-wheel drive, Kaiser-Frazer settled on a conventional body-on-frame, front engine, rear-wheel drive sedan. Their first slab-sided Kaisers and Frazers, launched as 1947 models, were quite successful for a few years in a sellers' market. They used a Continental "Red Seal" side-valve, six cylinder stationary engine, which saved K-F the expense of tooling up for its own engine. When it proved troublesome in

1947 Frazer – Kaiser-Frazer's assault on Detroit failed

1948 Tucker – radical attempt at new post-Second World War car

automotive use, K-F brought its production in-house.

A more flamboyant entrant was Preston Tucker, flush from a successful wartime business in which his Tucker Aviation Corporation built rotating gun turrets. In 1945 Tucker announced his "Car of the Future." It was a large, low, six-passenger sedan with a horizontally-opposed (flat) six cylinder helicopter engine mounted in the rear. The slow-turning engine gave the Tucker tremendous performance and a claimed 161 km/h (100 mph) cruising speed.

The Tucker Torpedo, later re-named the 48, also boasted such safety features as disc brakes, a pop-out windshield and padded interior. In addition to two regular headlamps, it had a central "cyclops eye" headlight that steered with the front wheels.

Tucker Corporation managed to acquire a huge war surplus bomber engine plant in Chicago and set up production. Unfortunately he was able to build only 51 cars before the Securities and Exchange Commission began investigating his practices. This led to rumours of fraud, and the enterprise collapsed. Tucker was exonerated in 1949, but it was too late; there would be no more Tucker cars. He died of cancer in 1956 believing that he was the victim of dark, conspiratorial forces in Detroit that were trying to sink him because he represented a threat to the Big Three. Many felt there was some justification for these suspicions.

Another enterprise that attempted to crack fortress Detroit was the Playboy Motor Corporation of Buffalo, New York. In 1947 it launched a small three-passenger convertible powered by a

1947 Playboy – another 1940s failure

four cylinder Continental engine. Playboy managed to produce 97 of its little cars over the next four years, before succumbing to bankruptcy.

There would be other attempts too, names like Bobbi-Car, Keller, Davis, Kurtis and Gregory. None survived. The Gregory was particularly interesting in that it had its Continental engine in the rear driving the front wheels, an unusual approach to say the least.

In Europe an Italian by the name of Enzo Ferrari, who had managed the Alfa Romeo racing team from 1930 to 1937, started a small car-making enterprise in 1940. This activity was soon interrupted by the Second World War, during which the Ferrari factory manufactured machine tools. When peace came Ferrari returned to automobiles. He began with racing cars, and gradually added road cars based on his racing car designs.

Ferraris became strongly associated with V-12 engines, and were fabulously successful in competition. The Ferrari company thrived making competition cars, while also becoming the quintessential manufacturer of exotic road cars. By the late 1960s it was under the control of Fiat.

In the late 1940s the imported cars that began landing in North America included the British Jaguar. The company had been founded as a modest motorcycle side-car manufacturer in 1922 by two Englishmen, William Walmsley and William Lyons. Walmsley would later leave the business, but Lyons would stay and nurture the company into a full fledged car builder.

The first Jaguars that arrived in North America in 1947 were powered by engines of pre-war design. This changed late in 1948 with the introduction of a car that would have a lasting impact. This was the 1949 Jaguar XK120, a low, sensuously styled sports roadster capable of sprinting to 96 km/h (60 mph) in 10 seconds, and reaching a top speed of 193 km/h (120 mph) in stock form. This sensational performance was provided by an equally sensational engine, a twin overhead camshaft, inline six. Its 3.4 litre (210 cu in.) displacement was smaller than a Chevrolet six, but it developed a hearty 160 horsepower at a high 5000 rpm, the same power as a Cadillac. The XK120 would establish Jaguar in North America, and although plagued for many years with poor assembly quality and spotty reliability,

1950 Jaguar XK120 – stunning styling, outstanding performance

Jaguar would manage to retain its exotic aura as a prestigious "Continental" car.

Station wagons had never achieved great popularity during the 1920s, '30s and '40s, mostly because they were clad with wood which made them expensive to build and maintain. This would change with the introduction of Plymouth's 1949 Suburban all-steel wagon. Although steel station wagons had been introduced earlier, notably by Willys in the Jeep in 1946 and Crosley in 1947, they did not provide passenger car standards of refinement. The Jeep, based on a utility vehicle, couldn't offer the comfort or driving sensation of a family sedan, and the Crosley was just too small to be practical. There had also been the 1935 Chevrolet Suburban Carryall, really a panel truck with windows, but it was more commercial vehicle than passenger car.

It fell to Chrysler Corporation's Plymouth Suburban (and its Dodge counterpart) to take the station wagon into the mainstream. The all-steel wagon quickly supplanted the "woody," and the station wagon would become the *de rigueur* family hauler in rapidly spreading post-war suburbia.

Near the end of the decade Oldsmobile, which had pioneered the fully automatic transmission in 1940, would share with Cadillac in another engineering milestone: the short-stroke, overhead valve, high compression V-8 engine.

Both Cadillac and Oldsmobile introduced their new V-8s for the 1949 model year. Their development had been inspired by the pioneering work on high compression and anti-knock gasoline conducted by GM's brilliant research chief, Charles Kettering. This new type of powerplant would go on to dominate the American industry for 30 years.

In addition to its overhead valve V-8, Cadillac would introduce tailfins to the world. Starting in 1948 as little more than raised taillamps, they became a much imitated styling cue for Cadillac, and would soon be copied by the rest of the industry. During the following decade fins would grow to grotesque heights before fading out in the 1960s.

In Germany the auto industry was struggling to recover from the war. The workers in Germany's car plants that had been damaged by

1948 Cadillac tailfins – a styling fad that swept the industry

Allied bombing were picking through the rubble. Daimler Benz, maker of Mercedes-Benz vehicles, found its factory in such an advanced state of destruction that its board of directors stated that the company "had ceased to exist." In spite of this, they were able to recover enough to begin rebuilding pre-war Mercedes 170V models, and then to begin building new 170V and diesel powered 170Ds. They brought out their first new post-war design 220 and 300 models in 1951. D-B gradually expanded its line, and returned to the preeminent position the company had enjoyed before the war.

Other Germany companies such as Audi and BMW found their car plants in the Russian Zone where they were promptly nationalized by Communist governments. They too managed to get going, however modestly, in the Western zone. BMW still had its motorcycle plant in Munich, and used this as base for getting back into auto production. It survived for a while by building the tiny Isetta Bubble Car.

The giant Volkswagenwerk in Wolfsburg near Hannover, was only 13 kilometres (8 miles) from the East-West border, but at least it was safe. It was badly damaged, although it had still been doing war work until near the end. Following the war it fell under the control of the British, specifically an engineer by the name of Major Ivan Hirst of the Royal Electrical and Mechanical Engineers. Under Hirst's direction the plant was gradually cleaned up and converted to civilian use. It served first as a truck repair depot for REME, but slowly the workers unearthed the Volkswagen tooling. With Major Hirst's help in obtaining needed supplies like coal and steel, they were able to return the Volkswagen Beetle to production, albeit slowly; 1785 VWs were built in 1945. They went to the occupying forces and the German Post Office. Production reached 10,020 in 1946; 8987 in 1947; and 19,244 in 1948, the year the 25,000th VW came off the line.

The British wanted to get rid of the VW plant, to see it up and running on its own. Its ownership was a murky issue that would take years to sort out; it had been built by a pre-war German government that no longer existed. In 1948 the Volkswagenwerk was placed under the general managership of Heinrich "Heinz" Nordhoff, an engineer who had been a pre-war Opel executive, and ironically, an implacable foe of the state sponsored Volkswagen at that time. Nordhoff was a dynamic and inspiring leader, and he took the Volkswagen cause to heart. Under his management Volkswagen grew and prospered. By 1955 the one millionth VW had been produced, and by 1961, the five millionth.

The Japanese auto industry was also struggling to get going after the war. It had been small in the 1930s, devoted mostly to building trucks. Following the war, truck building was again the main priority, but gradually car production was increased. Japan was under the control of the Supreme Commander for the Allied Powers, represented by U.S. General Douglas MacArthur, who was sympathetic to getting Japan back on its feet. In order to get into post-war car production companies resorted to building Japanese versions of such cars as the English Austins and Hillmans, and French Renaults. By 1958 the Japanese were producing cars of their own design.

The 1940s would see the passing of many automotive pioneers. Walter Chrysler, who had risen from roundhouse sweeper to president and chairman of his own company, Chrysler Corporation, died in 1940, as did the famous steam car building twins, Francis and Freelan Stanley. Louis Chevrolet died in 1941.

Henry Ford I, and William Durant, founder of General Motors, both died in 1947. Ford, a wealthy American folk hero, died a bitter old man. Durant was a poor but still enthusiastic bowling alley operator. Charles Nash went in 1948, as did William Knudsen.

The rising interest in cars brought a quest for more information about them. The popular American automotive tester and journalist following the Second World War was Tom McCahill. McCahill began writing road tests and car reports for a do-it-yourself craft magazine called *Mechanix Illustrated*. His first test, of a 1946 Ford, appeared in February, 1946, and Tom would soon build a large following of readers.

While Tom was one of the first, his tests, more anecdotal than scientific, were always laced with outlandish similes and unabashed hyperbole. A more analytical approach was brought to the road test craft by John Bond of *Road & Track*, a magazine launched in New York in 1947, but soon moved to California. Bond was a graduate in mechanical engineering from General Motors Institute in Flint, Michigan. His in-depth engineering analyses and carefully instrumented and authoritative road tests followed the English pattern, and set a standard that would be followed by other serious American automotive magazines.

The 1940s was a decade dominated by the Second World War, the remarkable contribution of the auto industry to the war effort, and its recovery. The American industry had demonstrated that it was truly the "Arsenal of Democracy."

1950 – 1960
OPTIMISM, FINS AND FLAMBOYANCE

The 1950s could be called the golden age of the North American automobile industry. Although the 1950 - 1953 Korean Conflict involved the auto industry, and caused some material shortages, auto production was not interrupted as it had been during the Second World War. With Depression and war-time memories fading, optimism was strong, and there was limited foreign competition. Styling rose to full flower, producing some of the most flamboyant cars ever.

It was a very prosperous period, especially for the Big Three, and even more especially for General Motors which produced almost half the cars sold in North America. It was the world's first corporation to make a profit of a billion dollars. In fact GM was so dominant in the marketplace that its greatest fear wasn't so much the strength of the competition, but the possibility that the U.S. Justice Department might decide that it was a monopoly, and step in and break it up. GM's size and economic influence were alluded to by GM president "Engine Charlie" Wilson (to distinguish him from "Electric Charlie" Wilson, the head of

General Electric) when he said that "We at General Motors have always felt that what was good for the country was good for General Motors as well." His words were often twisted and misquoted, and cited as an example of the consummate arrogance of the world's largest corporation. But Wilson was a plain spoken engineer, and in fact he was just stating the truth; if the country prospered, people bought more new cars.

Under the hoods, overhead valve, short-stroke V-8 engines proliferated. Cadillac and Oldsmobile had showed the way in 1949 with their efficient new V-8s. Chrysler was a little slower, but when its hemispherical combustion chamber "Hemi" V-8 came out in 1951 it was a sensation. Overhead valve V-8s came from Studebaker in 1951, Lincoln in 1952, and Buick and Dodge in 1953. Ford got its overhead valve V-8 in 1954 in the U.S., but Canadians had to wait until the following year.

Chevrolet's legendary "small-block" V-8 was introduced in 1955 in the extremely popular newly styled "Motoramic" Chevrolet, named after GM's annual road show extravaganzas that featured the newest models, as well as their latest "dream cars." The new Chevrolet V-8 set a benchmark for light, powerful, durable engines. Its derivatives survive in some GM vehicles .

The old reciprocating piston engine continued to improve, but there always seemed to be challengers in the wings. Rover in England, Chrysler in America, and several others experimented with gas turbine automobile engines, but they would come to naught. A revival of the steam engine was even tried by some brave souls, but that era was past. The only alternative powerplant that would have a future, albeit a limited one, was the Wankel rotary combustion engine introduced by German inventor Felix Wankel in the late fifties. It would appear in a production car in the 1960s.

After the Second World War the big automobile companies had considered producing lighter cars in addition to their main lines. One of these was the Chevrolet Cadet, whose chief engineer was Earle S. MacPherson. MacPherson was an ingenious engineer, and among the novel features he designed for the Cadet was a front suspension comprised of a shock absorber surrounded by a coil spring, with the anti-roll bar acting as the lower suspension arm. This elegantly simple invention was very effective, while still being economical to produce. It became known as the MacPherson strut.

The Cadet project was cancelled, and MacPherson moved on to Ford. His MacPherson strut made its debut on the new post-war 1951 English Ford Consul/Zephyr models. That strut would become popular beyond MacPherson's wildest dreams. Unfortunately he didn't live to see its almost universal adoption; Earle MacPherson died in 1960, two years after retiring from his position as engineering vice-president of the Ford Motor Company.

General Motors abandoned the light car project when it discovered that the cost of designing and building smaller cars was almost as high as it was for larger ones, as Ford had also discovered in 1936 with its smaller, and stillborn, model 92A. Smaller cars generated lower profits. This left the field open to the independent manufacturers, and imported cars.

But others, such as the visionary Nash president George Mason, and vice-president George Romney, were convinced there was a market for smaller cars. In 1950 Nash revived the Rambler name, one that could be traced back in its history to when it was still the Thomas B. Jeffery Company building Rambler bicycles, and later, Rambler cars. It was the first post-war American compact, an attractive little car with a 2540 mm (100 in.) wheelbase, which was 381 mm (15 in.) shorter than a Chevrolet's. It was powered by the side-valve, 2.8 litre (172.6 cu in.) six cylinder engine from the Nash 600, which provided quite acceptable performance and could achieve 25 to 30 mpg.

1951 Nash Rambler – first post-war compact enjoyed popularity

1951 Henry J – Kaiser-Frazer's answer to the Rambler

In spite of the failure of the tiny American Austin/Bantam in the 1930s, and the imminent demise of the Crosley, Nash still thought there might be a market for an even smaller car. It showed its NX1 prototype in 1950. This would evolve into the Metropolitan, a marriage of English Austin mechanicals and American styling. The Metro was built in England, but wasn't really English or American. Although its lack of a rear seat limited its popularity with families, it enjoyed modest sales, and lasted from 1954 to 1962.

The other independent auto companies followed with their smaller cars. Kaiser-Frazer brought out the Henry J, which the Sears-Roebuck Company also fitted with Sears tires, battery, etc, and sold as the Sears Allstate. Hudson's Jet and Willys-Overland's Aero vied for a place in the compact car market too, but were gone within a few years.

Sports car interest had begun stirring with the arrival of a few English MG TC models in the late 1940s. Sports cars were strictly for fun, offering little in the way of trunk space or weather protection. But they soon caught on with a sporty segment of the market. The TC was followed by the more modern MG TD model in 1950, and sports cars began to build a market niche as more English roadsters such as the Jaguar, Triumph, Jowett, Singer and Austin-Healey began arriving.

American manufacturers responded. Crosley Motors of Cincinnati, Ohio, was first with its tiny 1949 Hotshot. It had such advanced features as an overhead camshaft engine with an over-square design, and the world's first four-wheel disc brakes. Unfortunately these brakes were initially troublesome, and Crosley, lacking the engineering resources to fully develop them, kept discs for only one year. Perhaps the Hotshot's most outstanding feature was a price of under $1000.

Another early American sports car was the attractive Anglo-American hybrid Nash-Healey, created by marrying an English Healey chassis and body to a Nash Ambassador engine and driveline. Kaiser-Frazer joined the sports car movement with its fibreglass bodied Kaiser-Darrin that featured doors that slid into the front fenders. The Nash-Healey and Kaiser-Darrin were priced out of the market, and would soon leave the scene.

In 1950 Briggs Cunningham, a wealthy American sportsman, began a quest to win the classic French LeMans 24-hour endurance race in an American car. American cars had never won at LeMans, the world's most prestigious road race, although in 1928 a Stutz had finished second and a Chrysler third. Cunningham wanted to change that, and in 1950 entered two Cadillacs, one almost stock, and one with a special aerodynamic body. They finished tenth and eleventh, a respectable showing on the first outing. It proved to Cunningham that American components had the durability to compete against the best in the world.

He began to pursue his dream in earnest by setting up a factory in Florida to produce purpose-built Cunningham sports racers. The nucleus of the B. S. Cunningham Company, located in West Palm Beach, was the operation of a couple of speed specialists, Bill Frick and Phil Walters. Walters had raced under the name Ted Tappett, and their Frick-Tappett Motors on Long Island, New York, had made a name for itself installing Cadillac engines in Fords, which they called "Fordillacs," and in Studebakers to create "Studillacs." With Cunningham's money behind them they relocated the business to Florida to begin designing and building the Cunningham.

Cunningham came close but didn't quite realize his dream. Although Cunninghams finished as high as third in 1953 and '54, which were commendable performances against the might of the European factory teams, Briggs Cunningham would never hear the Star Spangled Banner played over his cars at LeMans.

There were also some non-racing Cunninghams. To satisfy the competition authorities that he was an automobile manufacturer, Cunningham produced 27 beautiful road-going C-3 Cunningham coupes styled and built by Vignale in Italy, and powered by Chrysler Hemi V-8s. They are highly prized collectibles today.

The Big Three entered the sports car business with the 1953 Chevrolet Corvette two-seater roadster. To hasten production it was fitted with a fibreglass body, the first in a large-production car. Fibreglass became a Corvette hallmark, and has been retained to this day.

1951 Cunningham sports racer – an American tries to win LeMans

1953 Chevrolet Corvette – the Big Three enters sports car fray

That first Corvette was powered by a Chevrolet "Blue Flame" six cylinder engine modified to increase its horsepower from 115 to 150. In the beginning the only transmission was a two-speed "Powerglide" automatic, much to the dismay of true sports cars aficionados. This deficiency would be rectified when a three-speed manual became available in 1956 models, and even better when a four-speed manual was offered in 1957 models. The Corvette began to carve out a reputation as a genuine sports and competition car with the arrival of a Russian-born engineer named Zora Arkus-Duntov, and the fitting of Chevrolet's new overhead valve V-8 in 1955 cars. Arkus-Duntov later became the Corvette's chief engineer.

Ford answered Chevrolet with its two-seater 1955 Thunderbird which had wind-up windows and a cosier cockpit, compared with the early Corvette's side curtains. Unlike the sportier Corvette, the Thunderbird was more of a cut-down large car than it was a purpose-built sports car. It was aimed at the more luxurious end of the market. Unfortunately for two-seater enthusiasts the Thunderbird would give up any sporting aspirations it may have had by becoming a four-seater in 1958. Ford Division's number crunching general manager Robert McNamara decided that there was more money to be made with a four seater T-Bird, and he was proved correct. But he was never forgiven by two-seater Thunderbird fans.

As the decade proceeded, sales competition intensified and the Big Three gradually became more dominant. It was becoming apparent that the independent automobile manufacturers were getting a smaller piece of the automotive pie; the last great consolidation of the industry was about to take place.

This led to the formation of American Motors Corporation through the amalgamation of Nash and Hudson in 1954. In spite of Hudson's fine history, and the Hudson Hornet's fabulous racing reputation, the Nash cars would predominate after the union. The Hudson and Nash names were continued until 1957, although the Hudsons were just Nashes with Hudson badges, and not very attractive cars at that. They were both replaced by the Rambler when AMC decided that its future lay in smaller cars.

Studebaker and Packard also joined in 1954 to become the Studebaker-Packard Corporation. "Real" Packards would continue to be offered for a couple more years, followed by 1957 and 1958 Packards that were Studebakers with a Packard name, derogatorily called "Packabakers." It was a sad fall from grace for a grand old marque that had once been one of America's leading prestige cars. Packard was dropped from the corporate name in 1962.

Another casualty of the decade was Kaiser-Frazer, the company established in 1945 by construction magnate Henry Kaiser and Graham-Paige Motors president Joseph Frazer. K-F had prospered in the sellers' market for a few years after the Second World War, but when the marketplace turned around and there were lots

1951 Kaiser – lovely styling failed to save Kaiser-Frazer

of cars available, K-F's fortunes began to fade. Its newly styled 1951 Kaiser was a lovely car, and it almost doubled Kaiser sales to 231,000. But its side-valve six cylinder engine was becoming dated and demand soon began to slide. K-F couldn't afford to develop a V-8, so in 1954 it resorted to fitting a McCulloch, belt-driven centrifugal supercharger to boost the six's horsepower from 118 to 140.

In spite of Kaiser acquiring Jeep-maker Willys-Overland in 1953, which it renamed Willys Motors, Kaiser cars left the American scene in 1955. Car production was moved to Argentina.

Crosley production, which began in 1939, finally stopped in 1952, the tiny cars being just too small and under-engineered to flourish.

By 1957 the small raised taillights, soon to be called tailfins, that had first appeared on 1948

Cadillacs, had inspired the Chrysler Corporation's products to sprout fins of gigantic proportions. Not to be outdone, Cadillac mounted fins on its 1959 models that were so high and pointed they became a lasting symbol of that garish period of wretched excess. Others weren't paragons of good taste either. Such cars as Buick and Oldsmobile displayed vast areas of chrome, massive grilles, and sweeping spears. Three-tone paint schemes were common, and the Lincoln grew to over 5867 mm (19 feet) long.

All was not poor taste and too much chrome, however. Such cars as the Studebaker Starlight/ Starliner coupes, which evolved into the Hawk series, and the 1955-57 Chevrolets, were beautiful cars.

A popular item of the era was the wraparound windshield, a styling favourite of GM's styling chief, Harley Earl. He had introduced it on the 1951 Buick LeSabre and XP-300 concept cars, and brought it to production on the 1954 Cadillac. Like his beloved tailfins, it would also turn out to be a fad. They would fade away in the early sixties, but not before enticing many other manufacturers to fit them.

Toward the end of the decade, the traditional popular priced cars, Ford, Chevrolet and Plymouth, began to grow larger and more powerful. In the process they began crowding into the medium priced market, while at the same time creating a gap at the bottom. The increasing size of

1959 Cadillac tailfin – fins reach their apogee, then fade into oblivion

the popular sized cars put pressure on mid-priced cars. This would contribute to the death of the DeSoto, and hasten the demise of the Edsel which arrived in 1958. The Edsel also suffered from controversial styling, which didn't help sales. Its name would forever become associated with failure.

With all of the American compacts gone except the Nash Rambler, and a little later the Studebaker Lark, a market opened up for small, economical imported sedans. They had started to appear in the late forties and early fifties with a trickle of marques such as Austin, Morris and Hillman from England, Renault from France, Fiat from Italy, and Volkswagen and DKW from

1959 Edsel – its name became synonymous with failure

1954 Mercedes-Benz 300SL gullwing coupe – fuel injection for four-stroke gasoline engine

Germany. Volvo and Saab joined a little later from Sweden. There were also myriad other obscure nameplates like Goliath, Deutsch-Bonnet, Lloyd and Wartburg that would take a fling at the North American market, and soon disappear.

One of these little known marques did, however, introduce the world's first fuel injected gasoline automobile, sending a signal that Europe was threatening to pull ahead of America in technology. The German Borgward Group of Bremen began fitting fuel injection to two of its models, the tiny two-stroke Gutbrod and Goliath, in 1950. Some Goliaths were imported into North America. The more significant fuel injection development would come from Daimler-Benz who would pioneer it in four-stroke automobile gasoline engines with its 1954 Mercedes-Benz 300SL Gullwing coupe.

Another unusual automotive species, which came to be known as the Bubble Car, made a brief appearance on the North American scene. Such cars as the BMW Isetta and the Messerschmitt had been developed following the Second World War to satisfy Europe's pressing need for economical personal transportation. These tiny two seaters were a step up from a motorcycle and side-car combination in that they at least offered some weather protection. They would find very limited success in the New World, and would fade out in Europe in the 1960s when "real" cars, such as the Austin/Morris Mini, Fiat 500 and others became available.

The first German Volkswagens were imported into the U.S. in 1949, and to Canada in 1952. This off-beat little beetle-shaped sedan with an air cooled engine in the rear turned out to have a heart of gold. Designed in the 1930s by the Porsche Design Office, its overdrive fourth gear enabled it to cruise easily at 100 km/h (62 mph) on Germany's high-speed autobahn highway system. This made it well suited for North American driving conditions. Backed by excellent service, and some extremely clever, self deprecating advertising, the simple but sturdy Beetle's sales rose quickly. In 1958 100,000 Volkswagens were sold in the U.S., and 28,000 in Canada. By then it was the dominant import.

Another significant straw in the wind was the appearance in the late fifties of a small number of Datsun (now Nissan) and Toyota cars in the California market. Although initially unsuited for North America, the Japanese engineers gradually adapted them to our conditions, and sales were extended across North America.

As the decade wound down it was becoming apparent that in spite of Detroit's love of big cars, there was also a growing market for those that were small, economical and manoeuvrable. After a two year hiatus, American Motors revived the original 2540 mm (100 in.) wheelbase Rambler in 1958, and called it the American. It was an immediate success in a recession year. Studebaker responded with its smaller Lark in 1959.

Since imported cars had nibbled their way up to ten percent of the market in the U.S., and higher in Canada, the Big Three decided to act.

The result was the introduction of the 1960 compacts, the Chevrolet Corvair, Ford Falcon and Chrysler (soon to be Plymouth) Valiant, in late 1959.

In England, a gifted British Motor Corporation engineer by the name of Alec Issigonis created a car that was truly a harbinger of the future. Whereas Dr. Ferdinand Porsche had led much of the industry down the rear engine garden path with his Volkswagen in the 1930s, Issigonis would bring them back with his brilliant Austin/ Morris Mini in the 1960s.

The Mini was a marvel of packaging. In an overall length of just 3048 mm (10 ft) it accommodated four passengers and a reasonable amount of luggage. Issigonis's insight was to place the engine cross-ways in the front of the car, and drive the front wheels. This freed up most of the Mini's diminutive 2032 (80 in.) wheelbase for passenger and trunk space.

It would take the automobile industry several years to recognize the significance of Issigonis's layout. When it did, such cars as the 1973 Honda Civic and 1975 Volkswagen Rabbit (Golf in Europe, and later in North America) legitimized it to the point that it became the most popular method of sending power to the wheels.

The increasing volume and speed of motor vehicles following the Second World War demanded more efficient highway systems. Tentative steps to this end had been taken in the late thirties and early forties, but the war had turned attention from infrastructure to military needs. In 1939 Canada had opened its first controlled-access, multi-lane highway, the Queen Elizabeth Way between Toronto and Niagara Falls. A decade later, in 1949, Canada passed the Trans-Canada Highway Act, designed to produce a first-class, but not limited-access, all-weather highway across the country.

The Trans-Canada Highway Act specified a two-lane, hard surface, coast-to-coast highway with the cost split equally between the federal and provincial governments. An added wrinkle was that the federal government would pay 100 percent of the cost where the road traversed national parks. This led the wily Joey Smallwood, premier of Newfoundland, which had just joined Canada, to ensure that the Trans-Canada passed through the recently created Terra Nova National Park. In spite of a few remaining gaps, the Trans-Canada was declared officially open in 1962.

Ontario had been planning its limited access, multi-lane Highway 400 between Toronto and Barrie since 1945. It was completed in 1952, and Ontario's 400-series highways would eventually stretch from the Quebec border to Windsor, with several spurs to other centres. It would even ultimately include, in Highway 407, the world's first electronic toll collection system, which was privately owned, and opened in 1998.

The United States opened its first modern limited-access, multi-lane toll highway, the Pennsylvania Turnpike, in 1940. It stretched from near Pittsburgh on the west, almost to Harrisburg on the east. It utilized an unused railway right-of-way, and passed through seven tunnels under the Allegheny Mountains.

The PA Turnpike would become part of America's mighty 68,800 km (43,000 mi.) Interstate, controlled-access, multi-lane highway system that makes it possible to drive from Sault Ste Marie, Michigan, to Miami, Florida, or New York, New York, to Los Angeles, California, without encountering a stoplight. The Interstate system, which has been called the world's largest single civil engineering project, was the result of the Federal-Aid Highway Act signed by President Dwight Eisenhower in 1956.

This Act authorized the construction of a 66,000 km (41,000 mi.) highway network, officially named the National System of Interstate and Defense Highways. It was to be completed by all states by 1972, but with delays and additions, it was just reaching completion by the end of the century. It's difficult to imagine North America today without its controlled-access, multi-lane highway system.

Controlled-access, multi-lane highways were not, of course, limited to North America. Several European countries had fine high-speed road systems. France had long been famous for its excellent highways. In the 1930s the Hitler government in Germany had constructed its outstanding limited access Autobahn highway network, although Chancellor Hitler's agenda was far more sinister than just accommodating motorists and commerce. The Autobahns were used to speed armaments quickly to the German borders during the Second World War.

Improved standards of living following the Second World War led to more travel for both business and pleasure. And since flying was still expensive, and trains were in decline, the family car became the overwhelmingly popular method of travel. This dovetailed perfectly with the construction of the Interstate highway system.

Those travellers required accommodation beyond the basic 1930s-type road-side tourist cabins with names like "Bide-A-Wee" and "Dew-Drop-Inn," or the sometimes seedy, and often expensive central city hotels. To satisfy this need a more convenient type of accommodation emerged. It was known as the motel, and it was located beside the highways, offering easy entry and exit to accommodate travellers in a hurry.

The motel idea was not new. In the twenties a man named Arthur Heineman had such a vision, and in 1925 he constructed his pioneering Milestone Motel in the town of San Luis Obispo, California. Heineman envisaged a chain of these motels, but before he could realize his dream the Depression, and then the war, intervened.

Motels started to become popular following the Second World War, but their quality was spotty, often leading travellers to request to view the rooms before committing themselves. A man named Kemmons Wilson became irritated by the lack of motel quality standards, and the fact that he had to pay extra for his children. Wilson, a home building contractor in Memphis, Tennessee, concluded that there was a need for a franchised chain of clean, good quality, motels with reasonable prices. And he vowed that kids would stay free, and that the motel would include a family restaurant.

Wilson constructed his first Holiday Inn, which he named after a 1942 movie, in 1952. Located between Memphis and Nashville, it was as successful as Wilson expected it would be. Tourists and business travellers alike welcomed the reasonable rates, the convenience of parking their cars near their rooms, the adjacent dining facilities, and best of all, that kids stayed free. Wilson began offering Holiday Inn franchises to other entrepreneurs, and within a few years the Holiday Inn's tall, distinctive neon signs were dotting the Interstates, always at interchanges, and other main highways across the United States and Canada. The chain motel business had been launched.

The Interstate highway system and high speed automobile travel wasn't kind to merchants located along old established routes. One of these businesses was the Sanders Court and Cafe in

Corbin, Kentucky, operated by a man named Colonel Harland Sanders. Sanders was not a war veteran; Colonel was an honourary title conferred by the State of Kentucky for his outstanding contribution to the food service industry.

The Sanders Court and Cafe was located on U.S. route 25, a well travelled road between the Midwest and Florida. Sanders came to specialize in breaded fried chicken cooked with his own secret recipe containing "11 herbs and spices." He fried the chicken in a special pressure cooker that reduced the cooking time from 30 minutes to nine. The cafe became so famous for its "Finger Lickin' Good" Kentucky fried chicken that it was recommended by Duncan Hines's *Adventures in Good Eating*.

Then disaster struck Colonel Sanders's business with the announcement in 1956 that Interstate highway 75 would be passing within two miles of Corbin. With most of the highway 25 business expected to be bled off by the Interstate, the value of his restaurant and motel plummeted. At age 66 most men would have given up and retreated into retirement to live on their social security, but not Sanders. He auctioned off the business, receiving barely enough to cover outstanding debts. He had been franchising his 11 herbs and spices recipe and special cooking method with modest success. Now, with his restaurant business gone, he decided to try in earnest to market his recipe and process.

Colonel Sanders's Cafe – birthplace of Kentucky Fried Chicken

Colonel Sanders and his wife loaded their car with seasonings, cookers and his carefully guarded recipe and hit the road to peddle franchises. By 1964 there were more than 600 establishments selling Kentucky fried chicken. By turning adversity into success Sanders became a wealthy man. He sold the Kentucky Fried Chicken operation, and it has subsequently gone through several owners. It went on to become one of the most successful fast food franchises ever, with many of them located along the Interstate system. Travellers can visit the Colonel Sanders museum housed in the Colonel's restored restaurant in Corbin, Kentucky, just off I-75.

Another fast food chain called McDonalds

came to prominence in the 1950s, thanks to easy automobile travel and the increasing desire for quick service, and even for people to eat in their cars. Not surprisingly it began in car crazy California. Maurice and Dick McDonald opened a drive-in restaurant in San Bernardino in 1940. They evolved into specializing in hamburgers, milkshakes and french fries, and gradually learned how to streamline and speed up the preparation process. They made each hamburger patty exactly the same size, and standardized everything, right down to the amount of ketchup and onion. They used single service containers to eliminate dish washing. Through a process of trial and error the McDonald brothers had developed their operation into a highly efficient fast food service, one so successful that it was serving a customer every 15 seconds. The drive-in fast food restaurant and California were a perfect match.

The McDonalds ventured timidly into franchising, but their hearts weren't in it and they sold less than a dozen. Then in 1954 an ambitious go-getter named Ray Kroc from Chicago, who sold milkshake mixers called "Multimixers," came on the scene. At a time when sales of his mixers were flagging, he noted that this McDonalds restaurant out in California was ordering more and more of them. With his usual nose for business, Kroc made a visit to McDonalds in San Bernardino. He stayed for an afternoon and saw his future. Kroc convinced the McDonalds to make him their franchise salesman. He opened his first franchise in 1955 and eventually bought the McDonald brothers out. Through hard work, thrift and strict adherence to standardization, cleanliness and good service, Kroc nurtured McDonalds hamburgers into an international fast food success story.

Kroc insisted in locating his McDonalds near the suburbs because it was filled with the young families that he wanted to attract. Suburbia was largely a product of the post-Second World War when returning service men and women were starting families and looking for pleasant affordable housing. The car made the suburbs possible because public transit there was either thin or non-existent.

It was a condition made to order for Bill Levitt, a New York home builder. He had recognized that the future growth pattern of North American cities would be to suburbia, and he had figured out a way to standardize home building, just as Henry Ford had standardized Model Ts and McDonalds had streamlined the hamburger. He obtained 1000 acres of farmland in Hempstead, on New York's Long Island. By carefully scheduling construction methods, pre-assembling components, moving specialized teams of workers from house to house, and eliminating basements, Levitt was building 36 houses a day by 1949. Levittown became the largest suburb in America.

The same thing was happening elsewhere, always driven by the automobile. Just west of

Toronto, beside the Queen Elizabeth Way in the Township of Toronto, now the City of Mississauga, a builder named Gordon Shipp assembled large parcels of land north and south of the QEW. The Applewood Acres subdivisions constructed by G.S.Shipp and Son in the late 1940s and fifties were representative of the new Canadian suburbia. They were like little towns complete with schools, churches and shopping.

As the decade closed it was more than ever apparent how significantly the automobile had altered the landscape. And an American automobile industry that had entered the 1950s with a sellers' market and unbounded optimism now began to face changing conditions. With imports on the rise it no longer enjoyed the monopoly that it had at the start of the fifties. Also, environmental and safety concerns would soon emerge. The next decade would see them flourish to the point where they would bring the government into the boardrooms of the automakers.

1960 – 1970
COMPACTS, MUSCLE CARS, PONY CARS, SAFETY AND EMISSIONS

The fifties were a period of free-wheeling optimism, garishness and little competition for the North American auto industry; the sixties would see that begin to change. The decade started with the beginning of the breakdown of the automobile hierarchy that had been so carefully crafted in the 1920s by GM's legendary president/ chairman, Alfred P. Sloan, Jr. It witnessed the creation of several specialty car segments in the marketplace. And it saw, rather belatedly, rising concerns over automobile safety and emissions, which led to safety and pollution control legislation. This would cause an unprecedented government incursion into the boardrooms of the car companies, and change the automobile and the industry forever.

With the introduction of its import-fighting compacts from the Big Three, the 1960 Chevrolet Corvair, Ford Falcon and Chrysler Valiant (which became the Plymouth Valiant in 1961), the industry began moving away from the traditional market positioning of cars that had evolved over the years.

In the fifties such cars as Chevrolets, Fords,

Buicks, Dodges, Cadillacs, Chryslers, Lincolns and Plymouths had their respective places in the automotive pyramid. Each conferred its own status and prestige, and the measure of a neighbourhood could be taken by driving through and noting the kinds of cars parked outside the homes.

In the 1950s the Big Three had been content to leave compact cars as the preserve of the so-called independents. Nash/American Motors had its Rambler, Studebaker its Lark, Kaiser-Frazer its Henry J, Hudson its Jet, and Willys-Overland its Aero. There were also a few imports, but they were not present in threatening numbers until near the end of the decade.

But those rising import sales would change this orderly and established market. When foreign car sales, led by an unorthodox rear engined car from Germany called the Volkswagen, whose success was a mystery to Detroit, began approaching 10 percent of the market in the late fifties, the Big Three responded with their compact cars. Their mission was to "drive the imports back to their shores." And they were successful in reducing import penetration for a few years.

But these compacts became afflicted with "Detroititis," growing gradually larger, more powerful and less fuel efficient. This allowed the imports to again move in to fill this gap, and by the end of the 1960s they would be back up to over a million annual North American sales. They were led by the Volkswagen, making the sixties its golden decade.

When the Big Three's compacts arrived they were quite different from one another. The Falcon was a conventional shrunken large car with traditional front engine/rear drive, plain styling, and a prosaic overhead valve, inline six cylinder engine. It was like a modern Model A Ford, and the true incarnation of the mindset of Robert McNamara, Ford Division's general manager, later Ford Motor Company's president, and still later the Secretary of Defence in the Kennedy and Johnson administrations. He was undoubtedly brilliant, but he was also truly conservative and bottom line oriented. He would have been just as effective and happy selling refrigerators or cereal, and the Falcon exemplified his philosophy of a no nonsense, efficient, cheap-to-build car.

The Valiant was a little more daring both in appearance and engineering. Its "European" styling featured an eggcrate grille, sculpted sides, and a fake spare tire moulded into the deck lid. It was powered by Chrysler's new "slant six" engine that would prove to be a robust corporate work-

1960 Ford Falcon – Ford joins the compact wars

horse for many years. Front suspension was by torsion bars, an unusual and somewhat exotic feature for American cars.

Chevrolet's Corvair was the most daring. Chevrolet's brilliant, hard driving general manager Edward Cole, a future General Motors president, came up with an "American Volkswagen." Its horizontally-opposed (flat), overhead valve, six cylinder engine was located behind the rear axle, just like the Volkswagen's four. Undeterred by the ghost of GM's disastrous experience with its 1923 air cooled Chevrolets, all of which had to be recalled, Cole gave the Corvair an air cooled engine. And the Corvair, like the VW, had four wheel independent suspension, although with coil springs rather than the VW's torsion bars.

When the Corvair fell behind the Falcon in sales, Chevrolet launched a sporty coupe version

1960 Chevrolet Corvair – GM's unorthodox star-crossed compact

called the Monza, and sales took off. And in 1962, along with Oldsmobile, the Corvair pioneered turbocharging in production cars, almost doubling its horsepower in the process. General Motors would keep turbocharging for a few years, but in a period of low cost gasoline it was easier and cheaper to obtain more power by just building a bigger engine. Thus the increased efficiency of turbocharging, although popular in racing circles and on trucks, was abandoned in production cars until it was resurrected by Porsche and Saab in the 1970s. GM would come back to it in 1978.

The compacts inspired others to begin producing "mid-sized," or "intermediate" models. In 1961 Oldsmobile brought out its F-85, Pontiac its Tempest, and Buick its Special, all mid-sized, and based on the same platform, although with different drivelines, such as the Tempest's "hanging rope" driveshaft. The Buick Special introduced America's first production car V-6 in 1962, although GMC had introduced a truck V-6 in 1960. The Buick V-6 was refined over the years until, like the 1955 Chevrolet small-block V-8, it would truly assume the mantle of venerability. At the end of the century this mundane pushrod, iron-block, 12-valve V-6 would still be found powering GM's family cars, quietly soldering on in a sea of overhead cam, alloy engines with four-valve cylinders, variable valve timing and other advanced technology.

Ford responded to GM's intermediate car challenge with its 1962 mid-size Ford Fairlane and Mercury Comet. The Fairlane would introduce Ford's answer to the Chevy small-block V-8. The Fairlane's V-8 featured thin-wall construction which produced a light, compact engine, and it became a Ford staple in various displacements for several decades.

The arrival of the compacts and intermediates was the beginning of a proliferation that would see almost all marques striving to be all things to all buyers. The ultimate absurdity would be reached in 1982 when GM's five divisions all offered versions of the new front-wheel drive "J-Cars," from the Chevrolet Cavalier to the Cadillac Cimarron.

Into this sixties mix came two new classes of cars in 1964: the Pony Car and the Muscle Car.

The Pony Car was spawned by the Ford Mustang that was introduced in April, 1964, as an early '65 model. By using the inexpensive driveline and underpinnings from the Falcon and Fairlane, and draping them in a stylish long-nose, short-deck body, a new sporty type of car was developed. The Mustang came in coupe and convertible forms (a fastback soon followed), and could accommodate two adults, plus two children in a small back seat, which enhanced its appeal for families.

The availability of a wide range of options kept the Mustang's base price under $2400, while allowing buyers with sporting pretension to add items like V-8 engines and four-speed manual transmissions.

The Mustang was an instant success, with sales of more than 264,000 by the end of 1964. In the process it made Ford's general manager Lido (Lee) Iacocca into a household name, getting his picture on the covers of both *Time* and *Newsweek*. This would ultimately be both good and bad for Iacocca. The good was that it stroked his huge ego and consolidated his reputation as a shrewd "car guy." Unfortunately for Iacocca, the bad was that the fawning media coverage would put him on a collision course with Ford chairman Henry Ford II. It would finally reach its denouement in 1978 with Ford's firing of Iacocca.

Mustang sales continued so strong that, in addition to its Dearborn factory, Ford had to convert two other plants to Mustang production to

1965 Ford Mustang – Ford Pony Car scoops the industry

meet the demand. Ford had the Pony Car market to itself until Chevrolet unveiled the 1967 Camaro. This was followed by others such as the Pontiac Firebird and AMC Javelin.

The other trend setting car that arrived in 1964 was the Pontiac GTO. By making a large V-8 engine available in the light intermediate Tempest body, and calling it the GTO option, Pontiac's general manager Elliott "Pete" Estes, and chief engineer John DeLorean, created a car for a youth market craving high performance at a reasonable price. It was soon dubbed the Muscle Car.

Others soon followed the GTO in the Muscle Car craze with such models as the Chevrolet Chevelle SS-396, Ford Fairlane GT, Mercury Cyclone GT and Oldsmobile 4-4-2. It culminated in the audacious high-winged 1969-70 Dodge Charger Daytona and Plymouth Superbird, which

1964 Pontiac GTO – starts Muscle Car craze of the '60s

1963 Studebaker Avanti – futuristic styling can't save Studebaker

were really just National Association for Stock Car Auto Racing racers made available to the public in limited numbers. Chrysler had to build enough to make them qualify as "stock" cars. Muscle Cars died in the early 1970s, killed by galloping insurance rates and rising safety concerns.

By the early sixties the venerable old Studebaker Corporation of South Bend, Indiana, was on the financial ropes. In spite of the lovely Hawk series and the futuristic fibreglass-bodied Avanti, intense competition and falling sales forced Studebaker to close its South Bend operation in 1964.

Studebaker production was then concentrated in its Hamilton, Ontario, facility until it ceased in 1966. This left American Motors Corporation (formed through the amalgamation of Nash and Hudson in 1954) as the only surviving non-Big Three car builder.

While Muscle Cars and Pony Cars had arrived in 1964, something different and entirely unexpected occurred the following year. That's when the auto industry was rocked by the publication of a book by a young Washington, D.C. lawyer and consumer advocate named Ralph Nader. In *Unsafe At Any Speed*, Nader launched a withering assault on the American automobile industry. The first chapter singled out the Chevrolet Corvair for a particularly scathing attack.

Nader alleged that the rear swing axles used on the 1960 to 1964 Corvair made the car dangerously unstable, and prone to rollover due to rear wheel "tuck-under" while cornering. He cited several examples of horrible Corvair accidents said to be caused by this design. Although GM had rectified the situation with fully articulated rear axles in the 1965 Corvairs, it was soon flooded with lawsuits regarding those early Corvairs. Sales went into immediate decline, although in the face of the falling demand GM would bravely carry the Corvair on until 1969.

But Nader didn't stop there. He went on to charge the industry with knowingly condoning unsafe cars, in effect killing its own customers to save money and avoid criticism. He cited the new power assisted brakes on the 1953 Buick Roadmaster. The power assist was provided by engine vacuum, and the brakes had a nasty habit of sucking the hydraulic brake fluid into the engine through a faulty O-ring, where the fluid was silently burned. Unknown to the driver the car gradually became a brakeless rolling time bomb.

Nader wrote that General Motors did not make a public announcement about this, or recall the Buicks, but instead quietly asked dealers to repair the problem when the cars came into the shop for service. In fact the problem was brought into sharp focus when such a brakeless Buick was brought to the Lawless Buick dealership in Ferndale, Michigan. As it was being driven into the shop by the assistant service manager Clifford Wentworth the brakeless car hit a mechanic, crushing his leg. In the ensuing lawsuit against Wentworth and General Motors the whole unfortunate episode of the failing brakes became part of the public record in the Wayne County Circuit Court, which Nader chronicled in his book.

Other areas addressed by Nader were automobile air pollution, expensive styling excesses that added nothing to utility, and the whole traffic safety administration. It was a wide ranging condemnation of the automotive establishment, and although widely ridiculed and disparaged by the car companies and the auto enthusiast press, known as "buff books," Nader's book rang alarm bells in Washington.

Unsafe At Any Speed was a seminal book. It did for the auto industry what Upton Sinclair's 1906 book *The Jungle* did to clean up the meatpacking industry, and Rachel Carson's *Silent Spring* of the 1960s did to raise the awareness of the dangers of pesticides. *Unsafe* resulted in a cascade of safety legislation that led to the much safer cars we have today.

Unsafe also added impetus to a pollution control movement already stirring in California, the bellwether of new trends. In the 1950s a prescient California Institute of Technology scientist named Dr. A.J. Haagen-Smit had described smog (a combination of smoke and fog), and named its three most prevalent constituents: carbon monoxide, nitrogen oxide, and hydrocarbons.

The automobile was a large emitter of these pollutants, and the geography of the Los Angeles basin, with mountains to the east and a prevailing west wind, made smog accumulation particularly acute. With its high automobile concentration and this unusual geography, California was forced to become a leader in emission controls. New American and Canadian nation-wide emission laws would build on initiatives taken in California.

Nineteen-sixty-five was also the year in which the Canadian and American governments enacted the Automobile Products Trade Act, commonly known as the Auto Pact. Under this Act the auto companies, in return for virtually free trade, i.e., elimination of tariffs in automobile and parts between the two countries, agreed to make Canadian production at least equal to Canadian sales.

The result was that the companies were able to gain efficiency by rationalizing production among all of their Canadian and American plants. It made the North American automobile industry much more closely integrated. The Auto Pact would be judged to be illegal by the World Trade Organization in 1999, and was eliminated in 2000.

On the other side of the world, a famous motorcycle manufacturer named Soichiro Honda decided to expand into automobiles. Honda's first car, the S500, bowed in 1962 as a tiny, two-seater sports car whose mechanicals, right down to the chain drive, were clearly based on motorcycle technology. It was an ingenious design, but too small and specialized to command much of a market.

From this start Honda moved on to a small front-wheel drive sedan in 1966, but it was also too small and underpowered to sell well in North America. Gradually Hondas evolved into the outstanding 1973 Civic. The Honda name was already well known in North America for light, easy-to-ride motorcycles, and for vastly improving the public image of motorcycling. They were promoted by some clever advertising such as: "You meet the nicest people on a Honda."

In 1963 Germany's NSU introduced the first genuine challenger to the traditional reciprocating piston engine with its Wankel rotary powered NSU Sport Prinz Spider. It was the world's first rotary powered production car. In 1968 NSU would bring out the NSU Ro80, a large, very advanced sedan powered by a two-rotor Wankel.

The rotary combustion engine showed promise, and such companies as Daimler-Benz and General Motors bought licences to manufacturer it. But the rotary had some initial problems such as rotor sealing difficulties, and some disadvantages vis-a-vis the reciprocating piston engine. Its exhaust tended to be dirtier, and its fuel economy was poorer for a given displacement, although not for a given power. These were difficult to overcome, and all except Japan's Toyo Kogyo Company, manufacturer of Mazda cars, would abandon the Wankel. Mazda gradually made the rotary a viable alternative to the piston engine, thanks to a brilliant and determined Mazda engineer by the name of Kenichi Yamamoto who persisted until he overcame the rotary's problems.

Another type of engine that was being pur-

1963 Chrysler Turbine Car – fails to displace piston engine

sued for the automobile was the turbine which was in the process of dominating aviation. Many companies had been working on turbine engines for cars for several years, including General Motors, Fiat and Ford, but the two that had been most aggressive were Rover of England and the Chrysler Corporation. Rover tested a very high performance turbine car in 1950, and followed it with several later generations, but none was brought to market.

Chrysler showed its first turbine powered car, a Plymouth, in 1954. Its turbine also went through several iterations, and by 1964 Chrysler felt confident enough to allow turbine cars to be tested by the public. Fifty Chrysler prototype turbine cars were loaned to 203 drivers randomly chosen from the general public. They covered 1.7 million kilometres (1.1 million miles) from 1964 to 1966, and their comments were generally

favourable. They particularly liked the smoothness of the turbine engine.

Chrysler would continue experimenting with the automobile turbine until 1980, by which time the company was more concerned with surviving than with bringing out a new type of engine. The turbine was up against a well entrenched and constantly improving piston engine that was a formidable moving target.

America also returned to front-wheel drive after the disappearance of the Cord almost 30 years earlier. The 1966 Oldsmobile Toronado packaged a huge V-8 engine and an automatic transaxle under its long hood, and eliminated the transmission hump, thereby offering full six-passenger seating. It was followed by the front-drive Cadillac Eldorado in 1967. These would provide GM with the front-wheel drive experience and confidence to proceed with its 1980 front-drive X-Cars (Chevrolet Citation et al.), and its eventual switch to front-wheel drive in virtually all of its cars.

While the 1960s had been generally good for the North American automobile industry, the earth had begun to shift as emissions and safety concerns started to surface, and import sales recovered. But the changes were not yet alarming, and the sixties could be called the last really prosperous decade for the North American industry. But if it thought it had faced some difficulties in the sixties, they would prove to be only a prelude for what was to follow.

1970–1980
OIL CRISES, EMISSIONS, FUEL ECONOMY AND DOWNSIZING

After two good decades, the 1970s were turbulent times for the American automobile industry. It was the dawning of a new uncertain world in which the industry would come under increased pressure on several fronts: from the government for improved fuel economy and safety, and decreased emissions; from rising foreign competition; from a concerned consumer movement; and from two oil crises that swung the public's buying mood back and forth between big cars and small ones. The flash and fins of the 1950s, and the fun and performance of Muscle Cars and Pony Cars of the 1960s, gave way to a much more serious tenor in the 1970s.

Tightening emission standards prompted a variety of technical responses, including leaner burning engines, retarded ignition timing, air injection pumps, and exhaust gas recirculation. In the struggle to produce cleaner exhausts, performance suffered. Engines coughed and stalled, bringing a new word, "drivability," into our vocabulary.

The most promising solution to exhaust emissions reduction was the catalytic converter, developed by General Motors and brought to market in the mid-1970s. It was a small muffler-shaped, stainless steel canister inserted into the exhaust system, and had as its active ingredients the precious metals platinum, palladium and rhodium. These were coated onto a ceramic honeycomb mesh, and acted as catalysts to facilitate the process of cleansing the exhaust, but were not consumed by it. Through chemical reactions the pollutants were almost completely changed into carbon dioxide (what we expel when we exhale) and water. Some sulphur was produced, which gives the characteristic "rotten egg" smell when the car was first started.

The catalytic converter became the main contributor to an amazing reduction in gasoline automobile exhaust pollutants that by the late 1990s would see hydrocarbons lowered by 97 percent, carbon monoxide by 96 percent, and oxides of nitrogen by 95 percent, compared with uncontrolled 1960s levels. In addition to lowering pollution, a bonus was that the "cat" allowed the engine to be tuned for better fuel economy. But the cat could not tolerate leaded gasoline, and in preparation for the converter's arrival, oil companies had to begin phasing tetraethyl lead out of gasoline in the early seventies. In addition to saving the converter, the removal of lead lengthened spark plug life considerably.

Tetraethyl lead had been considered a breakthrough when it was first added to gasoline in the mid-twenties to raise octane and reduce the engine knock caused by some of the fuel exploding in the combustion chamber, rather than burning at a progressive rate. It allowed higher compression ratios, which gave added power and improved fuel economy. With the lead being taken out, car manufacturers began lowering compression ratios in 1971, which added to the degradation in power and economy that the emissions hardware was already causing.

Removing the lead, plus the change in 1972 from quoting engine output as Society of Automotive Engineers *gross* horsepower (measured in the lab), rather than SAE *net* horsepower (measured installed in the car), brought a drop not only in real, but in quoted power ratings. The Chevrolet 5.7 litre V-8, for example, was rated at 250 horsepower in 1970; by 1972 it was down to 165.

In addition to these technical challenges, American manufacturers again faced import sales that had rebounded from the impact of the Big Three's 1960 compacts. The American industry's

second major response was another round of small cars for 1971, this time called sub-compacts. GM's was the Chevrolet Vega and Ford's was the Pinto. American Motors, by using the expedient of lopping the back end off its compact Hornet, was able to be a little quicker off the mark with its Gremlin, launched in 1970-1/2.

Chevrolet would again be more daring than the rest with the Vega, although not as radical as it had been with the Corvair. The Vega, originally intended to be powered by a Wankel rotary combustion engine, ended up with an overhead camshaft, four cylinder aluminum block engine with the pistons running directly on the aluminum. The engine was noisy and the block was sensitive to overheating, and prone to early bore wear, which hurt the Vega's reputation.

Ford stayed with a more conventional approach as it had with the Falcon. The Pinto's well proved English overhead valve four from the Ford Cortina and Capri had a cast iron block. The Pinto would, however, suffer its own disaster beginning in 1972 when it was discovered that rear end collisions could cause it to burst into flames. This was apparently because the fuel tank was too close to the rear bumper, and was not sufficiently protected. Ford was deluged with lawsuits, which were often successful. Although the problem was subsequently rectified, Ford suffered serious public humiliation.

Chrysler chose to fight the imports with its

1977 Ford Pinto – Detroit's second attempt to stem import tide

own "captive imports," cars brought in from Mitsubishi in Japan, and its European arms.

Late in 1973 North America suffered the first of the decade's two "oil crises" when the Arabs, furious at the United States for supporting Israel in the Yom Kippur war, launched an oil embargo. Suddenly the precious gasoline supply was threatened. The price shot up, and there were lineups at gasoline stations, particularly in the United States. Economical cars became sought after overnight, and small American and imported car sales flourished.

The oil scare brought into sharp focus the West's heavy dependence on oil from a volatile and unstable Middle East. In an attempt to reduce this dependency the United States government enacted legislation that imposed a Corporate Average Fuel Economy (CAFE) gasoline mileage standard on car manufacturers. It required a sales weighted fleet average of 18 mpg (U.S.) in 1978, rising to 27.5 mpg in 1985. The Canadian government didn't pass similar legislation, based on a promise from the manufacturers that they would meet the same standards in Canada.

Aware that cars were getting too big and thirsty, General Motors took the courageous step of "downsizing" its full line of large passenger cars, which would be marketed as 1977 models. The Chevrolet Impala/Caprice Classic was typical of the new smaller size. Its weight fell from 1950 kg (4300 lb) to 1656 kg (3650 lb), and overall length was reduced by 279 mm (11 in.) to 5387 mm (212.1 in.).

GM also began converting its 5.7 litre Oldsmobile V-8 gasoline engine to a diesel. This became optional on the 1978 Oldsmobile, and soon in the rest of the GM large car line. Unfortunately for General Motors their diesel would turn out to be a mixed blessing. Although it was 30 to 40 percent more fuel efficient than a comparable gasoline engine, it proved troublesome in service. In spite of this, in the quest for better fuel economy diesel engines gradually became available from many manufacturers, and would reach their peak in 1985 with 15 makes offering them in North American.

In 1972 Volkswagen passed a milestone when the 15,007,034th Beetle was built, surpassing the 1908-1927 production record for a single car model held by the Model T Ford. In what could

1978 Chevrolet Caprice Classic – "downsizing" from Detroit

1972 Datsun 510 – "poor man's BMW" helps consolidate Japanese in North America

be called a replay of the Ford Model T, which stubborn old Henry Ford stayed with for too long, the Beetle was also becoming obsolete. By the mid-seventies its sales would be overtaken by the rapidly rising Japanese with such well built and economical cars as the Honda Civic, Datsun 510, and Toyota Corolla.

Honda, only 11 years after building its first car, launched its Civic in 1973. While its transverse engine in the front, driving the front wheels, was thematically related to the 1959 Austin/Morris Mini, it was more advanced both technically and in its quality and amenities. Its overhead camshaft alloy four cylinder engine was smooth and economical, and provided very acceptable performance. It was light and nimble to drive. And by a stroke of luck for Honda, its arrival coincided with the first oil crisis. While Detroit sneered at the Civic's tiny size, consumers snapped them up.

The Civic would also prove that Japanese engineering prowess was now equal to the best in the world. In 1972 Honda announced that it would be introducing a new emission control system that would meet 1975 Japanese and American emission standards without the use of a catalytic converter. This was called CVCC, for Compound Vortex Controlled Combustion. The heart of CVCC was a stratified-charge combustion process achieved by using a third small intake valve to admit a rich air-fuel mixture into a compact auxiliary combustion chamber. Once this rich mixture was ignited it flowed into the main chamber where it lit off a lean mixture.

The Civic CVCC was introduced to North America as a 1975 model, and it did meet the emissions standards without a converter. When

1973 Honda Civic – Honda comes of age in automobile market

1980 Honda Accord – the new compact benchmark

Detroit's engineers opined that this system would work on a small four cylinder engine, but not on a big American V-8, Honda quietly fitted a 5.7 litre Chevrolet V-8 with the CVCC system, and it also met the 1975 standards without a converter. Needless to say, there were some red faces around Detroit. But as good as the CVCC idea was, tightening emission standards would eventually force Honda to resort to the use of a catalytic converter.

The Civic would prove to be only the first of Honda's one-two punch. To prove how fast it, and indeed the Japanese industry, was advancing in the automotive arts, Honda followed the Civic with its jewel-like Accord in 1976. It was a larger evolution of the Civic, and it proved to be a world class car.

The first Accords were two-door hatchbacks,

but in 1978 it expanded its market appeal with a little limousine-like four-door sedan. Here was a small car with the luxury and driving characteristics of a large one. Its slick five-speed manual transmission, high tech overhead camshaft aluminum engine, and ergonomically excellent interior made the Accord a revelation to North American drivers. It offered virtually everything that bigger cars did, but with much better fuel economy and crisper handling. It quickly became the small car benchmark for other manufactures to emulate.

The aging Volkswagen Beetle was finally replaced in 1975 by the new front-wheel drive Rabbit (Golf in Europe), although the Beetle-based Cabriolet would continue being built until 1980. Volkswagen became the first modern foreign manufacturer to establish a U.S. assembly plant when it started Rabbit production in an ex-Chrysler factory in New Stanton, Pennsylvania, in 1978. It had considered an American plant as far back as the 1950s, to be located in New Jersey, but had abandoned the idea.

Importers had been earlier in establishing plants in Canada. Sweden's Volvo, for example, began assembling cars in Dartmouth, Nova Scotia in 1963. It moved across to Halifax in 1965. Peugeots, Renaults, Toyotas and Datsuns were also assembled in eastern Canada in small numbers in the sixties and early seventies. These plants would prove uneconomic, however, and most would soon cease operation. Volvo lasted the longest, but announced in 1998 that it was closing its Halifax operation.

The Rabbit's creased-and-folded style, and cross-engine, front-drive, hatchback configuration, became a kind of benchmark for other sub-compacts. Ford had its European arm design a new Rabbit clone called the Fiesta, and Chrysler Corporation produced its Dodge Omni and Plymouth Horizon Rabbit lookalikes, the first small American cars with front-wheel drive. The Omni/Horizon even used a Volkswagen engine until its own 2.2 litre four cylinder K-Car engine became available. The Omni/Horizon and Fiesta arrived for 1978.

The quest for economy had also led GM to reach into its international parts bin and produce the sub-compact, rear-drive 1976 Chevrolet Chevette. Although not very exciting, it was serviceable, economical and reliable, and would be built until 1986.

While this activity was taking place to down-size large cars and produce small ones, the market was changing. The oil crisis gradually became an unpleasant memory. Motorists adjusted to higher priced fuel, and the demand for economy began to weaken.

The public was buying big cars again, and manufacturers were facing extreme difficulty meeting their CAFE requirements, some having to resort to rationing V-8 engines. And all of the research and emission control technology applied in the quest for economy and cleaner exhaust had to be paid for. Thus, another new term, "sticker shock," entered our vocabulary as motorists were jolted by the high prices they encountered in the showrooms.

Although manufacturers were using fewer V-8 engines, the public still expected them to maintain V-8 performance. This led General Motors to return to turbocharging, which it had pioneered in its Chevrolet Corvair and Oldsmobile F-85 in 1962, and used until 1966. Turbocharging had then languished in cars until Porsche brought it back in 1975, followed by Saab in 1976. For 1978 Buick fitted a turbocharger to its old standby V-6 engine, which did indeed give it eight cylinder performance with six cylinder economy.

The fierce competition and barriers to entry into the automobile industry still didn't deter some would-be auto moguls from trying to shoulder their way in. One of these was John DeLorean, a seasoned automotive engineer who had risen through the General Motors hierarchy to the point where the presidency was in sight. Then in 1973 he resigned his $650,000 job because his personal philosophy and behaviour had become incompatible with GM's conservative ethos.

DeLorean established the DeLorean Motor Company to produce what he called his "ethical car." He convinced a British government desperate to create jobs in Northern Ireland to fund a new car plant in Belfast. The two-seater, rear engined, stainless steel clad, gull-wing doored DeLorean coupe would start rolling off the assembly line in January 1981. But there were rumours of questionable business practices, and DeLorean kept asking the British for more money. When the British finally called a halt the company went into receivership in February, 1982, after some 7500 DeLoreans had been produced. In a bizarre twist, John DeLorean was arrested in Los Angeles in an alleged drug deal in October 1982; this was presumably an attempt to refinance the company. He was later exonerated based on an entrapment defence, but would not return to the automobile industry. He would declare personal bankruptcy at age 75 in 1999.

Another aspiring auto mogul was Malcolm Bricklin. After several questionable ventures, Bricklin decided to become an automobile manufacturer. Unlike DeLorean, he knew little about cars; he was a promoter and an opportunist. Bricklin had a prototype Bricklin SV-1 (safety vehicle 1) constructed, made a video of its performance, and set out to sell his idea and drum up financing. His search eventually led to New Brunswick where he convinced premier Richard Hatfield's government to fund a plant with a loan guarantee of $2.88 million, and a purchase of 51 percent of Bricklin Canada Limited's shares for $500,000.

Bricklin production began in 1974. Like the DeLorean it was a gull-wing doored coupe, but the Bricklin had a front engine and its body was made of fibreglass. Unfortunately the car was under-engineered and fraught with problems, including Bricklin's beloved gull-wing doors. The company went into receivership in 1975 after producing 2857 Bricklins. The New Brunswick government stopped investing at $23 million, and the sad Bricklin tale slid into history. Malcolm Bricklin moved on to import re-badged Fiats, followed by Yugoslavian Yugos.

Another significant development was the gradual introduction of electronics to automobile engines and drivelines beginning in the 1970s. It began slowly, but picked up momentum as engineers learned how to adapt the computer to the harsh environment of the automobile.

The transition to electronics became necessary because it was becoming apparent that the old mechanical systems, such as distributors with ignition points, and carburetors, simply could not cope with the demands of the apparently conflicting requirements of lower emissions and higher fuel economy. Engine management via electronic ignition and fuel injection would prove to be the engineers' salvation in the quest for cleaner, more fuel efficient cars.

The sombre mood of motorists was evident in the declining sale of convertibles. From a high of six percent of the market in the 1960s, convertible sales gradually fell to one percent in the seventies. No longer profitable, American manufacturers stopped convertible production with the 1976 Cadillac Eldorado. Those seeking alfresco motoring would have to turn to imports.

Fuel economy would again become a real concern when the second Middle East oil crisis arrived in 1979. Fortunately the American industry was better prepared to meet this one. GM, for example, had its downsized large cars and its diesel engine. It was also poised to launch its more efficient compact front-wheel drive X-Cars (Chevrolet Citation, et al.) in mid-1979 as 1980 models.

The gyrations in the marketplace had contributed to bringing the Chrysler Corporation to the brink of bankruptcy. It badly needed a sav-

1981 Chevrolet Citation – GM's big plunge into front-wheel drive

iour, and fortunately, one was available. Lee Iacocca, who had joined the Ford Motor Company in 1946 as a trainee engineer, had risen rapidly through the sales side of the company. He made his biggest mark with the introduction of the Ford Mustang in 1964 when he was the president of the Ford Division. It gave him an aura that even outshone that of company chairman Henry Ford II.

Iacocca became president of the Ford Motor Company in 1970, and perhaps because of his sometimes brash manner and publicity-seeking personality, relations between him and Henry Ford II became strained. He was abruptly fired by Ford in 1978. It harked back to the manner in which Henry II's grandfather, the first Henry Ford, had summarily dismissed Charles Sorensen after 40 years of loyal service. Perhaps it was in the genes.

1972 Datsun 240Z – Japan begins take-over of sports car market

Iacocca was now a free agent, and a few months later joined the Chrysler Corporation as president; he was soon appointed chairman. Iacocca thus earned the distinction of being the only man to ever hold the presidency of two of America's Big Three automakers.

Although Chrysler was destined to lose a staggering $1.1 billion (U.S.) in 1979, with Iacocca's leadership, charisma, and a $1 billion loan guarantee from the U.S. government, Chrysler was able to bring to market its 1981 K-Cars, the Dodge Aries and Plymouth Reliant. The loans, and the unexciting but sturdy K-Cars, would save the corporation. But Chrysler would stay with the K-Car for so long, and would spin off so many derivatives, that it would again bring the corporation to the brink of bankruptcy in the late 1980s. Fortunately its minivan would save it until the all new "cab forward" LH cars (Chrysler Intrepid et al.) arrived in 1992.

The sports car scene also saw a transition in the 1970s. Largely dominated by the British in the 1950s and '60s, sports car leadership would gradually pass to the Japanese. The British brought few new models to market - the principal exception being the Triumph TR7 - and allowed their popular sports cars such as the MG to become obsolete. The Japanese stepped in to pick up the market.

Although other Japanese sports cars had arrived in the sixties, the one that really established them was the 1970 Datsun 240Z. Here was a snug, unit construction, two-passenger car with four-wheel independent strut-type suspension, rack-and-pinion steering, and a four- or five-speed transmission. Its 150 horsepower, 2.4 litre overhead cam inline six could accelerate the 1066 kg (2350 lb) coupe to 96 km/h (60 mph) in 8.7 seconds, and reach a top speed of 196 (122), all for about $4000.

The second Japanese sports car punch was the 1978 Mazda RX-7. Equipped with a Wankel rotary combustion engine, which Germany's NSU Spider had pioneered in 1963, the RX-7 offered technical novelty, sports car performance, good handling, and pleasant styling, all at a reasonable price. It was an immediate success.

As the decade came to an end it was becoming apparent that the American automobile industry was falling behind the rest of the world, particularly Europe, in technology, a trend that had begun in the 1960s. America had once been a technology leader. It pioneered such advances as interchangeable parts (Cadillac, 1908); the self-starter (Cadillac, 1912); four-wheel hydraulic brakes (Duesenberg, 1921); the fully automatic transmission (Oldsmobile, 1940); automobile air conditioning (Packard, 1940); the short-stroke, overhead valve V-8 (Cadillac and Oldsmobile, 1949); hydraulic power steering (Chrysler, 1951); and automobile turbocharging (Oldsmobile and Chevrolet, 1962). But the American industry was now being eclipsed. European manufacturers were showing the way with the proliferation of fuel injection, steel belted radial tires, rack-and-pinion steering, and high-output, light-weight, overhead camshaft engines.

There were probably several reasons for this decline. A monopoly is not conducive to innovation, and that's what the American industry had until the 1960s. Also, the American industry had started to fall under the control of accountants rather than engineers, a process that had begun with the appointment of accountant Harlow Curtis to GM's presidency in 1953. These "bean counters," as they were derisively called by the engineers, were often more concerned with quarterly earnings and the price of the company's stock than they were in producing industry leading technology. Another reason for the decline was that there seemed to be a resistance in Detroit to technology that was "Not Invented Here."

An additional factor was the somewhat isolated nature of the American industry, particularly its leader General Motors. Located in the American Midwest, the industry was insulated from the trends and sophistication of the more cosmopolitan coastal centres. Furthermore, its management was dominated by graduates of midwestern colleges such as the University of Michigan in Ann Arbor, and its own university, General Motors Institute in Flint, Michigan.

GMI had originally been started before the First World War by the Flint Vehicle Workers' Mutual Benefit Association to give evening classes to plant workers and supervisors. It was taken over by GM in 1926, becoming the General Motors Institute of Technology, and later the General Motors Institute. Although it was a fully accredited university, it was a very specialized one. Its main focus was automotive, and its principal purpose was to keep GM supplied with future engineers and executives.

By working in a co-operative program involving a few months of study sandwiched between a few months of working at GM, students could finance themselves through university while gaining valuable on-the-job experience. It was a wonderfully convenient arrangement for both parties, but it did tend to create an inbred mentality that was not so likely to be curious about the wider world. It favoured General Motors, and by extension, the rest of the

American industry. The Chrysler Corporation also had an in-house Masters of Engineering program.

The result of these company "trade schools" was that a certain isolation grew up around the industry. Perhaps recognizing the incestuous nature of the situation, General Motors no longer controls GMI. Its name has been changed to Kettering University in honour of the great engineer/inventor, Charles Kettering.

Not only did these executives come from similar schools, they also tended to live north of Detroit in enclaves like Bloomfield Hills or Birmingham where the population was dominated by automotive people. They worked together and played together, resulting in what Brock Yates, in his revealing 1983 book, *The Decline and Fall of the American Automobile Industry*, called The "Detroit Mind." He quoted an acid tongued New York advertising executive who had spent several years working in Detroit: "The place is packed with people who have upper-class money and middle-class minds."

This somewhat self centred perspective was reflected in a resistance to change. Steel belted radial tires are a good example. Introduced in 1946 by France's Michelin, it was soon recognized that radials were superior in traction, wear and handling to traditional bias-ply tires. Many European manufacturers began fitting them to their cars. Because radials were more expensive to make, American manufacturers insisted on continuing with cheap, bias-ply tires, followed by the compromise bias-belted tires, long after European carmakers were fitting radials. They were ultimately forced to accept the steel belted radial as the standard of the industry.

The same pattern was followed with fuel injection. Although the German Bosch company had developed fuel injection in the mid-1930s, and was the acknowledged leader in the field, it was foreign, and thus not very welcome in Detroit. It also cost more, a not inconsequential consideration to the accountants. While European cars, even small ones like the Volkswagen Rabbit (Golf), had fuel injection, American makers tried to soldier on with the carburetor, which was quickly becoming obsolete in a high-tech world. The result was carburetors that reached Rube Goldberg levels of complexity as engineers struggled to adapt them to meet emissions and fuel economy legislation.

When the American industry finally relented and accepted fuel injection, it tried to get by with a cheaper compromise, as it had with bias belted tires. This was something called throttle-body injection, a carburetor trying to act like fuel injection. It produced, as expected, only mediocre results principally because the gasoline still had to travel through a long intake manifold, rather then being injected just upstream of the cylinders. The American industry eventually had to accept fully electronic, multi-point fuel injection.

It wasn't as if North American engineers weren't capable of advanced technology. Given free rein they could be the equal of the best in the world. The 1957 Chevrolet, for example, offered fuel injection, and it would continue to be available on the Corvette until 1965. Overhead camshaft engines were not unknown in Detroit, and General Motors had led the world with turbocharged automobiles in 1962, as it had with the development of the catalytic converter in the 1970s. But the combination of an insulated monopoly, cheap gasoline, an emphasis on the bottom line, and a "Not Invented Here" mentality conspired to allow the American industry to lag behind the rest of the world's technology.

There was also Japan's superior lean production method to contend with. Lean production had been pioneered and brought to a high level by Toyota. It refined the whole production system from suppliers to inventory control to the workers' movements on the assembly line, and produced cars that were cheaper to build yet had superior quality. All of this did not bode well for an American industry.

The North American industry was glad to see the seventies come to a close. But the eighties would turn out to be almost as tumultuous, as foreign manufacturers began building their "imports" in North America, and the relentless competition continued.

1980 – 1990
FRONT-WHEEL DRIVE, MINIVANS, AND JAPAN'S MOVE UPMARKET

The North American automobile industry had troubles in the 1970s, and they weren't about to go away in the eighties. There was the continuing technical complexity of fuel economy, safety and emissions standards. Also, the new decade would see the industry facing a continuing rise in foreign competition, not only from cars built overseas, but also from "foreign" cars built right on their own soil by North American workers, who were proving to be just as adept at producing high quality cars as their off-shore counterparts.

The beginning of the new decade found Chrysler on the ropes, Ford struggling, and General Motors about to suffer its first full year loss since 1921. American Motors was so weak that it had been rescued by Renault of France in 1979, which was trying to improve its North American market share. It would mark the first time an American auto manufacturer had been controlled from outside the country.

Economic conditions weren't helping either. The early eighties found rampant inflation, sky high interest rates, and an economy in recession. Not surprisingly, auto sales were falling, but of those who were still buying, many were opting for imports.

With imports taking at least 20 percent of new car sales in North America, unions and auto executives began calling for import restrictions to protect the domestic companies. It was a mighty comedown for an industry that had always prided itself on its rugged individualism, entrepreneurship, and "survival of the fittest" philosophy.

In the interest of preserving their North American beachhead without unduly antagonizing their hosts, the Japanese government imposed "voluntary" export quotas on the Japanese car companies.

The Japanese were, however, rapidly becoming global market players. In the spirit of "if you can't beat them, join them," and "build them where you sell them," Honda established a car plant in Marysville, Ohio, in 1982, becoming the second modern importer, after Volkswagen, to manufacture in the U.S. A new word, "transplant," meaning a foreign owned factory operating in North America, entered our vocabulary.

It was only the beginning of the Japanese

assembly plant invasion. Before the decade was over, Toyota, Nissan, Mazda and others had factories either established or planned in the U.S. and Canada. It was an ironic twist that the import quotas had probably given the impetus to the Japanese manufacturers to establish their transplants in North America. Thus, while the quotas gave American manufacturers a temporary reprieve, the longer term result was that the enemy was now camped right in their back yard.

Some foreign companies were not successful with transplants. Volkswagen would find that its American plant in Pennsylvania was no longer viable, and would close it in 1988. Hyundai of Korea established a plant in the Province of Quebec in 1985, but it too would close a decade later.

In an attempt to understand the philosophy of Japanese management methods, General Motors formed a joint venture with Toyota. It was called New United Motor Manufacturing, Inc. (NUMMI), and would build cars in a GM plant in Fremont, California, that had been closed due to poor labour relations and quality problems.

NUMMI produced Toyota Corollas, which would be badged as Corollas by Toyota, and as Novas by Chevrolet. Under Japanese management the improvement in plant morale and build quality was dramatic.

Factors such as build quality (fit and finish), and reliability and production efficiency were starting to receive increased attention. And much to the chagrin of the American manufacturers, consumers were coming to the conclusion that imported cars, particularly those from Japanese companies, were better built and required less warranty and maintenance attention. Also, the American companies were finding that it was costing them more to build their cars than it cost the Japanese on an hours-per-vehicle basis.

The quality and reliability factors were made public by such organizations as Consumers Union, publisher of the respected *Consumer Reports* magazine, and J.D. Power and Associates, a California-based private survey company that constantly polled new car buyers' satisfaction, and regularly published the results. Added to this was the fact that government mandated new car recall notices were now public information. There was really nowhere to hide if a manufacturer produced a troublesome model.

Another new phrase entered the automotive lexicon: lean production. Formalized in a 1990 book, *The Machine That Changed The World*, by James Womack, Daniel Jones, and Daniel Roos of the Massachusetts Institute of Technology, lean production's genesis was credited principally to Japan's Toyota Motor Company.

Womack, Jones and Roos called lean production "...the most revolutionary change since Henry Ford's assembly line." They claimed that this "new" method of production was making

"Fordism" obsolete. While there is no denying that lean production is more efficient in terms of such things as worker hours required to build a car, it was perhaps an overstatement to say that it was making Ford's assembly line obsolete. The cars, after all, still moved along a line, and assemblers still attached various parts as the vehicles arrived at their work stations, just as they had back in 1913 when the Ford Motor Company pioneered the moving automobile assembly line.

Lean production was really a refinement of the assembly line concept. Building upon the assembly line system of production, it was expanded to encompass the entire production process, including vehicle design, component suppliers, inventory control, and the mechanics of the assembly methods. These were analyzed by efficiency experts to ensure that the vehicle was designed for the optimum in assembly ease, that every wasted motion was eradicated, and that any unnecessary buildup of inventory was eliminated. Just-in-time became their inventory control mantra.

One of the experts who contributed to the evolution of lean production was Dr. W. Edwards Deming, an American who had tried to sell his philosophy of statistical quality control at home after the Second World War. Unsuccessful there, he was invited to preach his philosophy in Japan where the auto industry was not only recovering from the war, but really just getting started in mass production. Dr. Deming's theories were enthusiastically embraced and applied by the Japanese. He became a national hero there, to the point that an annual quality award was named after him.

Under the lean production project team approach, the time required to develop a new car from concept to production was significantly shortened. *Machine* showed that on average it took the Japanese 46.2 months, while it took the Americans 60.4. Part of the reason was that the Japanese pushed more of the engineering "upstream" to their suppliers, a trend that would accelerate in the 1990s as suppliers became a more integral part of the design and production process. They would design and produce whole assemblies such as suspension or brake systems that the vehicle manufacturer would simply bolt on.

Faster vehicle development time gave the Japanese a marketing advantage because they could offer fresh new models more often, and respond to market changes quicker. It was also, of course, more economical to develop a new vehicle in a shorter time.

Toward the end of the decade, American manufacturers would begin using the "platform team" approach to develop new models. Chrysler, for example, assembled a platform team for its LH models (some wags said LH stood for Last Hope), the Chrysler Concord, et al., and completed them in just 39 months.

On the technology side, the 1980s would see a continuation of the requirement for cleaner and more economical cars. This would lead to some rather unusual approaches, such as the Cadillac V-8-6-4 "variable displacement" engine. By deactivating some valves under low load and light throttle conditions, the effect was to change the engine from an eight cylinder to a six, or even a four.

Unfortunately, what had seemed like a good idea on paper didn't work out so well in practice. The V-8-6-4 was abandoned in 1982, but not before doing some damage to Cadillac's vaunted reputation for engineering innovation, based on such breakthroughs as interchangeable parts, the electric self starter, the synchromesh transmission and the short-stroke, overhead valve V-8 engine.

To once more repel the imports, General Motors introduced yet another wave of small cars in 1982, this time with front-wheel drive. Called J-Cars, they spanned the corporation, and would be GM's ultimate expression of the body "shell game." They were the Chevrolet Cavalier, Pontiac 2000, Oldsmobile Firenza, Buick Skyhawk, and Cadillac Cimarron. Unfortunately, while sturdy and serviceable, they lacked the refinement and technical novelty of the Japanese competition.

The Chrysler Corporation, with the assistance of government loan guarantees, and its trusty K-Cars, was able to pay off its loans by August 1983. Buoyed by the K-Car's success, Lee Iacocca felt that Chrysler was ready for a little glamour. As a kind of experiment, he had a special LeBaron convertible built for his personal use. It proved so popular that Chrysler put it into production for 1983, with a first year target of 3000 sales. That turned out to be 23,000; the American convertible was back, and Ford and GM soon followed suit.

Chrysler continued its turnaround momentum with the introduction of the minivan, the most revolutionary new vehicle since the Ford Mustang. Chrysler's minivans, the Dodge Caravan/Plymouth Voyager (there would be a Chrysler version later), code named T-115, were an immediate success in the market. They largely replaced the station wagon as the family vehicle of choice. Although competitors came on the scene, none had Chrysler's touch with the minivan. It would sell over 3.7 million during its first decade, controlling 50 percent of the minivan market. Really competitive alternatives such as Ford's Windstar finally arrived, but as Chrysler chairman Lee Iacocca loved to crow, "We showed them how to do it and they still couldn't do it."

Volkswagen had pioneered the minivan back in 1950, and the Big Three had joined in the 1960s with vehicles like the Corvair Greenbrier, Ford Econoline and Dodge A100. But those vans had not been as car-like as the T-115, and the market wasn't ready to move them into the mainstream. Station wagons were still the family

1986 Dodge Caravan – Chrysler popularizes the minivan

1987 Ford Taurus – Ford's aerodynamic gamble pays off

vehicle of choice. The credit for popularizing the minivan in the 1980s must go to Chrysler with its garagable "Magic Wagons."

Ironically, it could have been Ford's success story rather than Chrysler's. When Lee Iacocca was still president of Ford, he and product planner Harold "Hal" Sperlich, and some others, had developed a small front-wheel drive van-type vehicle in the mid-seventies. Although they were enthusiastic about it, Ford senior management vetoed the idea. After Iacocca moved to Chrysler, Sperlich soon followed, and they were able to bring their minivan idea to fruition.

But Ford would have its own success story with the daring new aerodynamic 1986 Ford Taurus and Mercury Sable models. Audi had blazed the trail with its remarkable 1983 5000 model, which pushed production car design to new levels of aerodynamic and space/weight effi-

ciency. But the Audi was an upscale luxury car aimed at a relatively narrow market niche. In a bold venture, Ford gambled $3 billion to develop and launch its wind-cheating Taurus/Sable right into the mid-size sedan segment of the market, the bread-and-butter of any manufacturer which hoped to be a major market player. A mistake here could be disastrous.

But after a period of initial surprise and adjustment, the public enthusiastically embraced the Taurus/Sable in both sedan and station wagon versions. The Taurus became a top selling model for several years, and the original concept proved so sound that it would last for a decade with only relatively minor revisions.

In the meantime, Japanese manufacturers left no doubt that they were well on the way to becoming a world automotive power. Honda was a good example. The foundation had been laid with several outstanding models. The 1973 Honda Civic, for example, was followed by the 1976 Accord, a model that seemed to capture the essence of what North Americans wanted in a car.

Datsun (now Nissan), picked up the sports car ball that had been dropped by the British with its stunning new 1970 Datsun 240Z. This snug, two passenger coupe with its overhead camshaft, six cylinder engine set new standards of performance, comfort and value. The Z-series would go on to become the best selling sports car of all time. And Datsun's sturdy and value-packed Datsun 510 compact sedan was judged by many to be a poor man's BMW.

Toyota's Corolla had become another very popular model, one that has stood the test of time. It survives to this day as one of Toyota's most popular and reliable models.

With this sound base, Honda, Toyota, Nissan and others began marching into the mid-size fray. Now it was no longer a question of whether the Japanese would tackle the luxury market, but when. The first signal, the Acura Legend, came in 1986.

Acura was an upscale division created by Honda because it realized that the Honda name conjured up images of lower priced economy cars; a new division would give it a fresh persona. To give the division more breadth and sales power, a lower priced version called the Acura Integra was introduced as the Legend's stable-

1991 Lexus LS400 – Japan is now firmly in the luxury league

mate. This name was for North America only; on other continents they were sold as Hondas.

The Acura Legend was Japan's first real incursion into the luxury market. It was a sleek, V-6-powered sedan in the same size category as the Audi 5000. It was smooth, quiet and civilized, an up-market evolution of the Accord sedan. It was to the Accord what the Accord had been to the Civic.

But the Legend was only the beginning of Japan's march toward luxury models. Both Toyota and Nissan would also create Mercedes-Jaguar-BMW competitors. In 1990 Toyota's Lexus division and Nissan's Infiniti division, both newly created entities, introduced their luxurious Lexus LS400 and Infiniti Q45. They were more than competitively priced, and were technically advanced and impeccably assembled. They were destined to change the whole dynamic at the luxury end of the automobile market.

The 1980s would see the last vestige of the North American independent auto manufacturers leave the scene with the purchase of American Motors Corporation by Chrysler in 1987. Formed by the amalgamation of Nash and Hudson in 1954, AMC's Nash roots extended back to 1902 when the Thomas B. Jeffery Company turned out the first Rambler. Its Hudson side dated from 1909 when department store magnate Joseph L. Hudson financed the launching of a new car company in Detroit.

Although American Motors had enjoyed a few good years in the late 1950s and early '60s, their existence had largely been a troubled one. They tried valiantly to go model for model with the Big Three, and in the process almost went bankrupt. AMC was bought by Renault of France in 1979, but it would turn out to be a difficult marriage. French-designed models like the Alliance and Eagle Premier enjoyed only limited success. By 1987 Renault decided to give up trying to sell cars in North America, a quest that had begun in the modern era with the tiny, rear engined 4CV sedan back in 1949.

Chrysler not only got the Nash and Hudson legacies, but a real jewel in the Jeep name, immortalized by the Second World War, and civilized to become the grand-daddy of all four-wheel drive sport utility vehicles. AMC became Chrysler's Jeep-Eagle Division. The deal also included a second jewel: the ultra-modern Bramalea, Ontario, assembly plant, which would produce the company-saving (again) Chrysler LH cars (Chrysler Concord, et al.).

Another significant purchase came when the Ford Motor Company bought Jaguar in 1989 for a healthy $2.5 billion (U.S.). It would prove to be a good move for Jaguar, giving it access to Ford's vast technical expertise, and added leverage when purchasing components. Ford would fold Jaguar into its Premium Automotive Group, which included Jaguar, Lincoln, Aston Martin, Volvo and Land Rover.

The 1980s, far from being an easier one than the seventies for the American automobile manufacturers, only saw competition intensify. But the news was not all discouraging. Out of all of this activity would come a leaner, more efficient industry producing cars that were more economical, cleaner, structurally stronger, safer, and more powerful. The consumer would be the winner.

1990 – 2000
SPORT-UTES, CROSS-OVERS AND ELECTRONIC WIZARDRY

The 1990s began with an economic recession that was even worse than the one that ushered in the eighties. It was not only the longest running post-Second World War downturn, but also the most severe since the Great Depression of the 1930s. Unemployment was high and buyer confidence was low.

But if the economy of the 1990s started out badly, it would recover dramatically. By mid-decade the stock markets were recording new highs, inflation and interest rates were low and stable, and unemployment was shrinking.

This newfound prosperity found the automotive market becoming dominated by vehicles that weren't automobiles at all; they were trucks. Sales exploded for pickups, vans, and most of all, for big, heavy, expensive fuel-hungry, four-wheel drive sport utility vehicles (SUVs). At the beginning of the decade annual SUV sales were one million in North America. By the end they would be three million.

Companies that had become famous for their luxury cars, and had never before thought of building trucks, succumbed to the lure of the

2000 Cadillac Escalade – Cadillac builds a truck

huge profits that could be made on SUVs and pickups. Thus we had such makes as Lincoln and BMW getting into the passenger truck business. Even Cadillac, that bastion of General Motors luxury automobiles, would finally acquiesce to the demands of the marketplace, and the siren song of the bottom line; it introduced its first truck ever, the Escalade SUV, for 1999.

This all came about because there was a marketplace eager to embrace the newest automotive fad: sport utility vehicles. SUVs became *de rigueur* among the country club set and soccer moms. Although their four-wheel drive, off-road capability would seldom be tested, it was always present, becoming a new kind of status symbol. Unfortunately all of this hardware added weight and complexity, and increased fuel consumption. The rising popularity of trucks was the reason that average vehicle fuel economy began to fall in the 1990s. As cars continually became more economical the improvements were being cancelled by greater numbers of trucks in the national fleet.

Cheap motor fuel was one of the principle reasons for this swing to larger, thirstier vehicles. With the weakening influence of the Organization of Petroleum Exporting Countries (OPEC) cartel since the mid-eighties, the inflation- adjusted price of gasoline fell to levels not seen since the 1950s. It had become cheaper than bottled water, and memories of oil crises were long gone.

Diesel cars also fell out of favour in North America, in spite of the fact that in addition to their vaunted fuel economy, they now offered performance equal to gasoline cars of just a few years earlier, not to mention cleaner exhausts, other than particulates. From a peak of 15 marques offering diesels in the mid-eighties, they fell back to just two, Mercedes-Benz and Volkswagen, in the nineties. And even Mercedes-Benz would abandon the North American diesel market by the end of the decade, leaving Volkswagen to carry the oil burner banner.

In spite of large advances in emission control in automobiles, environmental concern still moved the California Air Resources Board to try driving technology in the marketplace. It mandated that by 1998 two percent of each manufacturer's new cars sold there had to emit zero emissions.

General Motors stepped up to the plate, trying with little success to interest the public in electric cars. In 1996 it launched the electric EV1, for lease only, through selected Saturn dealers in the southwestern U.S. It met with an indifferent response. GM abandoned its EV1, and California dropped its "two percent by '98" rule because it was clearly unrealistic. But it stuck to the other part of the law which raises the proportion of zero emission new car sales to 10 percent by 2003. Like its earlier law, it too will almost surely prove unworkable.

As the state-of-the-art of electric cars, and the batteries to power them, existed at the turn of the century, motorists simply continued to have serious misgivings about a car with a driving range equivalent to two gallons of gasoline. And besides, unless the electrical power was coming from nuclear plants, which have special environmental problems of their own, the emissions were just being moved from the vehicle's tailpipe to the generating plant's smokestack.

Small two-seater sports cars made a comeback in the 1990s, the trail having been blazed by the 1989 Mazda Miata. Compact, fun to drive and affordable, it rekindled the spirit of British sports cars of the 1950s and '60s, as its predecessor the 1978 rotary-engined Mazda RX-7 had a decade earlier. But unlike the RX-7, the Miata remained truer to its affordable sports car mandate.

By mid-decade the success of the Miata would entice others such as Daimler-Benz, Porsche and BMW into this market niche, albeit at about twice the price. In an era that seemed to be turning to nostalgia, they would all have styling cues harking back to the 1950s.

Daimler-Benz's Mercedes-Benz SLK came with a retractable steel top, *a la* the 1950s Ford Skyliner convertible. Porsche's Boxster had some curves reminiscent of the famous racing Porsches of the 1950s and '60s, and was also the first rear/mid engined Porsche with a water cooled engine, moving it further from its Volkswagen heritage. The BMW Z3's front fender vents were direct descendants of those on the beautiful 1956 to 1959 BMW 507.

As the automobile market in developed countries matured to the point where sales were mostly replacements for scrapped vehicles, not an expansion of the total market, the problem of over capacity began to emerge. There were simply more factories than were required, with the result that the world's 600-plus car plants were producing at only about 75 percent of capacity. They were capable of building almost 20 million more vehicles than the market could absorb. This was

far from economical, but the political pressure to keep plants open was always strong.

General Motors was North America's highest-cost producer. Because it had not undergone such severe downturns as Chrysler and Ford had in the 1980s, GM had not cut staff or plants as drastically. Also, a newly invigorated auto workers union was mounting stiff opposition to work rule changes and job reductions.

As an example, during the summer of 1998 the United Auto Workers union struck GM's Flint, Michigan, metal fabricating plant for seven weeks. Exacerbated by just-in-time operation, its impact quickly rippled through the entire corporation, bringing GM's whole North American assembly operations to a halt, and costing it millions of dollars in lost production. It was evidence of how difficult it was for companies to rationalize production in the face of political pressure on one side, and militant unions on the other.

In the meantime, the American manufacturers' share of the car market continued to erode, while that of the "imports" from foreign based manufacturers, the majority of which were now built in North America, continued to rise. American makers still dominated the truck market, particularly pickups, where the Ford F-150 was the largest selling vehicle in the world, but Toyota was making threatening gestures here too.

Mergers, alliances and consolidation had been a mark of the automobile industry since the beginning, and they continued in the world-wide auto industry during the 1990s. In 1998 Volkswagen outbid BMW for England's venerable Rolls-Royce, but, ironically, it didn't get the vaunted Rolls-Royce name with the business, although it did get Bentley. An even bigger deal was what both sides called a merger of the Chrysler Corporation in the U.S., and Germany's Daimler-Benz AG, makers of Mercedes Benz vehicles. In reality the creation of Daimler-Chrysler was a take-over of Chrysler, not a merger. Many long time Chrysler executives would soon depart, and DaimlerChrysler quickly installed German management.

As noted, the domination of the market by trucks became even more pronounced during the 1990s. Vans, SUVs and pickups were all classed as trucks by the government, although most of them were used exclusively as passenger vehicles. As evidence that a more moderate approach might be taking over, the large, heavy SUVs such as the Jeep Grand Wagoneer, were joined by a new breed of SUVs. These were mini-SUVs such as the Suzuki Sidekick/GMC Tracker, Toyota RAV4 and the Honda CR-V.

The mini-SUV market had been pioneered by Suzuki some 20 years earlier with its tiny LJ80 four-wheel drive Jeep-type vehicle. Suzuki began importing them into Canada in 1980, and into the U.S. in 1985, and the little 4X4s gradually caught on and started to grow. As the decade wound down Suzuki was moving its SUV further upmarket; the 1999 Suzuki Grand Vitara came with a 2.5 litre V-6 engine.

Mini-SUVs offered many of the features of the large ones, such as, in most cases, a higher stance for better visibility, an aggressive looking body, and that touchstone of all sport utilities, four-wheel drive. In addition, they provided better fuel economy, and a much more convenient size for parking and garaging than their big brothers.

The latter half of the 1990s would start to see a blending together of the types of vehicles offered. Station wagons, mini-vans and SUVs began to overlap in what were called "cross-over" vehicles. Manufacturers started basing their smaller SUVs on car platforms. Honda's CR-V, for example, used the Civic as its foundation. Subaru took its Impreza four-wheel drive station wagon, jacked it up and beefed it up, and called it the Forester. And four-wheel drive was increasing in station wagons, mini-vans and even cars. All Subarus, for example, had all-wheel drive. And since Audi was strongly promoting its all-wheel drive quattro system, it was difficult to buy a new Audi with just front-wheel drive. (Also see chapter on four-wheel drive).

Convertibles had always been a niche part of the market since closed cars overtook open ones in 1925. They even faded out on the American scene in the mid-1970s, to be revived by the

Chrysler Corporation in 1983. But the late 1990s would see the return of a different type of convertible from such marques as Mercedes-Benz and Toyota, one whose folding top was made of metal, and thus provided open air motoring or the snugness of a hardtop car. It was an idea that had been pioneered by Peugeot in 1937, and had some popularity in the 1950s on Ford's retractable-hardtop Skyliner. But Ford's hardtop convertible was a troublesome mass of motors, circuit breakers and relays, and the top ate up most of the trunk space. It was only offered for three years.

Air quality in cities and high density areas continued to be a major concern in the 1990s, and motor vehicles were a significant contributor. In spite of the enormous advances that were made in the cleanliness, fuel efficiency and power output of the internal combustion engine over the past couple of decades, many observers felt that the automotive power of the future could be a hybrid system in which cars would be powered by a combination of an electric motor and an internal combustion engine. In less densely populated areas the engine could propel the car, while in cities the batteries and electric motors could take over

In 1998 the Toyota Motor Company announced that its Prius Hybrid Vehicle would be sold to the public. The Prius had a 1.5 litre gasoline engine with variable valve timing, and an

2000 Toyota Prius – gasoline-electric hybrid

electric motor. The engine and the motor shared in powering the car by way of a planetary gearset power splitter. This allowed the engine to drive both the generator and the car. It also enabled the electric motor to assist in driving the car, or to fully propel it under certain conditions.

The engine operated in its most efficient range, and did not exceed 4500 rpm; it stopped when the vehicle was at rest, or moving slowly, and the electric motor took over. Regenerative braking helped re-charge the batteries under braking and deceleration. Toyota claimed that its Prius offered twice the fuel economy of regular cars, and much lower exhaust emissions.

Honda also offered its Insight near the end of the decade, a gasoline/electric, two-seater hybrid car. The heart of the Insight was its "Integrated

Motor Assist" system that teamed an aluminum, three cylinder 67 horsepower gasoline engine with a 13 horsepower electric motor. The engine was the prime mover, with the electric motor coming in to assist as required. The motor was a circular type, and its 58.4 mm (2.3 in.) thickness allowed it to be mounted between the engine and the five-speed manual transmission. At the close of the century it was the most fuel efficient car available in North America, with the astonishing government ratings of 3.9 L/100 km (72 mpg) city, and 3.2 L/100 km (88 mpg) highway.

Another approach that was being vigorously pursued as the decade drew to an end was the fuel cell. Many observers felt that this would be the ultimate power source for the automobile, and that the hybrid would be only an interim step. Fuel cells convert chemical energy into electricity, thereby eliminating the typical heavy battery pack found in electric cars. The chemical energy comes from hydrogen, and it can be extracted from fossil fuels or ethanol. The world's leading fuel cell pioneer at the end of the decade was Ballard Power Systems of Vancouver, British Columbia. Ballard was working with Daimler-Benz and Ford, among others, to make fuel cells practical for cars.

Electronics continued to play a increasing role in the functioning of the automobile. By the 1990s the more mundane tasks of engine ignition, fuel management and transmission control had been well worked out, allowing the engineers to turn to increasingly exotic applications. This manifested itself in such features as "smart" airbags that tailored their deployment to crash severity and passenger weight, satellite navigation/communication systems, and vehicle stability systems that selectively braked appropriate wheels to coax an over exuberant driver's car back to the intended course. Cadillac's "On-Star" and "Stabilitrak" were pioneers in communication and stability systems.

So as the decade, the century, and the millennium were coming to a close, the automobile, the invention that had made the single greatest impact on humanity in the 20th century, was alive and well. But it was still under tremendous pressure to become cleaner and more economical. Undoubtedly the engineers in the next decade, and beyond, will continue to improve the car in incremental steps as they have for the last 100 years. The internal combustion engine is far from dead, and it has become better with each passing year. What Gottlieb Daimler and Carl Benz started in 1885 will continue to be humanity's main method of transportation far into the future.

Engineering and Evolution

Aerodynamics: The Quest to Slip Efficiently through the Air

When the Organization of Petroleum Exporting Countries plunged North America into two oil crises in the 1970s and quadrupled the price of gasoline almost overnight, it popularized the science of automobile aerodynamics, also referred to as streamlining.

Superior aerodynamics allows a car to slip more easily though the air, reducing the power required and saving fuel. Aerodynamics is important because above 80 km/h (50 mph) more engine power is used overcoming aero drag than all others combined. The term coefficient of drag was soon added to the lexicon of new car buyers.

Coefficient of drag is an abstract number invented by scientists. To give some idea of its boundaries, consider the worst aerodynamic shape as a flat plate, and accept that it has a Cd of, say, 1.15. At the other end of the scale, imagine an egg with a long tapering tale with a Cd of 0.05. Automotive Cd numbers will lie between these two figures.

Scientists and engineers point out that the Cd number by itself is only part of the story. To be truly meaningful the Cd and the frontal area of the vehicle, called the CdA, must be considered together. A Greyhound bus may have a reasonably good Cd, but its huge area still requires a lot of power to push it through the air. In an era of mass media marketing, however, the simple, easy to advertise Cd number has been popularized.

The science of aerodynamics dates back to the late 15th century when Leonardo da Vinci noted that air resisted the movement of bodies. Galilei Galileo later confirmed air resistance, concluding that it was proportional to the speed of the object. In Sir Isaac Newton's laws of mechanics he established the classical theories of aerodynamics by calculating that air resistance increased as the square of the velocity. In other words, there is four times more air drag at 120 km/h (74 mph) than there is at 60 (37), and nine times more at 180 km/h (112) than at 60 (37).

In spite of man's slow travel in those days, a few pioneers pursued the study. Englishman Francis Wenham designed the first wind tunnel in 1871. Russian Nikolai Joukowsky built a wind tunnel at the University of Moscow 20 years after Wenham. By placing an object, say a vehicle, in a tunnel, blowing air over it, and measuring the resistance exerted by the vehicle, its aerodynamic efficiency could be determined. A smoke stream blowing over the body, wool tufts attached to it, or oil flowing over it, identify the areas of eddies and turbulence that cause aerodynamic drag.

By early in the 20th century there were wind tunnels in England, Russia, France, Italy and Germany. In the United States aviation pioneers Orville and Wilbur Wright had one in Dayton, Ohio, directed almost exclusively toward aircraft aerodynamic research, which intensified during the First World War.

Germany was a hotbed of automotive aerodynamic leadership. The Treaty of Versailles following the First World War forbad Germany from developing or building airplanes. This freed up a lot of aircraft aerodynamicists and wind tunnels for other work. One of these, Austrian Paul Jaray, established himself as the father of automotive aerodynamics. His early work was with airplanes and Zeppelin airships, and following the war Jaray turned his talents to automobiles. He applied for his first automotive patent in 1922, an airfoil-shaped design with a rounded windshield and smooth underpan.

In wind tunnel tests conducted by colleague Wolfgang Klemperer the Jaray car was found to have a coefficient of drag of 0.28, a remarkable figure when the average sedan had a Cd of around 0.80.

In a more modern wind tunnel test in Stuttgart in 1939 the Cd was found to be an even better 0.245.

Jaray made a significant contribution to testing by demonstrating that full size vehicle evaluation wasn't required; scale models in small wind tunnels yielded valid data. He believed that an aerodynamic automobile had to be a totally integrated design, not one with a fin added here or a fender skirt there. His principles were applied to the 1934 rear-engined Czechoslovakian Tatra car.

Another former aircraft aerodynamicist, Edmund Rumpler of Germany, showed his Rumpler "teardrop" car at the 1921 Berlin Motor Show. Its lines were based on aircraft principles, and claimed a Cd of 0.28.

Probably the best know aerodynamicist in more modern times was Dr. Wunibald Kamm. Working at the Stuttgart Research Institute in the 1930s, Kamm's significant contribution was the routing of air through the car body as well as over it, and his use of the chopped off "Kamm" tail.

Kamm's genius was in discovering how to keep the boundary layer of air passing over the body from breaking away too soon and creating drag inducing eddies. He ducted the air entering the front of the car through the radiator, and exhausted it at the base of the windshield. This flow then blended with and energized the air passing up the windshield and over the roof, causing it to follow the contour of the body for a longer distance. The ultimate aero shape, a long tapering tail, is impractical for an automobile. Kamm's solution was to simply chop the rear of the car straight off where the boundary layer began to separate from the body. Thus evolved what is called the Kamm-back of modern automobiles.

Dr. Kamm demonstrated his theories in the 1930s by building BMW based specials, one of which, the K-5, achieved a top speed of 185 km/h (115 mph) with an engine of only 115 horsepower. It also got 29 mpg (9.7 L/100 km) at 96 km/h (60 mph), and 19 mpg (14.8 L/100 km) at 145 km/h (90 mph). These performance and economy figures were all excellent for that time.

North American automotive aerodynamic study began in the early 1930s. Two University of Kansas engineers tested a variety of cars, from a tiny 1930 American Austin to a 1934 DeSoto Airflow. The average Cd of 14 cars was 0.675, ranging from 0.51 for the DeSoto Airflow to 0.80 for a 1931 Chevrolet.

Chrysler had an early interest in auto aerodynamics and in Jaray's work. In their testing they discovered that cars of the "square" era were more aerodynamically efficient going backwards than going forward! Chrysler engineers tested a 1932 DeSoto for top speed and discovered that it would normally reach 121 km/h (75 mph). Mounting the body backwards increased the speed to 132 km/h (82 mph)!

1986 Audi 5000 – set new standards in aerodynamics

The Chrysler/DeSoto Airflow models of 1934-37 were the result of Chrysler's attempt to build an efficient and rational "engineer's car." The Airflow, unfortunately, failed in the marketplace, setting Chrysler into a conservative styling mode that would last into the 1950s.

In spite of its failure, the Airflow awakened interest in aerodynamics in other manufacturers. Ford's 1936 Lincoln Zephyr had a Cd of 0.47, which was better than the Airflow's 0.51. But Ford, being aware of Chrysler's lack of success, didn't advertise the fact. Chrysler's failure with the Airflow set auto aerodynamics back many years in North America.

Although post-Second World War cars were "streamlined," in reality their shapes were created in the stylist's studio not the aerodynamicist's wind tunnel. By 1960 Cds were still running in the 0.42 to 0.50 range, little better than the 0.47 of the Lincoln Zephyr of 24 years earlier. Better progress was made in Europe where fuel economy was much more important; some Citroens, for example, had Cds in the low 0.30s.

It took the 1970s oil crises to focus on auto aerodynamics in North America. Following the trail blazed by the 1983 Audi 5000, Ford stepped forth boldly with its aerodynamic 1986 Ford Taurus/Mercury Sable. After tentative steps with its '79 Mustang and '83 Thunderbird, Ford took a courageous plunge with the mid-market Taurus/Sable. Its Cd of 0.29 to 0.32 put it at the head of the aero class, and the market rewarded Ford by making the Taurus one of its best selling products ever.

Everyone is now fully into the aero wars. The 1996 Mercedes-Benz E-class had a Cd of 0.27. What is even more interesting is that M-B achieved this using a water tunnel, not a wind tunnel, pointing up the fact that to the scientist both air and water are liquids. M-B has used hydrodynamics for aero development for several years. Air bubbles replaced the wind tunnel's smoke or wool tufts to identify turbulence. Subsequent wind tunnel testing confirmed the water tunnel's results.

The quest for slipperier shapes will continue in automobile aerodynamics. It's a competitive world, and M-B's 0.27 was equalled by the 1998 Volkswagen Passat. Aerodynamics efficiency is benefitting all of us with quieter, more economical cars.

FOUR-WHEEL DRIVE – THE ULTIMATE IN TRACTION IS FAR FROM NEW

Propelling a vehicle via all four wheels has become very popular during the last couple of decades, led by the phenomenal growth in sport-utility vehicles. Four-wheel drive, once the realm of military and industrial applications, is now found in many garages and driveways of urban life.

Its current popularity could lead to the conclusion that 4wd is a relatively recent development. Such is not the case; the idea of driving all four wheels is almost as old as the car itself. But it took military conflicts to really bring it to the fore.

It should be noted that the terms four-wheel drive and all-wheel drive are often used interchangeably to describe 4wd vehicles. There can be a subtle difference. All-wheel drive means full-time four-wheel drive in which all of the wheels are receiving power all of the time. In vehicles described as having four-wheel drive, however, all wheels may be receiving power only *some* of the time, although four-wheel drive is always available if required.

In the early 1900s the Aultman Company of Canton, Ohio, built steam cars, and experimented with a four-wheel drive steam truck. Cotta Automobile Company of Rockford, Illinois, fitted 4wd to a light steam car, mounting the engine in the middle of the vehicle and driving all wheels via chains.

In The Netherlands, Jacobus Spijker began building his Spyker (he simplified the name for commercial purposes) cars in 1900, and by 1904 had produced an experimental all-wheel drive race car. It had a huge 8.7 litre, six cylinder engine (the industry's first six), and it had both four-wheel drive and four-wheel brakes. Although ahead of his time, Mr. Spijker built only a few of his 4X4 cars before going to more conventional designs.

In 1903 a heavy all-wheel drive truck called the Columbia was built, probably in Hartford, Connecticut. Electric motors mounted near each wheel drove the wheels through chains. It also had power steering using an electric motor to turn the front axle's "fifth wheel."

All of this 4wd activity was preliminary to what would soon take place in the small town of Clintonville, Wisconsin, where a local blacksmith, Otto Zachow, took a franchise to sell Reo cars in about 1904. While demonstrating a Reo he slipped off the road, and the only way he could get enough traction to get out of the ditch was by backing up. Zachow noticed that the car seemed to have better traction when the wheels were pulling than when they were pushing. Why not, he reasoned, build a car with front-wheel drive, or even better, four-wheel drive.

Zachow began designing and building his 4wd vehicle, and when he had a working prototype he approached a young local lawyer named Walter Olen. Olen recognized the design's potential, and not only helped Zachow obtain a patent in 1908, but also assisted in setting up the Badger Four Wheel Drive Auto Company, soon changed to the FWD Company. Olen would ultimately become president, a position he held until 1952.

The company was able to buy a White steam car which Zachow proceeded to fit with 4wd. Test drives were successful, but the price they would have to charge was so high that financial success eluded them. They persisted, however, and their next 4wd vehicle was a large gasoline powered car referred to as the "Tank." FWD challenged all comers by offering a $1000 prize to any car that could match its ability in mud and snow; none could.

Although the company persevered, orders were not forthcoming. Then in about 1912 British military personnel observed some of the tests, and ordered two four-wheel drive trucks. These proved satisfactory, and with war clouds gathering over Europe, they soon placed an order for 50 more.

The big order hit little Clintonville like a bombshell, but somehow the resources were assembled and the FWD Company was on its way. By 1915 some 400 FWDs had been built, and still the orders rolled in. FWD contracted with outsiders such as the Peerless Motor Car Company of Cleveland, Ohio, to meet the demand. They engaged the Kissel Motor Company, and the Mitchell Motor Car Company, to keep up when the U.S. entered the First World War in 1917. They also sold FWD trucks for the border skirmish with Mexico.

FWD's success prompted another Wisconsin firm, the Thomas B. Jeffery Company of Kenosha, Wisconsin, builder of Rambler cars, to enter the 4wd business. Jeffery supplied the military with a 4wd truck called the Quad.

When peace came in 1918 it ended the demand for FWD's military trucks. Jeffery, which had become the Nash Motor Company when ex-GM president Charles Nash purchased it in 1916, was able to fall back on its automobile business. Walter Olen managed to keep FWD going on a modest scale by providing parts for army surplus FWD trucks. He also set about designing and promoting a new generation of civilian 4wd trucks for use in such industries as construction and mining.

Four-wheel drive activity during the 1920s and '30s was pretty well confined to construction vehicles. Marmon-Herrington, an off-shoot of the defunct Marmon luxury car company, also entered the all-wheel drive business. One of its most popular products was 4wd conversions for Ford trucks.

It took war to again bring 4wd to the fore. With German Chancellor Adolf Hitler threatening Europe, astute American military men realized that they could again be drawn into war. Aware of the large role played by 4wd vehicles in the First World War, they wanted something similar, although smaller and nimbler.

The military tested Marmon-Herrington Ford trucks, and the tiny American Bantam's Americanized version of the English Austin Seven, but found that neither entirely met their needs. An army ordnance technical committee drew up the requirements for a general purpose 1/4 ton truck. Included were weight and size specifications, and four-wheel steering, which was later dropped. The principal requirement laid down by the committee was four-wheel drive.

In the summer of 1940 the U.S. army sent invitations and specifications to 135 automotive and related manufacturers asking them to submit a prototype vehicle in just 49 days. Due to the short deadline most dismissed the idea, but some began working on it even though they knew they couldn't meet the date requirement.

Among these were Willys-Overland and Ford. Only tiny American Bantam managed to produce the specified 4wd utility vehicle within the 49 day limit, delivering its "Bantam Recon Car" to Camp Holabird, Maryland, within one- half hour of the deadline.

Although the hastily assembled vehicle had some problems, the army found the little Recon Car to be just what they wanted. But with the Army's need in the tens of thousands, and Bantam's production capabilities not nearly in that league, it had little choice but to consider the designs of Willys-Overland and Ford. The army settled on the Willys, mainly because of its more powerful engine. American Bantam, naturally very bitter, did get an order for 1500 Recon Cars, and also built many military trailers during the war.

The Jeep, as the vehicle became known, probably a contraction of general purpose (although this is the subject of some dispute), was arguably the Allies' most valuable Second World War tool. Its toughness and go-anywhere capability endeared it to fighting troops everywhere. It served as everything from gun carrier, to ambulance, to general's limousine, and was the mechanical hero of the war. By 1945 some 600,000 of those little Jeeps had been built by Willys, and by Ford under licence. The Jeep was not the only 4wd wartime vehicle, but it was certainly the most famous.

1945 Civilian Jeep – its name became synonymous with 4wd

Willys-Overland didn't suffer the same market collapse after the Second World War that FWD had after the first one because they were able to create a civilian version of the military Jeep and successfully move it into peacetime production. It had worldwide goodwill and a ready-made reputation. It was the recognized leader in the sport utility field, although it did inspire competitors such as Britain's Land Rover and Japan's Toyota Land Cruiser. Then in the 1960s competition intensified when others such as International-Harvester's Scout, and Ford's Bronco entered the market.

Four-wheel drive was pretty well confined to utility vehicles until the 1960s. It was tried briefly in racing cars, and in 1966 an "FF" (Ferguson Formula) version of the Chrysler powered English Jensen Interceptor offered a 4wd system developed by Harry Ferguson of light farm tractor fame. It was available until 1972 but sold in limited numbers.

In 1974 the Japanese Subaru company introduced 4wd to the moderate price field and immediately became popular in places like the New England mountain states. Subaru has been the most tenacious proponent of all-wheel drive cars since that time. Others such as Audi's "quattro" drive, and American Motors' Eagle also contributed to 4wd's popularity. GM, Ford and Chrysler tried it on such cars as Tempos, Pontiac 6000s, and minivans, with limited market response. Four-wheel drive's greatest popularity remains in sport-utility vehicles.

The introduction of such advancements as liquid silicone viscous couplings and Mercedes-Benz's brakes-only 4wd system has made full-time 4wd possible without the disadvantages of the older, all mechanical systems. All-wheel drive is now so well engineered that drivers don't even realize they have it. In addition to the explosive growth of sport utility vehicle sales, 4wd is becoming increasingly popular in cars.

Front-Wheel Drive
Pulling Becomes the Norm

Front-wheel drive is far from new in automobiles, although its popularity in North America has been relatively recent. Pulling from the front instead of pushing from the rear, in fact, goes back to the very dawn of the motorised vehicle.

In 1769 a French army engineer by the name of Nicholas Cugnot built what is acknowledged as the world's first mechanically driven road vehicle. His invention was a heavy military tractor that had its steam engine mounted at the front, driving the single front wheel. Although it was capable of only four km/h (2.5 mph), needed to stop every 30 m (100 ft) to generate steam, and crashed on its maiden drive, the cumbersome machine was, nevertheless, successful enough to earn its place in history. It was a prescient development because France, while not the actual inventor of the automobile, would prove to be its cradle.

The genesis of the modern internal combustion engined automobile is credited to German engineer Carl Benz of Mannheim who built his Benz "Patent Wagen" in 1885, and patented it early in 1886. This little three wheeled machine (one in front; Carl apparently didn't know how to make a steering mechanism for a four wheeler) had its engine behind the seat driving the rear wheels. To give the three wheeler better stability, the engine and its large flywheel where mounted horizontally. The die had been cast for rear-wheel drive.

As other car designs evolved, the engine gradually moved under the seat, and then in most cases, forward to be housed inside a hood ahead of the driver. The drive, however, continued to be through the rear wheels. This was partly out of tradition, but also for the very practical reason that the universal joints of the day just couldn't reliably cope with the tasks of both steering and propelling the vehicle. It would take the sturdy constant velocity joint to solve that problem.

Dr. Ferdinand Porsche, the father of the Volkswagen, and later along with son Ferdinand, known as Ferry, the founder of the Porsche Car Company, would become famous for rear engine, rear-wheel drive cars. But, surprisingly, he started out as a front-drive pioneer because his very first car which he built in 1900 at the age of 25, had front-wheel drive. It was called the

Lohner-Porsche, and was propelled by electric motors mounted in each of the front wheel hubs. At about the same time, the Graf brothers of Vienna built a car with a one cylinder gasoline engine driving the front wheels. It didn't get into production.

In North America an innovative marine engineer by the name of Walter Christie was also exploring the merits of pulling instead of pushing for his race cars. His marine experience no doubt influenced his direct drive approach. He mounted a huge engine transversely in the front of his racer and drove the front wheels through a flywheel and clutch at each end of the crankshaft. Although quite fast, the Christies, which were built between 1904 and 1908, were not very successful in racing.

Front-wheel drive languished for several years, finding no manufacturer willing to bring it to production, although American race car designer Harry Miller engineered a number of successful Indianapolis type racers in the 1920s and '30s. Then in 1928 the Alvis company of England marketed what was apparently the world's first production front-wheel drive car. It was a sports car with four-wheel independent suspension and a 1.5 litre overhead cam, four cylinder engine that could be had with or without a supercharger. This was followed in 1929 by an eight cylinder version.

At about the same time, Tracta of France and its front-wheel drive expert, J.A. Gregoire, introduced a front driver. On this side of the ocean, Errett Lobban Cord's Auburn Automobile Company of Auburn, Indiana, brought out his large 1929 L-29 front-drive Cord using Miller patents. While other American manufacturers such as Chrysler and Packard experimented with front-wheel drive, none except the Cord, which would last until 1937, adopted it. The impetus then swung back to the Europeans.

The Germans picked up front-wheel drive in the early thirties when DKW introduced its aptly named 1931 Front model with front drive, a cross-mounted engine, and four-wheel independent suspension, the first production car to combine these features. Front-wheel drive would continue to be a DKW feature until the marque's demise 35 years later. DKW was followed in 1932 by the German Adler company with its Trumpf front-wheel drive model, and in 1933 by Audi with a front driver.

The stage was set for the appearance of the car that no doubt did more to popularize and legitimize front-wheel drive than any other. This was the 1934 Citroen Traction Avant model from France, a car so successful that it would remain in production in the same basic form until 1957, by which time more than 700,000 had been built. In addition to front-wheel drive, the Traction Avant had other advanced engineering features, including unit construction, torsion bar suspension, and wheels that were pushed out to the corners of the car for excellent stability. In appearance it somewhat resembled a 1934 Ford.

Following the Second World War the thrust was to get back into production to satisfy the pent-up demand for cars, even if the offerings were warmed over pre-war models. The emphasis was more on production than on technical innovation, although an upstart in America, Kaiser-Frazer, experimented with front-wheel drive and torsion bar suspension, but finally settled on conventional vehicles.

Then in 1959 the tiny English Austin/Morris Mini came on the scene. Designed by the quirky but brilliant Alec Issigonis, who had also created the successful Morris Minor, it would change the way people thought about cars, particularly small ones.

Issigonis resurrected the DKW Front idea, and mounted the four cylinder Mini engine transversely in the nose of the car in unit with the transmission and differential. He sent the power through the front wheels. It was such a compact and space efficient powertrain package that it allowed the accommodation of four adults, and a reasonable amount of luggage, in a car that was only 3048 mm (10 feet) long overall.

General Motors was trying some novel automotive layouts in the 1960s, and returned the American industry to front-wheel drive with its large 1966 Oldsmobile Toronado. This was fol-

1985 Dodge Omni – America's first front-drive sub-compact

lowed in 1967 by a Cadillac spin-off, the Eldorado. But the industry still loved its big rear-wheel drive automobiles, and in an era of cheap gasoline, it saw no need for the space and weight efficiency offered by front-wheel drive.

Front-wheel drive came of age in the 1970s. First there was the nimble and economical front-wheel drive Honda Civic that arrived in 1973. Many said it was what the Mini should have been. Then came the very successful front- wheel drive Volkswagen Golf (initially the Rabbit in North America), and its various imitators.

The rising price of oil, and even worse, the threat to its security of supply, finally brought the North American industry to the realization that the cars of the future would have to be lighter, and more fuel and space efficient. Front-wheel drive with its superior mechanical packaging made a significant contribution to this goal.

Chrysler was the first to market a small, domestically built, fuel efficient, front-wheel drive car, its Dodge Omni and Plymouth Horizon sub-compacts in 1978. They were unabashedly Rabbit influenced, and even used Volkswagen derived engines.

Ford's response was to import another Rabbit clone, the front-wheel drive Ford Fiesta from Europe. This was marketed until their home-grown front-drive Escort was ready in 1981. General Motors made the biggest entry of all, drawing on the expertise amassed with its Olds and Cadillac front drivers to develop its compact 1980 front-wheel drive X-cars, introduced in mid-1979. These were the Chevrolet Citation, Pontiac Phoenix, Oldsmobile Omega and Buick Skylark. They arrived, with exquisite luck, at about the same time as the second oil crisis.

The X-cars suffered some early quality problems, probably the result of being rushed to market, but these were eventually solved. General Motors committed itself to front-wheel drive, and the X-cars were followed in 1982 by the sub-compact J-cars. These were to be the real import fighters, although for years they seemed to be one step behind the best imports in performance, quality and refinement. Every GM division would have a J-car, from the Chevrolet Cavalier to the Cadillac Cimarron. Chrysler's corporation-saving K-cars and their many spin-offs were also front-wheel drive.

Although front-wheel drive is far from universal, it is the predominant way of driving today's cars. Even the Swedish Volvo Car Company, which for years maintained that rear wheel drive was the only way to go, although it marketed the small front-wheel drive 480ES in Europe, has finally changed to front-wheel drive. When someone as staid and conservative as Volvo adopts it, you know that front-wheel drive has been fully accepted.

Minivans: Invented by Volkswagen, Popularized by Chrysler

When the Chrysler Corporation advertised that it produced the "original" minivan, it was playing a little loose with history. Chrysler can be given credit for popularizing the minivan, and bringing it into the mainstream of motoring consciousness, but its birth goes back much further than the 1984 launch of Chrysler's "Magic Wagons," the Dodge Caravan and Plymouth Voyager.

The concept of the minivan is based on the goal of achieving the greatest passenger/cargo-carrying capacity within the shortest overall vehicle length. The idea isn't exactly new; a couple of forward thinking Americans, Buckminster Fuller and William Stout, set out to do this in the 1930s.

Fuller, a brilliant designer who is best known as the inventor of the geodesic dome, also applied his talents to a motor vehicle which he introduced to the world in 1933. He called it the Dymaxion, or more formally, the 4D Transport Unit.

The Dymaxion was shaped like a short, fat cigar, and it looked a little like an airplane without wings. It had two regular sized wheels positioned just forward of the vehicle centreline, which meant that the driver and front passengers rode ahead of the front axle.

The rear was supported by one small wheel, which gave the Dymaxion a nose-up attitude. This wheel was used for steering in the fashion of a boat rudder, providing the Dymaxion with the interesting capability of being able turn completely around in its own length.

Power came from a Ford V-8 engine mounted in the rear, but reversed to send its power forward to the front wheels. With an overall length of 5791 mm (228 in.) and a wheelbase of 3175 mm (125 in.), the Dymaxion could accommodate 11 people.

Fuller was invited to show it at the 1934 New York Auto Show, an invitation that was later withdrawn, probably at the insistence of the Chrysler Corporation out of concern that the Dymaxion would upstage its new Chrysler/-DeSoto Airflow models. In response, Fuller parked it in front of the main entrance where it generated tremendous public interest. In spite of this attention, the Dymaxion was never a financial success, and only three were built.

1936 Stout Scarab – early minivan idea

William Stout's van-like vehicle, which he called the Scarab, was not as radical as Fuller's, but was nevertheless unusual and ahead of its time. Stout was a remarkable engineer; one of his many accomplishments was the designing of the famous Ford Tri-Motor airplane.

Stout decided to turn his aircraft knowledge to the design of a road vehicle, completing his first prototype in 1932. It had a steel space frame and an aluminum body, and aircraft influence was evident in the lack of fenders or hood. In fact, like the Dymaxion, it somewhat resembled an airplane with no wings. Also, *a la* the Dymaxion, it was powered by a Ford V-8 mounted in the rear. It had four wheels and rear-wheel drive, however, which gave the Scarab a low, flat floor.

The wheels were pushed out to the corners of the Scarab, and this, combined with a very long wheelbase, gave it almost room-like accommodation. The rear seat, for example, was a full 1829 mm (six feet) wide, and the only seat that was anchored was that of the driver. The others could be moved around, and a small table could even be set up.

Stout built his second prototype in 1935, and established the Stout Motor Car Company to manufacture the Scarab. Alas, the price of $5000 was very high, and only nine Scarabs were built before production ceased. They were sold to people of wealth such as Harvey Firestone of tire building fame, chewing gum magnate Philip Wrigley, and Willard Dow of Dow Chemical.

It was after the Second World War that the first real minivan appeared, and it came from an unlikely source: Volkswagen. In the early 1930s Germany had commissioned engineering consultant Ferdinand Porsche to design a small, affordable car for the German masses. The result was the well known Volkswagen Beetle. A giant state-owned factory was constructed to manufacturer it, but by the time this was completed the Second World War was imminent, so the plant was used to build Volkswagen-based military vehicles called Kubelwagens, and other war materials. The end of the war found the plant badly bomb-damaged, and in the hands of the British.

The British gradually got the plant back to

producing Volkswagens, and returned it to Germany. A trickle of VW Beetles turned into a flood, and with production well under way in the late 1940s, VW's management and engineers turned their thoughts to the development of a light commercial vehicle. Since a "box-on-wheels" is the most space efficient package, that's what the practical Germans devised. The VW Transporter as it was called, although it went under many names such as van, window van, Kombi and microbus, was really just a metal box set on a sturdy frame. A very versatile pickup version was also offered.

The Transporter was powered by the Beetle's flat, air-cooled, four cylinder engine, although reduction gears in the hubs, originally used in the Kubelwagen, gave it the pulling power necessary for commercial applications. The engine was located behind the rear axle, as in the Beetle, and drove the rear wheels through a four-speed manual transmission.

The front seat was directly over the front wheels, the ultimate in "cab forward" design, which freed the remainder of the van for passengers or cargo. Access to the carrying area was via two swinging side doors, supplemented by a huge hatch at the rear. What Volkswagen had accomplished was a vehicle that, while only a few inches longer than the Beetle, could accommodate up to seven passengers, or carry 3/4 of a ton of cargo.

The first Transporter came off the Wolfsburg

1961 Volkswagen Van – Volkswagen invents modern minivan

assembly line early in 1950, and it was immediately apparent that VW had invented a whole new type of vehicle. With no competition, the VW van soon became very successful for both passenger and light cargo hauling.

Within a few years some competition would appear in the form of such models as the Fiat Multipla from Italy and the DKW Karavan from Germany. Neither, however, had the versatility and all-round practicality of the Volkswagen, nor the world-wide service network, with the result that the VW van prevailed over all others.

As would be expected with such a small engine pushing a large box-like body, the performance was very modest. *Road & Track* magazine tested a VW van in December 1956 and recorded a top speed of barely 60 mph (96 km/h), and a zero to 60 mph acceleration time of 75 seconds.

The VW van was so unusual, and so easy to maintain and economical to run, that in the 1960s and '70s it became a favourite vehicle of hippies, or the beat generation. Usually decorated in psychedelic colours and garish painted flowers, its large volume made it an ideal home on wheels, the ultimate antiestablishment machine.

Volkswagen had the market it had created virtually all to itself for more than a decade. Then in 1961 Detroit finally responded with its own van-type vehicles, the Ford Econoline and Chevrolet Corvair Greenbrier. Both followed the VW's box-on-wheels theme, but with a different approach. Ford's used a conventional front-engine, rear-drive configuration using components from the compact Ford Falcon. The six cylinder, water cooled engine was located between the driver and passenger seat.

The Greenbrier was a much more radical design. Its powertrain was based on the Corvair car, which had a flat, six cylinder, air cooled engine located in the rear, an unabashed copy of the Volkswagen Beetle. It's not surprising that the Greenbrier came out looking like a more stylish version of the VW van. The Chrysler Corporation would enter the field in 1964 with its flat-nosed Dodge A100 model.

With their larger engines the American vans had much higher performance than the VW. The Greenbrier's 80 horsepower was more than double that of the Volkswagen's 36, for example, although the VW was still the most economical on fuel. The concepts were very similar and the VW now had some serious competition. But while the minivan market was growing, station wagons were still the vehicle of choice for the majority of buyers who wanted more carrying capacity than provided by a regular car.

This competition would only last for a few years. As seems inevitable in Detroit, the Ford and Dodge grew larger and more powerful. The Chevrolet Greenbrier, on the other hand, simply disappeared in 1964 when Chevrolet decided that sales did not warrant continuing it.

Through the 1970s and into the '80s, Volkswagen had the minivan field largely to itself again as other manufacturers made their vans larger, heavier and thirstier. The VW van was revised and enlarged in 1967, and again in 1979, when it became the Vanagon. Each new generation received important mechanical and utility upgrades, and by the time the Vanagon came along in 1979 its 2.0-litre, 67 horsepower engine (still an air cooled flat-four in the rear; water cooling would come in '83) was capable of pushing it to 142 km/h (88 mph), and could accelerate it to 96 km/h (60 mph) in 21 seconds.

In 1984 the whole minivan world changed with the introduction of Chrysler's T115 compact vans, the Dodge Caravan and Plymouth Voyager.

Using the K-car (Dodge Aries/Plymouth Reliant) front-wheel drive engine and driveline allowed Chrysler to create a vehicle that was seven passengers large on the inside, yet small enough on the outside to be stowed in the average suburban garage. Chrysler advertised it as the "garagable" van.

Chrysler's minivan was a sensation. It took the market by storm and quickly replaced the conventional station wagon as the family hauler of choice. It also marked Chrysler as a product innovator to be reckoned with.

In spite of Toyota's mid-engined Van Wagon coming on the scene at about the same time, the Dodge Caravan/Plymouth Voyager immediately dominated the minivan market, and would continue to do so for a decade. Ten years later, and after many imitators, it was finally seriously challenged by Ford with its Windstar, and General Motors with its Chevrolet Venture and Pontiac Trans Sport.

It is ironic that it had taken Ford 10 years to fully respond to this challenge because Ford had the idea in its hands back in the 1970s. That's when Ford president Lee Iacocca was still flying high on his Mustang reputation. His chief product planner was a man named Harold "Hal" Sperlich, and they had another idea that they thought would be even hotter than the Mustang.

Under the direction of Iacocca and Sperlich, Ford's styling department developed the garagable van idea in 1972-73. Code named the Carousel, it looked remarkably like Chrysler's Caravan/Voyager of 10 years later. Just as the concept was about to become a reality the first oil crisis arrived in 1973. This resulted in a stampede to small, fuel efficient vehicles, and the Carousel project was cancelled.

Lee Iacocca was fired by Henry Ford II in 1978 after 32 years of service. He surfaced a few months later as president of the ailing Chrysler Corp. He knew where the real talent was in Ford, and in the process of reviving Chrysler he took delight in making the Ford Motor Company his happy hunting ground for top flight executives. Among them was Sperlich, and when Sperlich and Iacocca got back together they proceeded to turn their stillborn Ford "better idea," the minivan, into one of the most outstanding marketing successes in history. But there are now many competitors in the minivan segment, and Chrysler no longer holds the commanding sales lead and outstanding owner loyalty it once had.

It's over 50 years since Volkswagen pioneered the "box on wheels" type of vehicle and began producing it. It was the concept that futurists like Buckminster Fuller and William Stout had been striving for. It's safe to say that even Volkswagen could never have envisaged how popular the minivan would eventually become.

Station Wagons: Elegant Roots for a Suburban Workhorse

The station wagon came of age in the burgeoning suburbia that followed the Second World War. Young families flocked to these developments in search of space, fresh air, and the dream of home ownership. The trappings of this new life had to be accommodated when the young family travelled. Since suburban public transit was virtually nonexistent, transportation revolved around the family vehicle.

The station wagon, a sedan with an elongated roof, evolved as the quintessential suburban hauler. It carried everything from two-by-fours, to fertilizer, and went to the grocery store and on vacation. It became both family car and status symbol.

But while post-war suburbia popularized it, the station wagon's history predated the automobile. It began when the train was the king of long distance land travel. The station wagon, also known as the estate wagon, depot hack, and in England, the shooting brake, got its name because the grand hotels met their guests at the railway station in horse-drawn passenger wagons, usually decorated with light wood framing and dark panelling.

As mechanical horsepower replaced livehorse power, motorized station wagons, usually on truck chassis, began to appear. But the station wagon was still so specialized that automobile manufacturers didn't offer production models until the 1920s.

The first was Durant Motors in its 1923 Star station wagon. Durant Motors was the creation of William "Billy" Durant, the charismatic entrepreneur who had formed General Motors in 1908. Through mismanagement he lost control to the bankers in 1910, formed Chevrolet and used it to regain GM in 1915, and lost it for good in 1920.

His enthusiasm and business contacts enabled Durant to form Durant Motors within six weeks of his GM ouster. The Durant car came first, followed by the Star in 1922, a light car to compete directly with the all-conquering Model T Ford.

The Star sold 100,000 in less than a year. To expand its appeal, a station wagon was added in 1923. Although the wooden body was supplied by an outside contractor, the Star station wagon was a factory model and qualified as the first production wagon. Ford's "optional" wagon required customers to arrange for bodies with independent coachbuilders.

Station wagon progress was slow and steady; in 1929, for example, Ford sold only some 4400 Model A wagons. Even at that, however, Ford would dominate the wagon market in the years leading up to the Second World War, and for many years after.

In 1936 Chevrolet introduced the Suburban, a panel truck with windows and seats. Since it had no wood, it could be called the first all-steel station wagon, but it was really more truck than car, and thus was not in the true spirit of the car-based station wagon.

In the decades following the Second World War station wagons came into their own. When auto production resumed in 1945-46 after the war-time shutdown, most manufacturers returned to wooden wagons. An exception was Willys-Overland. Instead of going back to cars it converted its famous war-time four-wheel drive military Jeep into a multi-purpose civilian utility vehicle. It added the all-steel Jeep station wagon in 1946, but like the 1936 Chevrolet Suburban, it was more truck than car.

Crosley Motors of Cincinnati, Ohio, followed Willys in 1947 with a tiny all-steel station wagon. In 1948 its sales of 23,489 of its Lilliputian simulated wood-sided mini-wagons made it the world's largest wagon manufacturer. But Crosley's

1949 Plymouth Suburban – all-steel body popularizes station wagon

prosperity was brief; with the return to a buyers' market its production plummeted, and it left the automobile business in 1952.

The all-steel station wagon was clearly the way of the future. Traditional woody wagons were expensive to build, prone to creaking, swelling, shrinking and groaning, and required regular varnishing. The real breakthrough in all-steel, car-based station wagons came from the Chrysler Corporation in 1949 as the Plymouth Suburban (there was also a Dodge version). In spite of coming initially only in what *Mechanix Illustrated* magazine's car tester Tom McCahill called "horse's hoof brown," sales flourished. Based on Plymouth's short-wheelbase sedan, the Suburban combined passenger car quietness, ride and handling, with station wagon utility. Other colours soon followed, but there was no simulated wood siding.

Traditional wood-clad station wagons gradu-

1956 Chevrolet Nomad – brought glamour to station wagons

ally gave way to all-steel bodies. Buick discontinued wood in 1953, and Ford in '54, the last to do so. Real wood was replaced by simulations as manufacturers competed to achieve the appearance of wood by cladding their wagons with fibreglass, plastic and other materials embossed to resemble wood.

They also competed in seating configurations. Nine passenger wagons were offered, with some lowering the third seat and facing it rearward. Others used two small, side-mounted seats facing each other. Third seats could be removed or folded down.

For all its convenience, a station wagon still was a boxy vehicle. Although it was difficult to make it look stylish, General Motors managed to do so with its Chevrolet Nomad and sibling Pontiac Safari.

The Nomad began as a small Corvette-based concept station wagon shown in the 1954 Motorama, GM's annual city-hopping new product and "dream car" exhibition. Audience response was so positive that in 1955 GM went into production with a larger version of the Nomad on a Chevrolet chassis.

These two-door wagons were lower than the regular ones, and featured a forward-slanting B-pillar and an almost uninterrupted expanse of glass that extended from door to door around the rear of the vehicle.

Unfortunately the Nomad and Safari lost some utility by having only two doors when the wagon market was shifting to four. Also, the steeply slanted rear window reduced carrying capacity. The Nomad/Safari two-door wagons were made for only three years, and are now one of those rarities: a collectible station wagon.

Other ingenious ideas were tried. In 1963 Studebaker introduced its "Wagonaire," in which the rear part of the roof slid forward, giving a sun-roof effect and allowing tall items to be carried. In 1964 Buick and Oldsmobile introduced their "Vista-Cruiser," a wagon with a raised roof area surrounded by tinted glass. Inspired by the "Scenicruiser" highway bus, it provided better visibility and increased rear head room.

For sheer brilliance, few ideas can match Ford's two-way, dual action "Magic Doorgate." Introduced in 1966, its clever arrangement of hinges, torsion bars and latches let the tailgate swing down in traditional fashion, or be opened from the side like a door. It facilitated rear seat entry and cargo loading. If Ford was the king of station wagons before, this consolidated that position; the Ford Country Squire with its simulated wood siding became the class of suburbia.

Another approach was General Motors' clamshell tailgate in which the glass retracted up into the roof, and the bottom part of the tailgate slid down under the floor. In spite of its novelty, the clamshell was not space efficient, and was soon discontinued.

A subset of the station wagon was the small sports wagon, exemplified by such cars as the MGB GT, introduced in 1965, and the 1970s Volvo sport wagon based on the P1800 coupe. These niche market vehicles combined sports car qualities with expanded luggage space.

With car sizes being driven down in the search for better fuel economy, station wagons came under increasing pressure. Each downsizing eroded the wagon's advantage, and in the late seventies, before the second oil crisis, the market began moving to large commercial vans that were custom equipped for passenger use.

But this was all preliminary to what would happen in 1984. That's when Chrysler Corp. introduced its minivans and changed the automotive scene. Volkswagen had originated the modern minivan back in 1950. But while VW evolved the concept, and GM and Ford picked up on it in 1961 with the Chevrolet Corvair Greenbrier and Ford Econoline, Chrysler deserves the credit for popularizing it with its Dodge Caravan and Plymouth Voyager.

The minivan combined car-like driving characteristics with greater carrying capacity than a car or wagon, and could be parked in the average suburban garage. The market responded spectacularly to this natural successor to the station wagon.

While the minivan has become the vehicle of choice for many families, the station wagon is far from dead. Such notables as the Ford Taurus and Volvo wagon are still selling in respectable numbers. While no longer the king of suburbia, the station wagon is still a part of the automotive scene. In fact, it began making a comeback in popularity in the late 1990s.

THREE-WHEELED CARS: FOR THOSE WHO THINK THREE WHEELS ARE ENOUGH

Three-wheelers have flitted in and out of the history of the mechanically driven vehicle since its very dawn. That dawn came in 1769 when French army engineer Nicholas Cugnot invented the world's first self propelled road machine, a heavy artillery wagon. It was motivated by a steam engine, and it had just three wheels.

The engine on Cugnot's wagon was mounted above the single front wheel, which was smaller than the rear ones, and steam was generated in a big acorn shaped boiler slung out in front. Although it was slow and ponderous – it crashed into a wall in an early test – it has nevertheless earned its place in history as man's first tentative step toward mechanically propelled land vehicles.

The dawn of time as far as the modern automobile is concerned took place in 1885 when a German inventer by the name of Carl Benz of Mannheim built and tested what is recognized as the world's first car powered by an internal combustion engine. It was also a three-wheeler. It became a three-wheeler by default. Because Benz apparently didn't know how to devise a mechanism to steer two front wheels, he used just one.

It was steered by a crank handle mounted atop a vertical steering column attached to a rack-and-pinion steering gear.

Benz soon switched to four wheels, but others continued to see a future for just three. One of these was Frenchman Leon Bollee, the son of France's pioneer in steam powered road vehicle, Amedee Bollee. He called his little machine a "voiturette," a term that would soon be adopted as a generic name for light motor vehicles. It appeared in 1895 with two wheels at the front and one at the rear. The single rear wheel was belt driven.

Perhaps the best known of all three-wheelers was the Morgan, originated by Harry Frederick Stanley Morgan in the spa town of Malvern Link, Worcester, England. H.F.S. Morgan's father was a clergyman and motor racing enthusiast, which no doubt influenced his son's future. After serving his engineering apprenticeship with the Great Western Railway, H.F.S. opened a garage selling Darracq and Wolseley cars.

It wasn't long before Morgan's inquisitive mechanical nature led to plans for the development of a motorcycle for his own use powered by a Peugeot V-2 engine. He enlisted the help of the engineering master at nearby Malvern College, but the influence of the emerging automobile soon modified his motorcycle idea. The vehicle that emerged in 1909 would become known as a cyclecar, a kind of amalgam of motorcycle and motor car. It was a one passenger, three-wheeler with the engine in front driving the single rear wheel through a shaft and chains.

Even this first prototype showed evidence of Morgan's ingenious mechanical approach. The frame's side members, for example, also did double duty as exhaust pipes. And the sliding pillar independent front suspension he used would prove such a sound design that it is still the basis for Morgans being built into the 21st century! It has finally deviated from its sliding pillars and gone with inboard coil springs over shock absorbers in the recently introduced Aero 8 model.

Although he had no real plans for production, H.F.S. did exhibit two of his little three-wheelers at London's Cycle and Motor Cycle Exhibition in 1910. The response was so positive that he decided to build them commercially. Thus, the Morgan Motor Company was established in 1912. The little machine was expanded to a two-passenger, and the great London retailer Harrods even agreed to carry them in their store.

The market proved receptive, and the tiny business gradually grew. Following a pause to make munitions for the First World War, Morgan continued to turn out its spindly three-wheelers, eventually making a snug back seat available for buyers with families. Being a three-wheeler meant it was classed as a motorcycle, resulting in an annual road tax that was half that of a comparably powered four wheel car.

Morgan power came from a variety of overhead and side-valve, air- and water-cooled motorcycle engines such as JAP and Matchless. In 1934 Morgan would make a four cylinder Ford engine available. When the three-wheeler lost much of its tax advantage in 1935, the three-wheeler went into decline.

The way to establish a reputation was through racing, and Morgan "trikes" were entered in many competitions, soon amassing an enviable list of victories. Morgan didn't have the three-wheel field entirely to itself, however; an active competitor was BSA.

Morgan added a four-wheel car in 1935, the Coventry Climax powered 4/4 model (four wheels, four cylinders), although they would continue to build the three-wheeler until the early 1950s.

Another English company that ventured into the three-wheeled field was Raleigh, famous for its bicycles. It introduced its four-seater "Safety Seven" model in 1934 with a layout that was quite different from other three-wheelers. Whereas

1940 Morgan F4 – a three-wheel pioneer

1961 Messerschmitt – three-wheel "Bubble Car"

Morgan and others had two wheels in front and one at the rear, Raleigh chose to put its single wheel in front. It was powered by a vee-twin motorcycle engine that fed its power through a three-speed car transmission, driveshaft and rear axle. The Raleigh's advantage was that its two rear wheels enabled it to carry four passengers without worrying about overloading a single rear wheel.

The taxing change caused Raleigh to discontinue car building in 1937, and it sold out to the Safety Seven's designer, T.L. Williams, who formed the Reliant Motor Company. Reliant would continue to build three-wheelers into the 1980s.

Following the Second World War the European need for cheap, motorized transportation spawned a variety of three-wheelers, referred to as "Bubble Cars." They were essentially replacements for the motorcycle and sidecar combination that was all many families could afford as transportation.

Among these were the Isetta from Italy, the Messerschmitt "Kabinenroller" and Heinkel from Germany, and the Bond from England. The Isetta came in three- and four-wheel versions, but even the four-wheeler had a rear track of only 508 mm (20 in.), so the effect was about the same as a three-wheeler. The manufacturing rights for the Isetta were bought by BMW of Germany, who built them from 1955 to the early sixties.

The configurations of these Bubble Cars differed. The rather egg-shaped Isetta and Heinkel, with their two wheels in front, carried two passengers abreast. To gain access the whole front of the car opened up as a door.

In the Messerschmitt the seats were in tan-

1948 Davis – American attempt to launch a three-wheeler

dem much like those in the fighter plane cockpit that inspired it (both Messerschmitt and Heinkel had been aircraft manufacturers). It had two wheels in front and one at the rear; later models would have four wheels.

The Bond seated two abreast, and had one wheel at the front and two at the rear. The engine was attached to the front wheel and turned as a unit when the wheel was steered. Although unorthodox, the Bond would continue to be made in updated versions until the 1970s.

These tiny three-wheelers pretty well faded out by the end of the fifties, to be replaced by much more practical four wheel cars like the British Motor Corporation's Mini, the Fiat 600 and the Hillman Imp. These "real" cars provided more space, better performance and safer motoring.

There was a sellers' market following the Second World War caused by the pent-up demand for new cars created by the war-time shutdown of the auto industry. This prompted a number of American entrepreneurs to try breaking into the automobile manufacturing business. Most used four wheels, but one, Glen Davis of California, tried to crack the market with a three-wheel car.

Davis organized the Davis Motor Car Company in Van Nuys, California, in 1947, and hired a number of engineers out of the aircraft industry. Not surprisingly, the Davis three- wheeler had some strong aircraft influences.

The Davis had one wheel at the front and two at the rear. The front one was mounted on a yoke suspended by two coil springs, aircraft style. The four cylinder Hercules or Continental engine was located in the front and drove the rear wheels through a Ford clutch, transmission and rear axle. Wheel changing was facilitated by built-in hydraulic jacks at each wheel.

Styling was also aircraft influenced, its sleek aluminum body smoothly enclosing the entire front of the car. The headlamps were hidden behind small doors, and cooling air entered under the bumper, eliminating the usual grille.

The Davis was a fairly large car, with a wheelbase of 2743 mm (108 in.), and an overall length of almost 4877 mm (16 ft). There was only one bench seat, and Davis claimed it would accommodate four passengers abreast, although they would have been a snug fit.

When the Davis made its public debut at the Ambassador Hotel in Los Angeles in November, 1947 it was enthusiastically received. Its projected price was to be under $1,000, and nearly 200 dealers paid almost a million dollars for the privilege of selling it.

Unfortunately Glen Davis didn't get his enterprise off the ground. The company suffered from lack of capital, and struggled through 1948 and into 1949. Amid charges of fraud, Davis was forced to close the doors in May 1949 after a total of just 17 Davises had been produced.

While Glen Davis's attempt to build and market a car was probably genuine, another three-wheel project that popped up in the 1970s was decidedly less convincing. This was the Dale car, brainchild of a burly lady by the name of Geraldine Elizabeth Carmichael and her Twentieth Century Motor Car Corporation, incorporated in Nevada and based in Encino, California.

The Dale, a stylish two-passenger runabout powered by a two cylinder portable electric generator engine, was unveiled in 1975. It had two wheels at the front and one at the rear. Although its body was to be constructed out of "Rigidex," a plastic claimed by Dale to be nine times stronger than steel, the prototype (there apparently was only one running) was made of fibreglass.

The Securities and Exchange Commission soon began to take an interest in the Dale operation, and when they began to make things hot for Twentieth Century, Dale decamped for Dallas, Texas, and set up her operation there. When the Dallas police became suspicious, the whole bizarre story started to unfold.

It turned out to be a giant hoax. Elizabeth Carmichael disappeared; it evolved that there was no such person. Carmichael was a transvestite named Jerry Dean Michael, a man who had been a 14-year fugitive from justice for counterfeiting and bail jumping. Needless to say, that was the end of the Dale three wheeler.

In spite of its fringe role in the automobile world, hardy three-wheel devotees persist. California was the source of yet another more recent three wheeler, the Trihawk, in the early 1980s. Manufactured by Trihawk Vehicles, Incorporated of Dana Point, California, its front wheels were driven by a 1.3 litre, flat, four cylinder Citroen engine hung out in front. It had a two passenger, fibreglass body, and would, according to *Road & Track* magazine (5/82), accelerate to 96 km/h (60 mph) in 10.2 seconds, and reach a top speed of 151 km/h (94 mph).

An even more recent three-wheel effort came out of Quebec in the form of the T-Rex from Campagna Motorsport of Plessisville. It was powered by a 1.1 litre 155 horsepower inline Suzuki four cylinder motorcycle engine mounted behind the two-passenger seat. It drove the single rear wheel via a chain, and the T-Rex was a real hot rod as far as three-wheelers go, accelerating through a quarter mile in under 14 seconds, and reaching a top speed of over 201 km/h (125 mph).

Although three-wheelers down through time have played a minor role in the grand scheme of automotive history, there always seems to be yet one more disciple willing to gamble that three wheels are enough.

Turbocharging: "Free" Horsepower From Thin Air

Using a turbocharger, short for turbine-driven supercharger, to recover "free" power from the stream of hot exhaust gas that flows out the tailpipe every minute we drive seems like such an elegant engineering achievement. Simply insert a gas turbine (the "hot" end of the turbocharger) into that exhaust stream, and use the resulting rotational motion to spin a compressor (the "cold" end) mounted on the same shaft. Using this compressor to pump more air and fuel into the engine means that more power comes out.

The compressor, or air pump, "boosts" more air into the engine than it would breathe normally. Since the turbine is driven by exhaust flow, it is free spinning, not attached to the crankshaft by the belts, gears or chains required by mechanically driven superchargers. It is an elegant engineering achievement, but not one without some compromises, most notably the time delay, called turbo lag, when the impeller is spinning up to the speed where it will produce more power.

Although the exhaust-driven turbosupercharger first appeared on production cars in the 1960s, it had already been around for many years. Its early principal application began in the late teens to help aircraft engines maintain sea level performance in the thin air of high altitudes.

While the turbocharger is said to have been invented by a Swiss engineer named Alfred Buchi in 1905, Dr. Sanford Moss of General Electric in the USA could be called the father of modern turbocharging. He dedicated his life to turbine machinery. Turbines were the subject of his Master's and Doctoral theses at Cornell University in Ithaca, New York. By 1903 he was working on various types of turbines, including gas and steam, and centrifugal air compressors.

During the First World War the American National Advisory Committee for Aeronautics became aware that French engineer Auguste Rateau had built a turbocharged aircraft engine. They knew that General Electric was experimenting with turbines, and asked it to work with U.S. military engineers in pursuing aircraft turbocharging. GE's expert was Dr. Moss.

Dr. Moss and associates applied a turbocharger to the First World War V-12 Liberty aircraft engine with excellent results. In 1918 a test was conducted on Pikes Peak at an altitude of 4267 m (14,000 ft), using a truck-mounted portable dynamometer. The turbo increased the Liberty's horsepower from 221 to 356. In 1921 a turbocharged Liberty engine powered a plane to a world altitude record of 12,435 m (40,800 ft).

With the end of the war, interest in aircraft turbocharging became less intense, although Moss and others continued to work on it. They tackled many problems, including the high temperature alloys required for the turbine wheels, the shape of the turbines, bearings and lubrication, the compressor and housing configurations, and the use of intercoolers to reduce the heat generated by compressing the air before it entered the engine. The wastegate, a valve that routes some exhaust flow around the turbo to prevent overboosting, was also developed.

It again took the impetus of war to spur turbocharger development. As war clouds gathered over Europe in the 1930s, the U.S. military wanted a heavy bomber that could fly at high altitudes. The Boeing B-17 "Flying Fortress" was the result, and turbocharging gave it the high altitude performance desired. It was so successful that during the Second World War most American military planes were fitted with turbochargers. The development of the pure "jet" engine flowed from gas turbine development.

Back on land, turbochargers were used on some commercial diesel engines before the Second World War. After the war they began to find more popularity on large industrial diesels in such applications as ships and construction equipment, where turbocharging was well adapted to the fairly constant operating speeds. It was also applied to large trucks, particularly for use in mountainous areas.

Performance and racing car enthusiasts began experimenting with turbochargers during the 1950s, but it wasn't until the 1960s that automobile manufacturers began offering turbocharging on production cars.

In the spring of 1962 Oldsmobile and Chevrolet introduced turbocharged models. Oldsmobile's F-85 "Jetfire" was first, with Chevrolet's Corvair Spyder coming a month later. Although they both used the same turbocharging application principles, their approach to engine detonation protection was different.

The Jetfire was a turbocharged version of Oldsmobile's 3.5 litre (215 cu in.) overhead valve aluminum V-8. In normally aspirated form it developed 155 horsepower, with 185 available in a high performance option. The turbo version produced 215 horsepower, or one for each cubic inch of displacement, so turbocharging gave a significant power increase.

Although supercharged engines normally have lower compression ratios to compensate for the increased cylinder pressures, Oldsmobile kept its Jetfire compression ratio at a high 10.2:1. To protect the engine from harmful detonation, an exhaust wastegate limited maximum boost to a moderate five pounds per square inch, and water injection (actually a mixture of 50% water and 50% alcohol) was used. This anti-detonation fluid was fed into the intake manifold when boost exceeded one psi.

Chevrolet's approach to detonation control in its turbocharged Corvair Spyder was different. It ran a moderate 8.0:1 compression, and by using a special ignition advance curve was able to run a boost pressure of 10 psi. The power output of the Spyder was 150 horsepower, compared with 102 for the high performance normally aspirated engine. With a displacement of 2.4 litres (145 cu in.), it produced slightly more than one horse-power per cubic inch.

The performance of both the Olds Jetfire and the Corvair Spyder were considerably improved over their non-turbo sisters. The Spyder, for example, was in the 10 second zero-to-96 km/h (60-mph) range, compared with about 18 for the normally aspirated model.

One of the problems of turbochargers had always been turbo lag. Early applications had fairly large turbine and compressor wheels, in the order of 152 to 178 mm (6 to 7 in.) in diameter. These typically spun to a maximum of about 35,000 rpm, and the inertia of the large wheels contributed to turbo lag.

1964 Chevrolet Corvair Spyder – turbocharging pioneer

To counteract this, the Olds Jetfire, for example, had a (61 mm) (2.4 in.) compressor wheel, and a 63 mm (2.5 in.) turbine. While not eliminating turbo lag completely, its low inertia allowed it to quickly spin up to the point where boost was produced. Maximum rpm of the Jetfire turbo unit was approximately 90,000.

For all of their engineering finesse, these turbo engines were more prone to trouble than non-turbo engines. Controlling detonation and keeping the turbo bearings cool and lubricated were on-going challenges. Always lurking in the background was the fact that an easier route to high performance in those days of cheap fuel was to simply build a larger engine. The result was that in spite of their engineering sophistication, turbos died out. Oldsmobile kept its turbo for only two years, while the Corvair Spyder was offered until 1966. Turbochargers on production automobiles would not be heard from for another decade.

Fuel economy and pollution control requirements combined to make the turbocharger look attractive again in the 1970s. The first energy crisis of 1973 had raised oil supply concerns, as well as prices, and resulted in fuel economy legislation. At the same time environmental awareness was dictating the need for lower emissions. These had the auto industry in a vise. Larger engines were required to counteract the power sapping impact of emission controls, but those larger engines used more fuel. It was a classic dilemma.

One avenue of relief was the turbocharger; it made a small engine act like a big one, yet burned less fuel. Porsche returned the turbo to the auto scene with the introduction of the Turbo Carrera in 1975. Its 3.0 litre single overhead cam flat six turbocharged engine produced 234 horsepower, compared with the normally aspirated 911S's 157 out of 2.7 litres. That was 78 horsepower per litre for the turbo engine, compared with 58 for the normally aspirated 911S. And in spite of that tremendous power increase, fuel economy didn't suffer much. Transport Canada's 1977 fuel economy combined city/highway figures were 22 mpg (Imperial) for the Porsche 911S, and 20 for the Turbo Carrera. The highway rating of 29 mpg was the same for both.

The next manufacturer with a turbo was Sweden's Saab in 1976. As a family car Saab's approach to the use of the turbocharger was more conservative. Using a relatively small 2.0 litre engine, it engineered the turbo to provide good mid-range torque rather than high rpm power. Saab would go on to become one of the leading innovators in turbocharging.

Diesel engines with their love of airflow are where turbochargers really shine. It's not surprising then that in response to fuel consumption legislation, Mercedes-Benz offered a turbocharged diesel car, the 1978 300SD. The 3.0 litre inline five cylinder Turbo Diesel gave the large S-series Mercedes very acceptable performance – zero to 96 km/h (60 mph) in under 13 seconds – combined with outstanding fuel economy. Transport Canada's 1979 guide recorded a combined urban/highway rating of 9.0 L/100 km, or 31.4 mpg.

General Motors also returned to the turbo arena in 1978, this time from the Buick Division. It offered such turbocharged models as the Regal and LeSabre sport coupes. By fitting a turbo to its 3.8 litre V-6, Buick was able to provide V-8 performance with six cylinder economy.

Through the 1980s most manufacturers would jump on the turbo bandwagon. Ford had its Mustang Turbo, Pontiac turbocharged its Trans Am, and Volkswagen obtained outstanding fuel economy with its turbo diesel Rabbit (later Golf). Turbos became particularly popular at Chrysler Corp. (it claimed to be the world's largest turbo user) as it powered heavier and heavier vehicles with 2.2 and 2.5 litre turbo fours.

Turbochargers and mechanically driven superchargers continued to be popular in the 1990s. Also, engineers learned to improve the airflow of naturally aspirated engines with such things as variable valve timing and multi-valve cylinder heads.

But while turbocharger popularity had waned, development didn't stop. Water cooled bearings and better materials and lubrication increased turbo life to virtually that of the rest of the engine. Light weight turbos – ceramics have been used – and clever routing of gases to keep rotors spinning fast have made turbo lag almost a thing of the past. They have become just one more technical weapon in the engineers' arsenal as they continue to wring more power and economy out of the old piston engine.

Not surprisingly, Saab, an early user, and the most loyal proponent of turbocharging, still offers it. Its 1998 9-5 model had what Saab calls asymmetrical turbocharging. A turbo was fitted to only one bank of its 3.0 litre V-6, but fed compressed air to all six cylinders. Maximum boost was only 3.7 psi, and no wastegate was used; an electronically controlled throttle managed boost. Using just "half" a turbo saves weight, plumbing and complexity.

After more than 80 years, there's still life in Dr. Moss's old turbocharger.

Ten Most Significant Automotive Developments

The number of technical developments, large and small, that have contributed to the improvement of the automobile over its 100-plus year history has been too numerous to count. But as the twentieth century drew to a close the Society of Automotive Engineers set out to produce some order out of this labyrinth. It asked the Fellows of the association to choose what they considered to be the 10 greatest automotive engineering achievements. Here are their choices in chronological order:

Pneumatic Tire - 1888

The pneumatic tire was originally patented by Robert William Thomson of Scotland in 1845 but the market was not yet ready for it and it faded into obscurity. In 1888 another Scot, veterinarian John Boyd Dunlop, who was practising in Ireland, patented an air-filled tire. This time it caught on, having arrived in the midst of a cycling craze spawned by the invention of the low-wheeled "safety" bicycle. Dunlop's name is now inextricably associated with the pneumatic tire.

Pneumatic tires were soon fitted to the emerging automobile, and were used on the first recognized production car in America, the 1896 Duryea Motor Wagon. The air-filled tire revolutionized land travel by providing a smoother ride, requiring much less energy input for a given speed and distance, and yielding outstanding traction capabilities. It has evolved through literally thousands of improvements to bring it to the reliable, long wearing, all weather tires that form the vital link between today's vehicles and the road. (Also see the section on John Boyd Dunlop in Twenty-Five Who Made A Difference.)

Electric Self-Starter - 1912

Before the invention of the electric self-starter, credited to Charles Kettering of the Dayton Engineering Laboratory Company (Delco), starting an internal combustion engine could be both difficult and dangerous. This became even more so as engine size grew. Kettering had been with the National Cash Register Company where he motorized the cash register. His genius was to recognize that an electric motor could be temporarily overloaded without damage, and thus he was able to use a smaller motor than conventional wisdom suggested. It worked for the cash register, so Kettering applied the same principle to the gasoline engine starter, also with successful results.

The electric starter, introduced on the 1912 Cadillac, was a milestone in automotive history. It gave the gasoline engine the decisive edge it needed to vanquish electric and steam powered cars, and expanded the use of the automobile by allowing it to be driven by people unable to operate a crank, including women and older people. It became universal in the industry within a few years.

Moving Automobile Assembly Line - 1913

The assembly of a car by moving it along from work station to work station, that is, bringing the car to the parts rather than the parts to the car, was first experimented with by the Ford Motor Company's production chief Charles Sorensen and some assistants in 1908. Henry Ford was skeptical but not opposed. It took five years before it would actually be used for the assembly of a whole car. Sorensen explained in his book, *My Forty Years With Ford*, that it was not implemented immediately because it would have been difficult at the Piquette Avenue plant in Detroit where car assembly took place on the third floor.

When the company had moved to its larger Highland Park premises, and demand for the Model T had proved to be extremely strong, they finally introduced the moving assembly line in the summer of 1913. It revolutionized the way cars were built, reducing production time for the Model T from 12-1/2 hours to 1-1/2. Ford production increased from 170,000 in 1912 to 500,000 in 1915. It also allowed Ford to increase its daily wage to five dollars in 1914, a radical step when the average industrial rate was about half that. It enabled the workers who built Fords to also afford to buy them.

Hydraulic Brakes - 1921

In the early days of the automobile, engineers were more concerned with getting cars to start and run reliably, than with making them stop. Brakes were crude affairs with levers or pedals actuating blocks, rods or cables acting on the rear wheels only, or on the driveshaft. They were usually of the external contracting type in which a friction band, usually asbestos, wrapped around the outside of a brake drum and squeezed against it. Moving the bands inside the drums improved effectiveness, but actuation via cables and rods was still inefficient; balancing brake pressure among wheels was a continuing problem.

As more reliable and powerful engines made cars faster, the need for improved stopping power increased. The Duesenberg Motor Company of Indianapolis, Indiana, decided to hydraulically actuate the brakes of its 1921 French Grand Prix racer. It used a master cylinder to deliver hydraulic pressure through pipes to slave cylinders at the wheels, where they pressed the brake shoes against the drums. The hydraulic pressure was the same to all wheels, thereby eliminating unequal brake application, and brake shoe pressure was greater. Duesenberg won the race, and its hydraulic brakes were a decisive factor in the victory. Duesenberg quickly applied them to their Model A production car which reached the market in 1921. Hydraulic brakes soon caught on in the auto industry. An early major adopter was Chrysler; they were fitted to the first 1924 Chrysler, and subsequently to all Chrysler products.

Automatic Transmission - 1940

A fully automatic transmission to replace the sliding-gear-and-clutch type was for many years one of automotive engineering's Holy Grails. Although engineers had been working on eliminating gear shifting since almost the turn of the century, and the synchromesh transmission introduced by Cadillac in 1929 certainly eased gear shifting, it took some 40 years to bring the full automatic to fruition. Among the attempts was the Carter friction drive comprised of drive wheel from the engine pressing at right angles against a large driven wheel covered with friction material. By moving the driven wheel back and forth across the drive wheel different ratios could be achieved. It failed due to excessive wear.

Another attempt, the Owen Magnetic, used electric generators and motors. General Motors tried rollers pressed between two wheels with curved surfaces. By altering the angle of the rollers, different ratios could be obtained. Like the Carter drive it failed due to excessive wear.

Moving the gears using pneumatic cylinders was also tried, but it was cumbersome and troublesome. Reo's 1933 "Silent Shifter" used a planetary gear-like system, and centrifugal weights to shift its two-speed transmission into high at 22 km/h (14 mph). A clutch was still required for startup, and the Silent Shifter suffered from roughness and slippage.

It fell to General Motors to develop the fully automatic transmission. Its first foray came in the 1937 Oldsmobile, comprised of a four-speed planetary transmission (the same principle as Henry Ford's Model T transmission) with a manual clutch. Once under way, using the clutch, the transmission shifted automatically by preventing different elements of the planetary gearset from turning. The next step was to replace the clutch with a fluid coupling which allowed slippage at low speeds, letting the car remain stationary with the engine idling, but gradually coupling up as engine speed increased. Eliminating the clutch brought fully automatic shifting. The planetary gear "Hydra-Matic" transmission was introduced on the 1940 Oldsmobile, and became available on the 1941 Cadillac. The automatic transmission is one of the most sophisticated components of modern cars, and is now fitted to some 90 percent of new passenger vehicles.

Air Conditioning - 1940

Refrigerated air conditioning is one of the modern marvels of automobile travel, and like other complex components, it had an evolutionary development. The working principle of refrigeration is that the refrigerant (initially a chlorine/fluorine compound with the trade name Freon-12, now replaced by more environmentally friendly compounds) absorbs a great deal of heat when it changes from a liquid to a vapour, and releases it when it is compressed and returns to a liquid. An air conditioner accomplishes this with three basic units: a compressor, driven by a belt off the crankshaft; an evaporator located in the cowl which cools the air coming into the car; and a condenser located in front of the engine's cooling radiator that dissipates the heat back into the atmosphere.

The air conditioners that auto manufacturers began experimenting with in the 1930s were bulky and heavy, weighing up to 136 kg (300 lb). Packard was the first automobile manufacturer to offer air conditioning in its 1940 models. In early systems some of the mechanism was under the hood, while the evaporator and blower were in the trunk. This added a lot of plumbing and complexity. The cool air entered the cabin through vents on the rear parcel shelf, or was sent forward through plastic tubes passing above the doors. It was better than nothing, but passengers would rather have had the air coming out of the cowl area.

By modern standards those early units were crude. Besides being heavy and large, there was no electromagnetic clutch on the compressor, with the result that it had to rotate all the time. This wore it out prematurely and caused a parasitic drag on the engine. Owners could remove the compressor drive belt during the winter, but this was an unwelcome nuisance.

General Motors made a considerable improvement in its 1954 Cadillac and Pontiac air conditioning by putting the evaporator in one of the front fenders. It used the heater's blower to move the cool air, but was not integrated with the heater. It fell to one of the independents, American Motors, to introduce the first truly integrated system. This combined the heater and air conditioning evaporator in the cowl area, and appeared in the "Weather Eye" system in AMC's 1956 products. It went a long way toward popularizing air conditioning in cars.

Air conditioning is now very popular, and very reliable compared with earlier systems. It will almost certainly become standard equipment in all cars, as ubiquitous as heaters. Modern automatic climate control systems that integrate the A/C with the heater to keep a constant cabin temperature make driving a pleasure in any kind of weather.

Fuel Injection - 1950

Rather than having the air and fuel mixed together in a carburetor, a fuel injection system metres the fuel into the engine under pressure just upstream of the intake valve (port injection), or directly into the combustion chamber (direct injection). An exception was the modified carburetor-type throttle-body injection used briefly by the American industry and some imports such as Nissan and Honda as a cost-saving measure. Along with more precise metering of fuel, injection eliminates the cylinder-to-cylinder air/fuel mixture variations that can be caused by a circuitous intake manifold.

Fuel injection was pioneered in diesel engines, with the first production automobile diesel appearing in 1936 from Mercedes-Benz. It had its fuel oil injected directly into the cylinders via a high pressure pump, and combustion was caused by the high cylinder pressure, not by an electric spark as in a gasoline engine.

Automobile gasoline engine fuel injection appeared in 1950 on the small German Goliath and Gutbrod cars. The fuel was injected directly into the combustion chambers of their two-stroke engines. This was followed in 1954 by the Mercedes-Benz 300 SL, which had a conventional four-stroke engine, and the fuel was again injected directly into the cylinders.

American Motors, in a significant harbinger of the future, announced that its 1956 Rambler Rebel would be available with Bendix electronic fuel injection. It wasn't really production ready, however, and very few, if any, were sold. The American industry introduced successful fuel injection in the 1957 Chevrolet. It was manufactured by the Rochester company, and was a very complex mechanical system of cams, levers and bellows. It was expensive to buy, and it was a rare technician who could repair and calibrate one successfully. Chevrolet discontinued fuel injection in sedans, where few had been sold, after a few years, but kept it in the Corvette until the mid-1960s.

Electronics would provide the real advancement in fuel injections. Volkswagen pioneered Bosch electronic fuel injection on its 1968 1600 series cars, and electronic injection would gradually displace mechanical systems. European manufacturers were ahead of American cars in adopting fuel injection, but the American industry was eventually driven to it by increasingly stringent emissions and fuel economy standards. By the 1980s fuel injection was virtually universal, and it has provided motorists with engines that start easily, run smoothly, and are both cleaner and more economical that they would have been with the now departed, but not lamented, carburetor.

Catalytic Converter - 1975

If there was a "magic bullet" in cleaning up automobile exhaust emissions it was the catalytic converter. Championed by General Motors, amid the dissenting voices of other automakers, the "cat" has accomplished everything that was envisioned for it. It allowed a return to cars with good drivability, and significantly reduced the three main pollutants from the internal combustion engine: carbon monoxide (CO), unburned hydrocarbons (HC) and oxides of nitrogen (NOx). NOx reduction by the cat was not immediate, but eventually did come under its control. And the cat did its job with 161,000 km (100,000 mile) durability.

The catalytic converter is a muffler shaped, stainless steel canister inserted into the exhaust system. Inside is a carrier, usually a ceramic substrate, which is coated with three precious metals: platinum; palladium; and rhodium. These act as catalysts, setting up the desired chemical reactions in the exhaust gases without being consumed themselves. Since the reactions generate high temperatures, the converter has to be shielded from the bottom of the car.

The converter brought with it a substantial change in the way gasoline was refined. Since lead "poisons" a converter, GM began warning oil companies as early as 1970 that they would have to start removing tetraethyl lead from their gasoline to accommodate the catalytic converter. This resulted in lower octane gasoline in which the octanes had to be "refined in" rather than leaded in. A side effect was that lead had acted as a valve lubricant, so that metallurgists had to learn how to retain valve life without lead. There was much grumbling from the oil industry about unleaded gasoline, but with the spectre of tightening government emission standards, which the cat promised to facilitate, they really didn't have much choice. Plus, eliminating lead had health benefits, and made spark plugs last much longer.

The use of the catalytic converter resulted in an immediate 10 to 15 percent improvement in automobile fuel economy by allowing engineers to tune the engines more efficiently. The converter couldn't do the entire cleanup job itself, but it certainly made a major contribution. In spite of its early detractors, the catalytic converter became universal, and was truly an engineering and scientific automotive breakthrough.

Electronic Engine Controls - 1970s

After American Motors Corporation's premature dabble with electronic fuel injection in 1956, electronics lay largely dormant in cars until electronic engine controls began appearing in the late 1970s. It was a happy occurrence because it was becoming apparent that the old mechanical systems were not precise enough to meet tightening emissions and fuel economy requirements. The silicone chip was about to wipe out 75 years of ignition and fuel control technology. Along with the increasing use of electronic fuel injection, it became necessary to use the computer to manage the engine's ignition timing, plus other functions such as exhaust gas recirculation and air-fuel ratio.

Chrysler began offering its "Lean Burn" engine system on some 1976 models which allowed it to meet non-California emission standards without the use of the still controversial catalytic converter. Traditionally an engine's ignition timing had been mechanically adjusted in response to engine speed and load, as signalled by intake manifold vacuum. Lean burn added to these factors such parameters as inlet air and coolant temperatures, and throttle position, to determine the optimum ignition timing. A computer enabled the timing to be adjusted in milliseconds to meet changing conditions, which allowed the use of ultra-low air/fuel ratios (lean burn) for much of the time. This attacked the emission problem right inside the combustion chamber, and had the benefit of lowering both emissions and fuel consumption.

Other manufactures quickly began adopting electronic engine control, and by the end of the 1980s computers were managing the complete powertrain, not just the engine. The "electronic revolution" was the engineers' salvation, enabling them to meet emissions and fuel economy legislation that would not have been possible with the old mechanical systems using vacuum and centrifugal ignition adjustment, and cam operated ignition points. Modern cars have more computing power than the original moon rocket, and it has moved well beyond its original ignition and fuel management chores to such areas as ABS brakes, stability control and navigation systems. Electronics have revolutionized the automobile.

Seat Belts and Air Bags

The seat belt has been the greatest single life and injury saver for automobile passengers since the invention of the car. Certainly developments such as hydraulic brakes, radial tires, precise steering, side impact beams and controlled deformation of auto bodies have all made significant contributions to preventing highway carnage, but the three-point lap-and-shoulder belt stands alone as the outstanding, easy-to-use, universal safety device.

It took a while for motorists to accept the critical protection provide by seat belts. Nash had offered them in 1950 but found little interest. Then in 1956 Ford tried to sell safety with such items as padded instrument panels and sun visors, recessed steering hubs, and seat belts. The public greeted them with a yawn, and Chevrolets outsold Fords.

The three-point safety belt was invented in 1958 by the late Nils Bohlin, a safety engineer with Sweden's Volvo Car Company. He had just arrived at Volvo from the aircraft industry where he worked on jet ejector seats and restraints. He transferred his expertise to automobile seat belts, and his three-point lap-and-shoulder belt was made standard in 1959 Volvos sold in Europe. In a study of 28,000 accidents following the introduction of the belt, they were found to be more than 60 percent effective in preventing deaths and injuries. They soon spread to the rest of the world, and their use is now legislated in many jurisdictions.

Safety belts began being supplemented by air bags in the 1980s. General Motors had tried to market them in the mid-1970s, but the public was not yet ready. They became more popular in the 1980s, and toward the end of the decade driver side airbag use was widespread. Front passenger bags soon followed, and automobile manufacturers began learning how to make them "smart" by tailoring the deployment to specific conditions, such as smaller or out of position passengers. By the end of the 1990s not only were driver and front passenger belts standard, but other side- and roof-mounted inflatable bags and air curtains protected passengers' heads and bodies.

CAR OF THE CENTURY
HENRY FORD'S UBIQUITOUS MODEL T

The twentieth century has produced a marvellous cornucopia of technology, inventions that have dramatically changed the way we live. But of all of those wondrous artifacts, such as the airplane, the television, the telephone, and the computer, none, arguably, has had quite the impact of the automobile. It literally transformed society.

The ability to go where and when one wanted gave personal freedom and independence never dreamed possible. It abolished rural isolation, and shaped our towns and cities. As the century drew to a close, it was deemed fitting to honour the automobile by selecting the one vehicle that best exemplifies the machine that has been such a powerful force in our society.

To be strictly accurate, the internal combustion engined car was a product of the late nineteenth century. Two Germans, Carl Benz and Gottlieb Daimler, both drove their gasoline powered cars in 1886, and Benz received a patent for his Benz "Patentwagen" on January 29, 1886. But although it was invented in the nineteenth, it wasn't until the twentieth century that the car became a practical conveyance, and gradually came into general use.

The idea for selecting a car of the century originated in the Netherlands. Two car enthusiasts, Dick Holzhaus and Michael Kalf, conceived the idea in about 1989, but couldn't bring it to fruition until the mid-1990s. At that time they were able to interest Fred van der Vlugt, a prominent Dutch automotive journalist, and the idea became a project.

In 1996 van der Vlugt set out to establish an organization to select the car of the century. The result was a Global Automotive Elections Foundation whose task was to co-ordinate the election process.

An Honourary Committee of internationally respected automotive experts formed part of the Foundation. This committee, through a secretariat based in Amsterdam, co-ordinated the world-wide jury of professional automotive journalists who voted on the cars.

The committee of experts was comprised of Thomas Bryant, editor-in-chief, *Road & Track* magazine (U.S); Paul Frere, independent auto journalist (Europe); Shotaro Kobayashi, editorial director, *Car Graphic* (Japan); Lord Montagu of Beaulieu, museum director (chairman of the honourary committee) (Europe); and Gordon Wilkins, independent auto journalist (Europe). Lorin Tryon, chairman, Pebble Beach Concours d'Elegance (U.S.) was also a member of the committee, but unfortunately he died before the end of the century.

Serving as the international jury for the COTC were 135 professional automotive journalists from 32 countries on all continents. There were three Canadians jurors: Alex Law of the Toronto Star; Jim Robinson of Metroland Newspapers; and the author.

To bring the huge number of nameplates down to a manageable size, the car distillation process was extensive. Of the thousands of brands that have marched through automotive history, 1500 were nominated by the industry, auto clubs and museums. Of these, 716 were confirmed as eligible by the committee of experts.

There were three eligibility criteria: The car must have been in series production with more than 50 built; It must have been designed for passenger transportation on public roads; And it must be a model of which at least three still exist.

The committee of experts then applied their knowledge and experience to shrink the original 716 down to 200 cars. The list of 200 was presented to the world-wide jury in Amsterdam in February 1997.

This eclectic and disparate collection ranged from the 1902-04 Lanchester to the Lexus LS 400, from the Model T Ford to the BMC Mini, from the World War II Willys Jeep to the Volkswagen Beetle. There were front engines and rear engines, gasoline, electric and steam (but no diesel) power, sports cars and sedans, and exotic marques such as Lamborghinis and Ferraris. They represented nine countries of origin.

The jury's job was to gradually reduce this group from 200 down to just one by December 1999. The jury's selection criteria were: General design; Historical significance; Handling and roadworthiness (compared with contemporaries); Performance (compared with contemporaries); and Technical innovation relevant to its period.

The 100 finalists that were announced at the Frankfurt Auto Show in September 1997, were varied and international, as would be expected of a world-wide jury. Nine countries and 57 marques were represented from Europe, Japan and the USA.

Every decade from the 1890s to the 1990s was included, with the 1930s to the 1960s predominating. Lancia of Italy had six nominees, followed by Alfa Romeo, BMW, Ford, Jaguar and Renault with four each. The jury then set to work reducing the 100 down to the 25 finalists, which were announced at the Geneva Motor Show in March 1999.

At the 25-car point the public was also invited to cast its votes, which had the potential of increasing the number to a maximum of 35. The 26 finalists were as follows:

Alfa Romeo Giuletta Sprint Coupe 1954 - 1968 Italy
Audi Quattro 1980 - 1991 Germany
Austin Seven 1922 - 1939 England
BMW 328 1936 - 1940 Germany
Bugatti Type 35 1926 - 1930 France
Chevrolet Corvette Sting Ray 1963 - 1967 USA
Citroen Traction Avant 1934 - 1957 France
Citroen 2CV 1948 - 1990 France
Citroen DS 19 1955 - 1965 France
Ferrari 250 GT SWB Berlinetta 1959 - 1962 Italy
Fiat 500 Topolino 1936 - 1948 Italy
Ford Model T 1908 - 1927 USA
Ford Mustang 1964 - 1968 USA
Jaguar XK120 1949 - 1954 England
Jaguar E-type 1961 - 1975 England
Mercedes-Benz S/SS/SSK 1927 - 1932 Germany
Mercedes-Benz 300SL Coupe 1954 - 1957 Germany
Mini 1959 - present England
NSU Ro80 - 1967 - 1977 Germany
Porsche 911 1963 - present Germany
Renault Espace 1984 - present France
Rolls-Royce Silver Ghost 1907 - 1925 England
Rover Range Rover 1970 - 1996 England
Volkswagen Beetle 1945 - present Germany
Volkswagen Golf 1974 - 1984 Germany
Willys Jeep 1941 - 1945 USA

The jury then made the selection on the final five, with the procedure now changed from a simple "yes-no" system, to a point allocation method, with 25 points to be divided among the five cars, with a maximum of 10 to any one car.

The crowning of the Car of the Century took place on December 4, 1999 in a special television presentation in Las Vegas, Nevada. The COTC also had a web-site on the internet (http:// www. cotc. com).

The winning Car of the Century was the American Ford Model T. It was a fitting choice because the "T" brought mass mobility on a scale previously unimagined. Widespread availability and affordability of the car would gradually spawn a variety of associated social developments such as suburbia, the drive-in theatre, drive-through restaurant, the motel and drive-in church. The ultimate manifestation of North America's automobile love affair is the drive-through wedding chapel.

The four runners up were the BMC Mini, Citroen DS19, Volkswagen Beetle, and Porsche 911. The Mini set the tone for the modern car's layout. Citroen's DS19 demonstrated innovative technology and aerodynamics. The Volkswagen Beetle is the closest to a world car that has so far been produced. And the Porsche 911 is indeed the evergreen sports car. Following are capsule descriptions of each one.

1911 Ford Model T

1959 Austin Mini

Ford Model T. Henry Ford's "Flivver" was sturdy, low priced, and universal, a social and industrial revolution that made Henry Ford an American legend, and the Ford Motor Company at its peak the largest automobile maker on the globe. The Model T put North America and much of the rest of the world on wheels, eliminated rural isolation, and ushered in the era of mass production with the pioneering of the moving automobile assembly line in 1913. The famous Ford five dollar day wage came in 1914. The T's use of vanadium steel made it extremely strong in spite of its spindly appearance. From 1908 to 1927 over 15 million Model Ts were built, a production record that stood until it was broken by the Volkswagen Beetle in 1972.

British Motor Corporation Mini. The Mini was a marvel of packaging, thanks to its front-wheel drive and cross-engine design. Although it wasn't the first with front drive, nor the first to use the cross-engine layout, it was the car that brought them together in an unbelievably space efficient manner. Although only 3048 mm (10 feet) long, it could carry four passengers and their luggage. Its tiny, rubber-cone suspension contributed to its surprising interior space. Conceived by a brilliant, if somewhat eccentric engineer named Alec Issigonis, the Mini demonstrated the effectiveness of the cross-engine, front-wheel drive layout, a system now used by the majority of the world's cars. Like the Volkswagen Beetle, it has inspired a modern version.

1955 Citroen DS19

1955 Volkswagen Beetle

Citroen DS 19. The Citroen DS 19's flowing aerodynamic lines and imaginative mechanicals were as advanced in 1955 as the Citroen Traction Avant's had been in 1934. The avant-guard unit construction body was made of steel (doors and fenders), aluminum (hood and trunk lid) and fibreglass (roof). The only carryover technology was the 1911 cc, overhead valve four cylinder engine. It had front-wheel drive, popularized by the Traction. The DS's "heart" was a belt-driven hydraulic pump for the central hydraulic system that operated the hydropneumatic suspension, and the brakes, clutch, steering and gear shift. The long 3124 mm (123 in.) wheelbase provided a cavernous interior, and the DS 19 was a superbly comfortable high speed cruiser.

Volkswagen Beetle. The Beetle is as close to a universal world car as we are ever likely to see. It was conceived in the 1930s by the Porsche Design Office. The mandate was to create an economical yet robust car that was affordable by the average family. The Second World War interrupted production, but it did begin slowly after peace came in 1945. The VW's basically sound design and sturdiness, and the Volkswagen company's diligent attention to sales and service, made it the world's predominant small car. It also formed the basis for the famous Porsche sports car. More than 21 million have been built, a production record for a basically unchanged car, and it is still being produced in Mexico. Its reservoir of goodwill was so deep that it inspired a New Beetle, which is also built in Mexico.

1966 Porsche 911

Porsche 911. The first Porsche Type 356 that emerged in 1948 evolved directly from the Volkswagen Beetle. Thus it had four-wheel independent torsion bar suspension, and an air cooled, horizontally opposed four cylinder engine behind the rear axle. The 911, which appeared in 1963 was a new design, but although it was moving away from its VW heritage, its basic layout was still a derivative of the 356. It had a crisper body design with larger windows, and the air cooled engine was now a flat six, still behind the rear axle. Torsion bars were retained all around, but with A-arms replacing the front trailing arms. The 911 amassed a prodigious competition record, and went through many permutations over its history, which continues to this day. Its horizontally opposed engine (now with water cooling) is still in the rear. The Porsche 911 is one of the great sports cars of all time.

Twenty-Five Who Made A Difference

GOTTLIEB DAIMLER – 1834 – 1900
Inventor - Daimler-Motoren-Gesellschaft and Others

Gottlieb Daimler and Carl Benz, both Germans, were the fathers of the automobile. Daimler installed an engine in a motorcycle and a boat in 1885, and then in a four wheel motorized carriage in 1886. Benz completed his motorized three-wheeled car in 1885, and patented it in January, 1886, so technically he was first.

Daimler was born on March 17, 1834, in the Village of Schorndorf, Kingdom of Wurttemberg, in southern Germany. After receiving a good basic education he was apprenticed to a gunsmith at age 14, then began working for a railway car and locomotive builder. At age 23 he began studying engineering at Stuttgart Polytechnic College.

Upon graduation Daimler returned to his employer, but becoming disillusioned with steam power, left in 1860 and travelled to Paris to see an internal combustion engine invented by Jean-Joseph Lenoir. He was not impressed. Daimler then went to England, the heart of the industrial revolution, and while working there was enthralled with the machinery. He returned to Germany in 1863, and took a job managing a vocational school that included a paper mill and sawmill. One of his students was a brilliant boy named Wilhelm Maybach, who would also become an engineer. They became inseparable both professionally and personally. Maybach would work closely with Daimler in the development of the high-speed internal combustion engine, and would later design some of Daimler's most famous cars. His son Karl would establish his own company to build luxury cars.

In 1868 Daimler was hired as general manager of Maschinenbau Gesellschaft Karlsruhe (Karlsruhe engineering works), a heavy engineering company. But he had never lost his passion for the internal combustion engine, and left four years later to become technical director of Gasmotoren-Fabrik Deutz (Deutz gas engine factory). Deutz manufactured Otto-Langen two-stroke, coal gas burning internal combustion engines. Daimler, and Maybach who had followed him to Karlsruhe, then to Deutz, reorganized Deutz into a successful and profitable engine maker.

By 1876 a German engineer named Nicholas Otto had developed a more efficient, coal gas fuelled four-stroke compression engine, and patented it in 1877. Daimler and Maybach refined Otto's engine, and envisioned it burning petroleum products, thus enabling it to operate anywhere. Unfortunately Daimler and Otto antagonized each other so much that one had to leave. Since Otto had the patent, Daimler was fired.

Daimler bought a house in Cannstatt, near Stuttgart, in 1882, and converted the greenhouse into a shop. He convinced Maybach to join him, and the two gifted engineers began exploring Daimler's dream of a smaller, lighter, higher revving engine than the Otto design, fuelled by a petroleum waste product, gasoline.

They were successful by 1883, and moved to larger premises in 1887. Daimler engines were soon powering boats, cars and trams, as well as being produced under licence by Panhard and Levassor in France. To meet the demand, in 1890 Daimler-Motoren-Gesellschaft, a public company, was formed. But the financial backers would not allow the two engineers the freedom they craved, and it was not a happy time; Maybach left in 1892, and Daimler in 1894.

DMG's progress declined, and under pressure from an English Daimler licensee, Frederick Simms, Daimler and Maybach were invited back to DMG in 1895. Under their management it became a successful engine and motor vehicle manufacturer, producing cars and trucks of high quality, as Daimlers until 1902, and then as Mercedes until 1926, when it merged with Benz & Cie. to form Daimler-Benz.

Unfortunately Gottlieb Daimler, one of the fathers of the automobile, did not live to see it come to full flower. He had suffered from a heart condition for several years, and died on March 6, 1900 at age 65.

JOHN BOYD DUNLOP – 1840 – 1921
Inventor - Pneumatic Tire

An automobile's tires are its vital link between the vehicle and the road, and without the pneumatic tire, high speed, comfortable car travel as we know it would not exist. For this remarkable device we can thank a man who, ironically, made his living treating horses, among other animals. That visionary was a Scottish veterinarian named John Boyd Dunlop.

John Dunlop was born to a farm family in Dreghorn, Ayrshire, on February 5, 1840, and graduated as a veterinarian in Edinburgh just short of his 21st birthday. He emigrated to Ireland and practised in County Down for a few years, and in 1867 established his busy and prosperous practice in Belfast.

The inventive Dunlop became adept at using rubber to make such equipment as gloves and tubes to aid him in administering medicine to cows and horses. Upon observing his young son bouncing over the rough cobblestones on his hard-tired tricycle, Boyd got the idea of somehow using rubber to cushion the ride. In 1887 he did some experiments with an inflated rubber tube wrapped around a wooden wheel. The rubber was protected with a layer of canvas. To test his new device he compared the rolling distance and energy required to that of a regular solid wheel, and found to his delight that his tire not only rolled more smoothly, but also travelled faster and farther for a given amount of energy input.

Dunlop then fitted his new tires to his son's tricycle and found that they did indeed provide a smoother ride. Also, not only was the ride better, his son was able to peddle faster and farther than with his regular solid tires, and with less exertion. Dunlop immediately saw the potential for increasing the speed and travelling range of horse-drawn vehicles, as well as bicycles, due to the decreased energy required.

Dunlop's next step was to try the pneumatic tire on a scaled-up tricycle to determine if it would carry the weight of an adult. The tire proved up to this task. Then, with the co-operation of Belfast bicycle manufacturers, he set out to see if his tires would support the weight of a person on only two wheels. This was also successful, and Dunlop knew he had made a significant discovery.

Although he obtained a patent on his pneumatic tire in July, 1888, it turned out that John Boyd Dunlop had not really invented it, he had re-invented it. The air-filled tire had originally been invented in 1845 by another Scot named Robert William Thomson who patented what he called "elastic bearings around the wheels of carriages" that would "present a cushion of air to the ground." They were tested on horse-drawn carriages, but the market was not ready to accept Thomson's invention and it lapsed into oblivion. It is unlikely that Dunlop was aware of Thomson's tire, so intellectual piracy is not suggested.

Dunlop's pneumatic tire had the advantage of more advanced rubber technology than had Mr. Thomson's, and it arrived into a much friendlier environment. By 1885 the "safety" bicycle, with its two equal or nearly equal sized wheels, had been developed into a practical conveyance by Englishman John Kemp Starley of Coventry. The Starley bicycles were called Rovers, and the company would later produce the Rover car. Since the Starley cycle was much safer and easier to ride than the big-wheel-small-wheel "penny farthing" type, it initiated a cycling craze in the 1880s and 1890s. This created a ready market for Dunlop's tire.

The pneumatic tire's advantages were quickly proved by bicycle racers, and they became accepted by the general public. With associate William du Cross of Dublin, Dunlop established the Dunlop Pneumatic Tire Company in Dublin in 1890 to manufacture and distribute tires.

Dunlop would have a disagreement with du Cross and withdraw from company operations within a few years.

Improvements to the tire came quickly, and it was a natural evolution that they would be fitted to the emerging automobile.

Although Dunlop lost the patent in 1892 with the discovery of Thomson's earlier invention, the Dunlop company had developed so many auxiliary changes and related patents that the company prevailed.

John Boyd Dunlop, whose name is inextricably associated with the pneumatic tire, died in Dublin on October 23, 1921, at the age of 81.

HENRY MARTYN LELAND – 1843–1932
Master of Precision - Cadillac and Lincoln

Although Henry Leland established and operated a renowned Detroit machine shop, reorganized one car company, and started another, his greatest contribution to the automobile industry was championing the cause of consistent, precise, manufacturing tolerances.

Perhaps it was his Quaker upbringing that made him such a stickler for precision. Henry Martyn Leland was born into a Quaker farm family near Barton, Vermont in 1843. He entered the workforce at age 11, and at 14 began his mechanic's apprenticeship. By the start of the Civil War he had demonstrated a high degree of skill, and was hired by the Springfield Armory. Gun manufacturing was very advanced, having adopted interchangeable parts in about 1800 when Eli Whitney, inventor of the cotton gin, began making muskets for the U.S. government. It was imperative that guns be repairable in the field with ready-made new or used parts, rather than depending on a skilled gunsmith.

When the war ended, the increasingly skilled Leland joined the Samuel Colt Armory in Hartford, Connecticut, inventor of the first successful revolver. He eventually landed at Brown & Sharpe, precision machine tool manufacturers in Providence, Rhode Island. Here the working tolerances were even more stringent than in gun making, and Brown & Sharpe's demand for precision in making products like micrometers and callipers suited Leland perfectly.

With Brown & Sharpe, Leland improved a hair clipper that they manufactured, and collaborated in the development of the Brown & Sharpe Universal Grinder that increased the speed and efficiency of steel-grinding. It was a major machine tool development.

By 1885 Brown & Sharpe made Leland a travelling sales representative, but after five years they parted amicably and he moved west to

Detroit, a bustling industrial town with an apparently boundless future and a severe shortage of skilled machine shops. Leland joined with lumber magnate Robert Faulconer, and ex-Brown & Sharpe associate Charles Norton to establish Leland, Faulconer & Norton, a high quality machine shop. One specialty was gear grinding, and Leland's son Wilfred, also a master machinist, managed the gear cutting operation.

When Norton left in 1894 the company became Leland & Faulconer. They established their own foundry, and were a major gear supplier to the bicycle industry. By 1896 L & F were making steam and gasoline engines for marine and other applications.

This operation had just been launched when Ransom Olds organized the Olds Motor Vehicle Company in 1897. It began in Lansing, Michigan, but soon moved to Detroit. When Olds's manufacturing methods proved too crude, he bought his car's gears and engines from L & F. The Olds Curved Dash model would become the first mass produced car in the world, with annual production reaching 6500 in 1905.

L & F's reputation was very sound, and Henry Leland was invited by the failing Detroit Automobile Company, whose superintendent was Henry Ford, to advise them on winding up the company. Leland's advice was to stay in business, and consider using an improved L & F engine. The owners agreed, and changed the name to the Cadillac Automobile Company with L & F supplying engines and transmissions.

Although L & F supplied its components on time, Cadillac's bottlenecks kept production well behind orders. Cadillac management again engaged Leland, this time to reorganize production. This was successful, and late in 1904 Cadillac merged with L & F to become the Cadillac Motor Car Company, with Leland in charge. Henry Ford departed.

In 1907 Leland imported the first Swedish Johannson gauge blocks, or "Jo-blocks" to America to achieve ultra-accurate parts production. The stage was set for the demonstration that would make Cadillac famous.

In 1908 England's Royal Automobile Club organized a demonstration of standardization at the new Brooklands race track. Three randomly selected Cadillacs were completely disassembled, the parts scrambled and some replaced, and the cars reassembled. They all then performed perfectly in an 800 km (500 mi.) test around Brooklands at an average of 55 km/h (34 mph).

This remarkable demonstration of interchangeable parts won Cadillac the RAC's prestigious Dewar Trophy. It was also stunning evidence of America's manufacturing prowess. With its enhanced reputation, Cadillac was purchased by General Motors in 1909, and the Lelands stayed on to manage it.

Henry Leland was instrumental in adopting

Charles Kettering's electric starter on the 1912 Cadillac, thereby revolutionizing the automobile industry, and winning a second Dewar Trophy. Another major advance was Cadillac's adoption of the V-8 engine exclusively for 1915.

Henry Leland and his son Wilfred stayed with Cadillac until 1917. When GM's William Durant refused to allow Cadillac to build First World War Liberty aircraft engines, the patriotic Lelands left and formed the Lincoln Motor Company. They manufactured Liberties until war's end, then switched to luxury motor cars. Unfortunately Lincoln was soon failing financially, and was purchased by Ford in 1922. The Lelands departed shortly after.

Henry Martyn Leland died in 1932 at age 89, leaving behind a legacy of precision manufacturing that was the foundation of automobile mass production as we know it today.

CARL BENZ - 1844 - 1929
Inventor - Benz & Cie. and Others

Carl Benz of Germany is recognized as the father of the internal combustion engine powered automobile. His first vehicle, a three-wheeler completed in 1885, is accepted as the world's first successful car.

Benz was born on November 25, 1844 in the Village of Pfaffenrot, in the Grand Duchy of Baden. He completed engineering studies at the Karlsruhe Polytechnikum, then worked in locomotive man-

ufacturing, weigh scale design and bridge building, none of which he found rewarding.

In **1871** Benz and August Ritter, a mechanic, opened a machine shop in Mannheim. Ritter soon departed, and Benz carried on, although the business was not very successful. He finally decided to pursue a long held interest in building an internal combustion engine. Since German Nicholas Otto held the four-stroke patent, Benz designed a two-stroke. By 1882 funding was arranged, and Gasmotorenfabrik Mannheim had been incorporated to produce Benz's engine.

Benz wanted to expand the application of his engine by installing it in a road vehicle. The principles of the company disagreed, and Benz soon resigned. He found new partners more amenable to a motorized vehicle, but only after the engine business was operating successfully. Benz & Cie. was formed in 1883. Sales of the two-stroke went well, but Benz began to have misgivings about the two-stroke principle. In spite of the Otto patent, he quietly began working on a four-stroke engine. The Otto patent was already being challenged because it was discovered that a French engineer, Alfonse Beau de Rochas, had patented the four-stroke principle in the 1860s.

By 1885 Benz had a successful four-stroke engine, and installed it in a 263 kg (580 lb) car he designed specifically for it; he did not use a converted buggy or carriage as would so many others. It had only three-wheels. The single cylinder engine was mounted horizontally in the rear, and drove the two rear wheels via a chain. It was fuelled by gasoline, and had electric ignition using a coil and battery.

Test drives began in the fall of 1885, and Benz received a patent for his car on January 29, 1886, one day before Otto's four-stroke patent was voided. Benz continued development, testing his car on short trips around home.

His wife Bertha was becoming impatient with Carl's reluctance to test the car on longer trips. One day the adventurous Bertha and her two sons stole out before Carl was awake, and set off with the Benz on an 80 km (50 mi.) journey. They completed it, albeit by pushing the car up the bigger hills. In proving the little Benz's reliability, Bertha Benz became history's first woman driver.

Benz built a few more cars, but they sold poorly in Germany. Then a Paris agent, Emile Roger, was appointed, and sales improved. Germany may have invented the car, but France would embrace it with greater enthusiasm. By 1892 Roger had sold about 25 Benzes. Carl then switched to four wheels, and sold even more. By the turn of the century Benz had built 2000 cars.

But Benz wasn't happy with the way things were going. He deplored the fact that increasing emphasis was being placed on speed. He resigned from Benz & Cie. in 1903. Benz & Cie. became a very successful automobile manufacturer, and in 1926 would join Daimler, manufacturer of Mercedes cars, to form Daimler-Benz. The father of the automobile, Carl Benz, died in 1929 at age 85.

WILLIAM CRAPO DURANT – 1861 – 1947
Entrepreneur - General Motors,
Durant Motor Company

William Crapo "Billy" Durant had the vision, drive and charisma that would lead him to found the world's mightiest enterprise, General Motors Corporation. But like many great organizations, it had modest beginnings.

Billy was born in the Durant home in Boston on December 8, 1861. Following a marriage failure his mother moved the family to Flint, Michigan where there was already an enclave of family members. Billy dropped out of high school before graduation and worked at a variety of jobs before becoming very successful in the insurance business.

At age 25 Durant was smitten by a small, two-wheeled, horse drawn road cart manufactured by the Coldwater Road Cart Company in Coldwater, Michigan. Durant journeyed to Coldwater with the intent of buying a share of the business, but ended up buying the whole thing from the discouraged owners. Durant and his business partner, Flint hardware merchant Dallas Dort, moved the little enterprise to Flint where they renamed it the Flint Road Cart Company.

In typical Durant fashion the enthusiastic Billy began visiting country fairs with his sample, and had soon sold 600 road carts, before the company had built even one! Undeterred, they hired a local carriage builder to make them, and were on their way. Renamed again as the Durant-Dort Carriage Company, it went on to become the largest carriage maker in the United States.

Billy was a millionaire by his early forties, but he was restless. After testing a Buick car in 1904 he decided to go into automobile manufacturing. The Flint-based Buick Motor Company had built its first car in 1904, but it wasn't prospering. With Durant-Dort's backing Billy took over Buick.

Billy's drive and enthusiasm, Buick's strong overhead valve engine, and the extensive Durant-Dort dealer network soon had Buick thriving. Billy organized a successful Buick racing team which included such outstanding drivers as Louis Chevrolet.

By 1907 Buick's annual production of over 4600 was second only to the Ford Motor Company. But Billy's automotive vision was much broader than Henry Ford's, and he incorporated a holding company in New Jersey called the General Motors Company on September 16, 1908. Billy brought Buick into GM on October 1st, 1908, and began assembling companies under the GM umbrella. He purchased Olds, Oakland (later Pontiac) and Cadillac. Within two years Durant acquired or had an interest in some two dozen car, truck and component makers, including the McLaughlin Motor Car Company of Oshawa, Ontario. Some were failures, but many, such as Oakland, Buick, Olds, Cadillac and McLaughlin, were sound investments.

By 1910 GM was financially over-extended due to Durant's haphazard management and he lost control of the company to the bankers, but remained on the board. Within weeks he had teamed up with ex-racer Louis Chevrolet and several Flint businessmen to form the Chevrolet Motor Company.

Louis Chevrolet designed a new car for Durant, which Chevrolet produced, along with a lighter car. Louis Chevrolet soon left the company, but Billy was on a roll again, and began quietly amassing General Motors stock. By September 16, 1915, exactly seven years after he had incorporated it, Billy regained control of his "baby," General Motors. With the assistance of Pierre S. duPont of the famous duPont chemical company, little Chevrolet had, in effect, swallowed giant General Motors, although it wouldn't officially be absorbed into General Motors until 1918.

Billy began another round of activity. He changed the General Motors Company to the General Motors Corporation, raised capitalization from $60 million to $100 million, and went on another buying binge. He formed United Motors Company to control several component manufacturers, including the Hyatt Roller Bearing Company that was owned by Alfred P. Sloan, Jr. Sloan would later become president and chairman of GM.

As General Motors grew, it again fell victim to Durant's loose management. The post-First World War recession found it in serious trouble with high inventories and falling sales. Led by duPont interests anxious to protect their GM investment, Durant was ousted for the second time in 1920. Pierre duPont became president, but Sloan was in effect running the company.

Within weeks Durant was back in the automobile business with his new Durant Motors, Incorporated. This lasted until 1932, then failed in the Depression. Billy Durant lost his fortune. When he died with little means on March 18, 1947 at age 85, it marked the passing of an automotive titan.

HENRY FORD – 1863 – 1947
Entrepreneur - Ford Motor Company

Henry Ford's birth on a farm in Dearborn, Michigan, in 1863, began a remarkable saga. The Fords were prosperous farmers but Henry disliked agriculture. He had an aptitude for machinery, and at age 16 began his machinist's apprenticeship in Detroit, becoming a journeyman in 1882. At his father's urging he returned to the farm, and also became a local service representative for Westinghouse threshing machines.

By 1891 the lure of the city drew Henry and his wife back to Detroit, and a mechanic's job with the Edison Illuminating Company. He soon became chief engineer, and in his spare time began building a gasoline engine. Ford wanted a car for his engine, and he and his assistant Charles King completed his first car at Ford's Detroit home in 1896. Henry called it a quadricycle, and his engine gave it reasonable performance. He sold it and built a second car in 1898.

The resulting publicity attracted William Murphy, a wealthy businessman who established the Detroit Automobile Company in 1900, with Henry Ford as superintendent. It was Detroit's first car manufacturer, but it lasted only nine months.

Ford then built a racing car which unexpectedly beat a Winton in 1901. This attracted new financing and in November, 1901, the Henry Ford Company was formed, with Henry as chief engineer. Henry soon split with his new partners, who hired precision machinist Henry Leland to run the firm, renaming it the Cadillac Automobile Company.

Ford built another race car, his huge "999" single seater in which bicycle racer Barney Oldfield beat all comers in an August 1902 race, averaging almost 96 km/h (60 mph). This attracted Detroit coal dealer Alexander Malcomson who partnered with Ford to finance the Ford Motor Company in June 1903. The first plant was on Detroit's Mack Avenue.

To gain further publicity, Henry Ford again tried racing with the Arrow, a twin of 999. He drove it on frozen Lake St. Clair on January 12, 1904, where, though badly frightened, he covered a mile in 39.4 seconds, a speed of 147 km/h (91.37 mph), establishing a new land speed record. It lasted just 10 days but it boosted his company's profile.

By 1905 the flourishing business moved to larger premises on Detroit's Piquette Avenue, but Henry was not happy. His backers wanted heavy expensive cars, while Henry liked light inexpensive ones. He was soon able to shake free and pursue his dream. Critically important to Ford's success would be three able employees, Canadian-born accountant James Couzens, Danish-born patternmaker Charles Sorensen, and engineer C. Harold Wills.

In the winter of 1906-07 Henry, Sorensen, and a few trusted assistants designed the Model T Ford. It looked tall and spindly, but it was sturdy and had a 20-horsepower four cylinder engine and foot-shifted planetary transmission. It was introduced late in 1908 and rising sales soon required a new larger plant in Highland Park. During 1910 19,000 Model Ts were built.

Henry was becoming an American folk hero, consolidated further in 1911 by defeating George Selden's patent for a horseless carriage driven by an internal combustion engine.

In 1913 Ford installed a moving assembly line and by 1915 annual production exceeded half a million cars. An even larger plant, the biggest in the world, was constructed on the Rouge River.

As production increased Henry Ford reduced the T's price, falling to $295. In 1914 he raised Ford's daily pay rate to five dollars. Business rivals predicted disaster, but the result was the opposite.

While Henry Ford was a mechanical genius, he was stubborn, and ignorant in matters outside his narrow area of expertise. And he could be mean and vindictive. His only child, son Edsel, became president of Ford in 1919, but Henry often undermined and countermanded him. Many believe this contributed to Edsel's early death in 1943 at age 50.

When Model T sales began slowing in the mid-twenties, Ford reluctantly agreed to replace it with the Model A in 1928. Chevrolet introduced its new six cylinder car in 1929, so Henry moved to a V-8 in 1932. It was his last technological triumph.

An aging Henry became senile and cantankerous. Upon Edsel's death he resumed control of the company, although not capable. His most trusted ally, Charles Sorensen, was forced out, and Henry came under the influence of the unsavoury Harry Bennett, head of Ford's internal police force.

The company was deeply involved in war work, and the family and the government were concerned about its chaotic management. Thus, Henry's grandson Henry Ford II, Edsel's son, was released from the navy and made president of Ford. Old Henry's objections were overcome by his wife Clara and Edsel's widow Eleanor.

Henry Ford died on April 7, 1947 at the age of 84. His legacy lives on in the great Ford Motor Company.

RANSOM ELI OLDS - 1864-1950
Entrepreneur - Olds Motor Works and Reo Motor Car Company

Entering the automobile business seemed like a natural thing for Ransom Eli Olds to do. His father had worked at a variety of mechanical jobs before establishing the P.F. Olds and Son machine shop in Lansing, Michigan, in the early 1880s (the Son was Ransom's older brother Wallace). They became prosperous manufacturers of steam engines.

Olds was born in Geneva, Ohio, on June 3, 1864, and joined the family company in 1883. He was industrious and thrifty, and was soon able to save enough money to buy out Wallace's share of the business. By 1887 the inventive Ransom - he received several patents over the years - had assembled a three-wheeled steam powered vehicle with the engine in the rear. It functioned reasonably well under test, but Olds thought he could do better. By 1892, using his three-wheeler as a base, he had built a four-wheeled steamer. It became the subject of a report in *Scientific American* magazine, and he sold it to a company that planned to ship it to India, although its final fate is unknown.

The Olds company began manufacturing

internal combustion gasoline engines, and in 1896 Ransom Olds completed his first gasoline powered car. This generated much good publicity, and Olds was soon in the gasoline automobile business. The Olds Motor Vehicle Company, which was separate from the engine company, was incorporated on August 21, 1897, with assistance from outside financing. It is recognized as America's oldest continuously operating automobile company, although General Motors has announced that it will end Oldsmobile production in approximately 2004.

Olds experimented with several designs, even trying electric power. Finally, by 1900, the now Detroit-based Olds Motor Works settled on the concept that would become the famous Curved Dash Oldsmobile. The two passenger Curved Dash was a basic design with a front-to-rear leaf spring on each side, which also acted as the frame rails. Its wheelbase was just 1676 mm (66 in.) and it weighed approximately 272 kg (600 lb). Its one cylinder, under-seat engine sent its power to the rear wheels via a chain and a two speed transmission. Tiller steering was used, and the front was dominated by a curved, toboggan-like dashboard that protected the passengers from road splash, and gave the car its name. Production of the car, officially named the Regular Runabout, but always called the Curved Dash, began late in 1900.

Curved Dash production was proceeding well until misfortune struck in the spring of 1901. A disastrous fire destroyed the factory, the only thing saved being one Curved Dash Olds.

A new factory was planned, but this time local business incentives brought it back to Lansing, the company's original home. They were able to resume production in 1901, making 425 cars. The Curved Dash received good publicity when a company employee, Roy Chapin, demonstrated its durability by driving one from Detroit to New York, where it was then placed on display at the New York auto show.

The Curved Dash became instantly popular, with production climbing to 2500 in 1902, 4000 in '03, and over 5500 in '04. This made Oldsmobile the first company to mass produce cars on a continuous and sustained basis in the United States. Many of the components such as engines, radiators and even bodies came from outside companies, an innovative policy that Olds promoted.

But there was trouble brewing in the successful Olds Motor Works. Fred Smith, who was secretary-treasurer of the company, and whose father had financed Ransom Olds, wanted the company to move into larger and more luxurious cars than the Curved Dash. Ransom Olds disagreed with this, and the split finally came early in 1904 when Olds "retired" from the company.

Ransom Olds was out of the automobile business, but only temporarily, and he was far from retired. His reputation was solid and his credit was worthy, and by August 1904 he had organized a new enterprise, the R.E. Olds Company, to manufacture cars. When the Smiths vigorously protested, Ransom changed the company name to Reo; he had sold the Olds name, he said, but not his initials.

Reo's first models were light cars, much like the Curved Dash Olds. But then Ransom apparently had a change of heart and the company was soon marketing larger cars. Ironically, while Reo was prospering - it built some 4000 cars in 1907 - the Olds Motor Works was declining. When Olds production slipped perilously close to 1000 cars in 1908, the company was bought by William Durant for his newly formed General Motors.

In addition to the Reo company, Olds had wide ranging interests. He gradually reduced his active company participation, and in 1936, left it entirely. This was the year in which Reo stopped building cars, although it would continue as a successful truck manufacturer.

Ransom Olds died on August 26, 1950 at age 86, leaving a significant legacy in the automobile industry. He had established two car companies, started automobile mass production, created a trend-setting supplier industry, and contributed significantly to making southeast Michigan the auto building capital of America.

SAMUEL MCLAUGHLIN - 1871-1972
Entrepreneur - General Motors Company of Canada

Robert McLaughlin operated a farm in the community of Tyrone in Ontario's Durham County north of Bowmanville in the mid-19th century. He loved wood, and as a boy had begun carving axe handles that were so exquisitely shaped they commanded a premium price. As he grew into manhood he built cutters, wagons and carriages in his spare time. He received so many requests to build them for others that in 1867 he gave up farming and went into the carriage business. He moved the company to Oshawa, Ontario, in 1878, and the McLaughlin Carriage Company prospered, gaining a reputation for well built vehicles.

Robert had three sons. The oldest, Jack, became a chemist, and invented a soft drink called ginger ale, and founded the Canada Dry Beverage Company. Second son George joined the carriage company, and Sam, born September 8, 1871, also went into the family firm in 1887. He served his apprenticeship as an upholsterer, then moved on to drafting, and was soon designing all of the company's products.

Shortly after the turn of the century Sam observed the emergence of the automobile and was sure it had a future. He convinced brother George that they should go into the car business. Robert wasn't persuaded, but he didn't stand in the way of Sam's drive to explore automobile production.

Sam toured several American car factories looking for a suitable vehicle to build. When he failed to make a deal for one he considered worthy, he tried to have a car designed in Oshawa. This also failed, and in search of help he turned to William Durant, an old carriage making acquaintance who was now building Buick cars in Flint, Michigan. McLaughlin and Durant had tried earlier to strike a deal, without success, but this time a 15 year agreement was reached in which Durant would supply Buick engines and chassis, and McLaughlin would fit them with bodies and sell them as McLaughlin-Buicks. The McLaughlin Motor Company began assembling cars late in 1907.

The McLaughlin Motor Company flourished in Canada. In the U.S. Durant went on to found General Motors, which took a financial interest in McLaughlin. As president of the Canadian operation, Sam was made a vice-president of General Motors. The McLaughlins continued to make carriages and sleighs until 1915, when Sam sold that business to take on the manufacturing of Chevrolets, again in a deal with his old friend Durant.

The end came for the McLaughlin Motor Car Company name in 1918 when General Motors bought the rest of it on the condition that Sam and George stay on and run the business, which became General Motors of Canada. With George's retirement from the vice-presidency in 1924, Sam became the last McLaughlin in the business that his father had started 57 years earlier in his drive shed.

When George retired Sam became chairman of the board of GM of Canada, while still remaining a vice-president of the U.S. parent organization. He retired in 1967, but remained honourary chairman of GM of Canada. Sam McLaughlin never forgot his loyalty to Oshawa, which benefited greatly from "Mr. Sam's" philanthropy. He funded the McLaughlin Planetarium in Toronto, and was an active supporter of the Boy Scouts.

Robert Samuel McLaughlin lived in his beautiful and beloved "Parkwood" home in Oshawa until the end. When he died on January 6, 1972, in his 101st year, Canada lost its greatest automotive pioneer.

WALTER P. CHRYSLER – 1875 – 1940
Entrepreneur - Chrysler Corporation

Walter Percy Chrysler's Chrysler Corporation, along with the Ford Motor Company and General Motors Corporation, comprised what became the Big Three American automobile manufacturers. It was a long journey for the boy who was born in 1875 on a farm near Ellis, Kansas.

Walter's railroad engineer father helped instill an avid interest in machinery in young Walter. Following high school he joined the railroad, becoming a journeyman machinist in 1895. In 1908 when he was with the Union Pacific in Olwein, Iowa, Walter was smitten by a big Locomobile at the Chicago auto show. Although it cost $5000, he bought it, not to drive, but to take apart and learn how it was made. It would shape his future.

Chrysler's skills and leadership qualities served him well with several employers, and he become manager of the American Locomotive Company's plant in Allegheny, Pennsylvania. One of the board members, James J. Storrow, a Boston banker and also a General Motors board member, was impressed with Chrysler's management of the plant. When the bankers took over GM from its founder William Durant in 1910, Storrow recommended that Buick general manager Charles Nash hire Chrysler as the works manager for Buick, GM's most profitable division. Nash soon became GM president, and Chrysler was made Buick's general manager.

By 1915 Durant had regained control of GM, and Nash resigned in 1916. Walter Chrysler was becoming increasingly dissatisfied with Durant's management, and departed in 1919.

Chrysler's reputation was well known and he was approached by the bankers to manage the failing Willys-Overland Company of Toledo, Ohio. Through staff cuts, equipment sales, negotiations with suppliers, and sharp cost control, Chrysler got W-O on the road to health. He was then hired to reorganize the floundering Maxwell-Chalmers partnership, both of which manufactured cars in the same Highland Park, Michigan, plant.

Chrysler signed a two-year deal to manage troubled Maxwell-Chalmers. He took a relatively low salary, but would receive generous stock options. Chrysler's first step was to replace the Maxwell Motor Company with the Maxwell Motor Corporation, with himself as chairman.

Chrysler spruced up the huge inventory of Maxwell cars and sold them at a profit, while continuing to improve the Maxwell, particularly its fragile rear axle. He also set out to develop a new car, hiring consulting engineers Fred Zeder,

Owen Skelton and Carl Breer for the job. The result was the 1924 Chrysler, a car of advanced design.

Although Walter Chrysler now had a fine new car bearing his name, he wanted his own company. By selling his General Motors stock, marshalling other assets, and obtaining bank loans, Chrysler managed to gain control of the Maxwell Corporation. In June, 1925, it became the Chrysler Corporation.

Chrysler didn't slacken his pace, but began expanding and diversifying his products. The Maxwell car's last year was 1925; it reappeared in 1926 as the four cylinder Chrysler 58. There was also a Chrysler 70, and a luxurious Imperial 80.

By 1928 Chrysler was able to purchase Dodge Brothers, a respected Detroit car and truck maker. He also launched his own mid-market car, the DeSoto, and the low priced Plymouth. These were bold moves for a relatively small company, but Chrysler pulled them off.

The Dodge acquisition gave Chrysler extensive production facilities, an established dealer network, and a line of trucks. The new Plymouth was well engineered and gave strong competition to Ford and GM in the low priced field. By 1932 it was third in sales behind Ford and Chevrolet.

The Chrysler Corporation survived the Depression, thanks to a broad product line, a sound engineering reputation, and Walter Chrysler's management ability. In 1935 he handed Chrysler's presidency to assistant K.T. Keller and moved up to chairman. He ceased active participation in 1938 for health reasons, and died in 1940 at the age of 65.

FERDINAND PORSCHE – 1875–1951
Engineer - Volkswagen, Porsche and Others

Ferdinand Porsche was one of the most innovative engineers of the 20th century, yet he didn't graduate from a university. His genius was innate, a gift that produced a prolific lifetime portfolio of imaginative and daring engineering designs. He conceived everything from luxury cars to Grand Prix racers, but his most lasting legacy was the humble Volkswagen Beetle.

Porsche was born in Maffersdorf, Bohemia, in the Austro-Hungarian Empire on September 3, 1875. His father was a tinsmith and young Ferdinand served his apprenticeship in that trade. But his first passion was electricity, and while still a teenager he wired the family house for electric lights.

At age 19 Porsche joined the United Electrical Company in Vienna, and, although not registered, quietly attended evening engineering classes at the Vienna Technical University. Within four years Porsche headed United's experimental shop.

In 1898 Porsche moved to Lohner, a carriage maker that was interested in the emerging automobile. Porsche mounted an electric motor in each front wheel hub of a carriage, creating the Lohner-Porsche. It won a gold medal at the 1900 Paris Exposition; young Porsche was on his way.

To overcome the limitation of batteries, Porsche designed a hybrid using a gasoline engine to generate electricity for the motors. It was called the "Mixte." Lohner was content to build Mixtes, but Porsche wanted to pursue gasoline engined cars, and in 1906 joined Austro-Daimler, an offshoot of Germany's Daimler company. He designed some outstanding Austro-Daimler gasoline cars, rising from technical director to chief executive. He favoured powerful engines in light cars, and as a result they excelled in competition. During the First World War he designed aircraft engines and a wagon train with hub-mounted motors. Porsche's professional recognition came in 1917 when Vienna Technical University awarded him an honourary engineering doctorate.

Porsche's interest had turned to producing an economical car for the masses, much like the Ford Model T idea. Although technically gifted, Porsche could be brusque and profane. When Austro-Daimler refused his small car idea, he left in 1923.

He next job was technical director for Daimler in Stuttgart, Germany, builder of Mercedes vehicles. Although Porsche designed big powerful cars for Daimler, including the SS and SSK, and the first production supercharged car, he was still interested in smaller cars. When Daimler-Benz (it had merged with Benz in 1926) also resisted his small car idea, Porsche left in 1928.

Porsche joined Steyr in Austria but it soon went broke, so on January 1, 1931, he opened a consulting business, the Porsche Design Office, in Stuttgart. An early client was the Zundapp motorcycle company which wanted to start building cars. Porsche offered Zundapp a small car idea they had been working on. It had a backbone frame and floorpan, an air cooled rear engine, and four wheel independent suspension using Porsche's recently patented torsion bars.

Zundapp pulled out after three prototypes were built, and Porsche's next small car customer was NSU, also a motorcycle maker. Porsche again brought out his rear engined car. NSU liked it, but in a replay of Zundapp, NSU dropped out.

Porsche's small car break finally came when German Chancellor Adolf Hitler announced in 1934 that he wanted Germany to build a "People's Car." When the industry demurred, Hitler took Porsche's design as a state sponsored project. That car became the Volkswagen, and a huge factory was completed for it in 1938, although few cars were produced before it was converted to war work.

Following the Second World War Ferdinand Porsche was detained several months by France on trumped up war charges. Although quite frail, when he was freed he managed to work with his son Ferdinand "Ferry" Porsche in launching the Porsche car in 1948. Ferdinand Porsche lived long enough to see his Beetles pouring out of VW's mile-long Volkswagenwerk in Wolfsburg, and his Porsches start to make their mark in competition. He died in 1951 at age 75.

ALFRED P. SLOAN, JR. – 1875–1966
Entrepreneur - General Motors

Alfred Pritchard Sloan, Jr., was not the father of General Motors; that honour belongs to its founder William Crapo Durant. But Sloan could certainly be called its stepfather. Without his administrative genius it's safe to say that the world's largest auto manufacturer wouldn't exist today.

Sloan was born in New Haven, Connecticut, on May 23, 1875. He received a degree in electrical engineering from the Massachusetts Institute of Technology in 1895, his graduation coinciding almost exactly with the emergence of the motor car in the United States.

Following graduation Sloan went to work for the Hyatt Roller Bearing Company of Newark, N.J., as "a kind of office boy, draughtsman, salesman and general assistant to the enterprise," as he recounted in his 1963 autobiography *My Years With General Motors*. Seeing little future at Hyatt, he joined an electric refrigerator company that manufactured central refrigeration for apartment houses.

When Sloan became aware that Hyatt was on the verge of bankruptcy his father and an associate invested $5,000 to rescue it, on condition that young Alfred would take it over on a six-month trial. By the end of the period Hyatt showed a $12,000 profit, with prospects for continued expansion. As Sloan said in his book, "I could not know then that through Hyatt I had entered one of the headwaters of General Motors."

The growth of Hyatt and the motor industry paralleled each other. In selling to the industry Sloan became acquainted with many of the early giants of the business such as Walter Chrysler, William Durant, Henry Ford and Sam McLaughlin. By 1916 when Hyatt was flourishing through its substantial business with the motor industry, Sloan got a surprising phone call from William Durant, now back in charge of General Motors.

Durant, on another expansion binge, wanted to know if Sloan would consider selling Hyatt to GM. After reviewing his options, Sloan accepted, and in 1916 Hyatt became part of United Motors, a subsidiary of GM.

It didn't take Sloan long to realize that Durant was the empire-building entrepreneur he had always been, with the same disdain for administrative matters. Since Sloan had a flair for orderly business, he was soon Durant's trusted aide and confidant and was virtually running the company.

The lack of organization in GM was anathema to the logical Sloan so he set out his ideas in what he called his Organization Study, completed in late 1919. It covered such matters as return on investment, profit centres, central control and the allocation of resources based on the most efficiently operated divisions.

While not hostile to the study, Durant didn't get around to acting on it. Then a frenzy of overproduction in 1920 in the face of a post-First World War economic downturn once again found Durant out, and the company in the hands of the bankers, as had happened in 1910. Pierre du Pont of the du Pont Chemical Company was named president and Sloan was appointed vice-president; in 1923 he was made president.

This was the beginning of the Sloan era and GM's climb to supremacy. He correctly identified that the automobile business was changing from a "mass" market (i.e., the Model T) to a "mass-class" market (more diversity and luxury, his aim for GM).

To accommodate this trend, he rationalized the overlapping GM makes, organizing the company's line of cars into five progressive models from the popular Chevrolet to the luxurious Cadillac. The annual model change that evolved under his reign made buyers want to trade in their cars every few years, and the hierarchy of marques encouraged them to move up the luxury ladder as their careers progressed.

Under Sloan GM prospered greatly, eventually bringing some 50 per cent of the North American automotive market under its control. His study formed the basis for the operation of the corporation, emphasizing as it did autonomous divisions building cars and components, guided by a central coordinating authority. It would prove to be a sound business model for large, diversified corporations.

Sloan moved from GM president to chairman in 1937, a post he held until 1956 when he became honourary chairman. During his lifetime he amassed a huge personal fortune, much of which he used to set up the Sloan Foundation, which established such organizations as the Sloan-Kettering Cancer Center.

A giant of the industry, Alfred P. Sloan, Jr., died on February 17, 1966 at age 90 in the Sloan-Kettering Center in New York.

CHARLES KETTERING – 1876–1958
Inventor - General Motors

Motorists owe a great deal to Charles Franklin Kettering, a farm boy born in Lundsville, Ohio in 1876. He graduated from a one-room school, and after high school would teach in one until he could afford to attend Ohio State University in Columbus. He was a brilliant student, and graduated in electrical engineering.

Upon graduation Kettering was hired by the National Cash Register Company in Dayton, Ohio. One of his early assignments was to electrify the cash register the company was producing. Kettering realized that an electric motor could be temporarily overloaded without damage, and he applied this idea to successfully motorize the cash register.

In 1908 Kettering improved the ignition on his personal Cadillac by adding a condenser, a device that stores an electrical charge. He brought this to the attention of Henry Leland, head of the Cadillac Automobile Company, and soon the Dayton Engineering Laboratory Company (Delco), established by Kettering and friend Edward Deeds, was supplying Cadillac with ignition systems.

When Leland wanted an electric self-starter to replace the difficult and dangerous hand crank on the Cadillac, he again turned to Kettering. Applying the same logic that he had to the electric cash register - a small powerful motor temporarily overloaded - Kettering developed a successful starter for the 1912 Cadillac. It was combined with the generator until the following year when Vincent Bendix invented his Bendix drive that allowed the starter to detach from the flywheel when the engine started. The self-starter was a watershed invention, giving the gasoline car the last push it needed to vanquish those powered by steam and electricity.

In 1916 Delco was purchased by General Motors, bringing "Boss" Kettering into the GM fold, where he would become research director. Kettering's next major project was the investigation of engine knock, or "ping." He and engineer Thomas Midgley, Jr., discovered that the knock was related to fuel composition, and was not mechanical as had been thought. After much experimentation they discovered that adding tetraethyl lead to gasoline increased its octane, or resistance to knock. "Ethyl" gasoline went on sale in the mid-1920s, and made an invaluable contribution in the form of higher compression ratios and smoother, more powerful engines. It was used until the early 1970s when it was phased out to accommodate the catalytic converter.

In the late 1920s Kettering and Midgley attacked the problem of producing an effective refrigerant for GM's Frigidaire Division. They developed Freon-12, a chemical that became the standard refrigerant of the industry by the mid-1930s.

Kettering was also largely responsible for the development of the two-stroke diesel engine that led to the dieselization of railways, and contributed significantly to the change to dieselizing line-haul trucks and other industrial applications. He also contributed to such diverse fields as aviation, and his "Delco System" generating sets brought electric power to farms before rural electrification.

But even the brilliant Kettering could produce a flop, the most famous of which was the air-cooled Chevrolet of 1923. Rather than a novel counter to Henry Ford's ubiquitous Model T, it proved to be a disaster. General Motors had to recall every one of them.

Some of Kettering's developments, such as leaded gasoline and Freon-12 refrigerant, turned out to be harmful to the environment and to human health. But in the context of their era they were outstanding engineering achievements.

Charles Kettering retired from GM in 1947, and died in 1958. As well as being a talented and innovative inventor whose legacy lives on, he was a generous philanthropist. In his honour the General Motors Institute in Flint, Michigan, was recently renamed Kettering University.

HARLEY EARL – 1893 – 1969
Stylist - General Motors

During his reign as General Motors' chief stylist for over 30 years, Harley Earl bestrode American automobile styling like a colossus. A big, imposing, strong willed man, he formalized the birth of auto styling, and nurtured it through its formative years. His genius came to full flower in the optimistic 1950s.

Earl arrived on the Detroit scene in 1926 during a period of significant change. The utilitarian Model T Ford was about to be replaced by the stylish Model A, and closed cars had taken over from open ones. General Motors, under the presidency of Alfred P. Sloan Jr., was evolving the annual model change to entice motorists to trade in their used cars. Earl would initiate the process in which styling would gradually replace engineering as the automobile's major selling point.

Harley Earl was born in Hollywood, California, on November 22, 1893, the son of J.W. Earl, a prosperous coachbuilder whose Los Angeles shop built wagons and carriages for local farmers and ranchers. Recognizing the car's potential, he renamed the company the Earl Automobile Works in 1908.

After attending Stanford University, Harley joined his father's business. He soon demonstrated a flair for style as the company progressed from making add-ons for standard cars, to building custom bodies. The business flourished with first generation, nouveau riche Hollywood movie stars like cowboy Tom Mix and comedian Roscoe (Fatty) Arbuckle, who were anxious to show off their wealth with a distinctive automobile.

The Earl firm was bought by Don Lee, the West Coast Cadillac distributor, in 1919. Lee catered to the movie establishment, and the Earl business, which became the company's custom body wing, was a perfect fit for Harley's styling flair.

Earl's introduction to General Motors occurred in the mid-1920s when he met Lawrence P. Fisher, general manager of the Cadillac division. Fisher recognized Earl's talent. He was, for example, using clay to model his cars rather than the traditional wood or metal. And he was employing smooth lines and contours to mould the hoods, fenders, headlamps and running boards into integrated, organic shapes.

The Cadillac division was in the process of developing the LaSalle, a less expensive "companion" car for the Cadillac. Fisher was sure that Earl was the man to design it, and convinced Sloan of Earl's skill. In 1926 Earl was contracted to style the LaSalle, and the automobile business would never be the same.

When it was launched in March, 1927, the LaSalle was a sensation with its imaginative use of colour and line. The low silhouette and seductively curved fenders ushered in a dramatic new influence on the American automobile.

Sloan immediately recognized the value of styling, and hired Earl to join GM as head of a newly created "Art and Colour Section," reporting directly to Sloan. It was the first formal styling department in an automobile company. But the first design out of Art and Colour, the 1929 Buick, was not the success the LaSalle had been; it was fat and bulbous. Earl claimed that the engineers had altered his design, but he had learned a valuable lesson: don't get too far ahead of public taste. Changes must be incremental and evolutionary.

To test public opinion, Earl developed the 1938 Buick Y-Job "dream car." Generally accepted as the first concept car, its long, low silhouette, horizontal grille, elongated fenders, concealed running boards and wraparound bumpers set the American car styling tone for more than a decade.

Following the Second World War Earl again startled the world with his seminal 1951 Buick LeSabre concept car. Like the Y-Job, the LeSabre was very advanced, and its fins, slots and jet plane-inspired styling set the automobile styling trend for another decade. It also influenced manufacturers around the world.

Earl is most remembered, however, for a feature that became known as the tailfin, inspired by the twin tail-boom vertical stabilizers of the P-38 Lockheed Lightning fighter plane. The 1948 Cadillac appeared with modest little rear fender kickups housing the taillamps. The public reacted favourably, and fins became a Cadillac trademark, setting in motion a styling cliché that would reach grotesque proportions on, appropriately, the 1959 Cadillac, before receding into oblivion.

The tailfin was not Earl's only mark. He inaugurated such features as the wraparound windshield, the hardtop "convertible" (not a convertible; it just looked like one) and multi-toned paint jobs. The man who influenced countless millions of cars, and was GM's most celebrated stylist, retired in 1959, and died in 1969.

KIICHIRO TOYODA – 1894–1952
Entrepreneur - Toyota Motor Company

Although Japan imported European and American cars during the early part of the century, and both Ford and General Motors set up knockdown automobile assembly plants there in the 1920s, the indigenous Japanese automobile industry didn't really flower until after the Second World War. Some of the seeds were sown before the war, however, and one of them was the Toyota Motor Company, which dates its history to 1937. It was the outgrowth of the Toyoda Automatic Loom Works, and its founder was Kiichiro Toyoda, son of Sakichi Toyoda, inventor of Japan's first automatic loom.

Kiichiro Toyoda graduated in mechanical engineering from Tokyo Imperial University in 1921, and joined his father's Toyoda Spinning & Weaving Company. He became chief engineer, and made valuable contributions in improving the automatic loom, and to the development of other equipment such as a carding machine.

Toyoda was interested in exploring the production of a Japanese automobile, and in 1929 toured some American car plants. In 1930 he set up an experimental shop in the loom works and had his engineers begin developing a gasoline engine. He also imported high quality European and American machine tools, ostensibly for the loom works, but also with automobile production in mind. At the same time the presence of Ford and GM was leading to the evolvement of a Japanese component supplier industry.

Kiichiro continued to research automobile production in Japan, and by 1933 his engineers had designed and built 10 prototype 50 cc motorcycle engines. An Automobile Department was set up at this time, and experienced engineers were recruited to begin designing and building a prototype car. They also began setting up a steel making plant. Although unaccustomed to designing cars, by 1935 they had produced a prototype sedan, the A1, powered by a 3,389 cc six cylinder engine. Its styling resembled the American Chrysler/DeSoto Airflow model.

This was followed by the model AA in 1936, the year in which Japan passed a new law increasing the import tax on car parts, effectively bringing to an end the Japanese operations of Ford and GM. In 1937 the Toyota (not Toyoda; they did not wish to emphasize the family name) Motor Company was established in the town of Koroma, later re-named Toyota City. Risaburo Toyoda, Sakichi Toyoda's son-in-law, and the managing director of Toyoda Spinning & Weaving Company, was named president, and Kiichiro Toyoda vice-president. Kiichiro also headed the research department. Automobile production began in 1938.

The impending war soon started to impact car and truck production. Since there was a greater demand for trucks, car making was gradually reduced while truck and bus production increased. Kiichiro Toyoda became president of Toyota Motor Company in 1941. By war's end much of Japanese industry had been badly damaged, although the automotive plants were more worn out than bombed out. Following its loss of the war Japan came under American control.

Toyota gradually recovered, building smaller cars, but in the early 1950s it went through a difficult financial period. It tried to compensate by laying off workers, but the union objected. As is Japanese custom, Kiichiro took responsibility for mismanagement of the company and resigned as president in 1950. He then engaged in technical research, and the hope was that he would be able to return to the presidency. Unfortunately this did not happen. Kiichiro Toyoda died on March 27, 1952 at the age of 57.

HEINRICH NORDHOFF – 1899–1968
Executive - Volkswagen

Heinrich "Heinz" Nordhoff was not a fan of the mighty Volkswagen company or its philosophy in the 1930s. In fact as a member of automaker Adam Opel's board of directors he was strongly opposed to Hitler's dream of his low cost car for the masses, and the construction of the giant factory where it was to be manufactured. He felt that the state had no business competing with the established automobile industry. But that would all change following the Second World War when the resourceful Nordhoff was chosen to manage the badly damaged mile-long Volkswagenwerk.

Heinrich Nordhoff was born on January 6, 1899 in the town of Hildesheim in the state of Lower Saxony, Germany. The family soon moved to Berlin where he attended a technical high school before entering the army during the First World War. When peace came he attended the Berlin-Charlottenburg Technische Hochschule (technical university), graduating as a mechanical engineer in 1927.

Nordhoff joined the Bavarian Motor Works in airplane design, but soon decided that he had more interest in the automobile industry, and that it offered a better future. His hope of getting work with an American company in the United States was dashed with the onset of the Depression in 1929, but he did manage the next best thing, a job with the Adam Opel company, recently acquired by General Motors.

Deciding that he preferred management rather than engineering, within a year Nordhoff was in charge of Opel's customer service. He was identified as a high potential employee, and by 1936 was on the Opel board of directors. Opel was planning to produce a small car of its own, and Hitler's car, eventually dubbed the Volkswagen, was strongly resented.

By 1942 Nordhoff had become general manager of Opel's Brandenburg truck plant in Berlin, now under Nazi control, where he stayed until almost the end of the Second World War. Following the war Nordhoff was able to return to

Opel in Russelscheim, but was soon out of a job when the American occupiers charged all German wartime managers, including Nordhoff, with being Nazis. Nordhoff was able to move to the British Zone in Hamburg where he got a job managing an Opel dealership.

As Nordhoff had been general manager of a large truck factory, his reputation as an able administrator was well known. But his wartime activities meant that he could never return to an American owned company. Thus when the British occupiers were seeking a person capable of heading the huge Volkwagenwerk in Wolfsburg, Nordhoff's name came up. He was hired, and on January 1, 1948, began his new job as Volkswagen's director general.

He found a war-torn plant and a company struggling to rebuild. Volkswagen production had tentatively resumed in 1945 with the production of 1785 cars. This rose to 10,020 in 1946, then fell back slightly to 8987 in 1947.

Any reservations that Nordhoff may have had about the Volkswagen were quickly overcome and he adopted it as his own. He lived at the plant for the first six months, moving a cot into a room near his office. He took command, his obvious enthusiasm giving the company hope and direction, and his infectious dedication raising the morale of the dispirited workforce of 7000.

Nordhoff established clear administrative responsibilities. He had the plant repaired as quickly as possible. Recognizing the Volkswagen's inherent technical merit, he set out to improve it. He established an inspection department to ensure quality control, and began organizing a sales and service organization. He was an indefatigable worker.

Under Nordhoff's leadership Volkswagen began to prosper. Exports started very modestly. In 1949 two Beetles were shipped to the United States by way of the Netherlands.

Production rose, and by May 1949 it had reached a total of 50,000 since the end of the war, and 100,000 by May 1950. By July 1953 it was 500,000, and by August 1955, one million.

Heinz Nordhoff's drive and dedication had been just what Volkswagen needed to make it a viable enterprise after the British relinquished control. He moulded it into the world's premier small car company with sales virtually around the world. This was the legacy Heinz Nordhoff left when he died on April 12, 1968 at age 69.

W. EDWARDS DEMING – 1900 – 1993
Quality Control Guru

With the encouragement of American General Douglas MacArthur, Supreme Commander of the Allied Powers, the Japanese were able to gradually rebuild their country after the Second World War. But the war experience which had brought vast numbers of high powered Western planes and ships, had taught them that their tech-

nology lagged far behind. When they were able to return to civilian industrial production their merchandise established a reputation for being cheap and shoddy.

The Japanese knew they needed help, and while MacArthur gave them the impetus to restore their society, it was another American, W. Edwards Deming, who would put them on the road to world quality leadership in their products.

Deming was born in 1900, and would prove to be a formidable intellect, graduating from Yale University in 1928 with a doctorate in mathematical physics. He evolved a system of statistical quality control, but became frustrated when American manufacturers didn't seem interested. After the Second World War he came to believe that the material abundance of America was making it wasteful of both its human and physical resources. He particularly disliked the American practice of interchangeable managers, the MBAs, lawyers and accountants who knew little about the core business, and whose only focus was on the bottom line and the share price.

W. Edwards Deming was a prophet without honour in his own land. The post-war United States economy was humming along briskly.

Consumer demand was so high that the cry was for more production, not better products. It was disheartening to Deming because he knew that poor quality would eventually catch up with America.

Feeling thwarted in his quest to convince American managers of the need for better quality, Deming joined the United States Census Bureau as a statistician. The Census Bureau was aware that Japan needed reliable demographic data to cope with providing appropriate social services for its people after the war, so in the immediate post-war years the U.S. government sent Deming to Japan several times to provide census expertise.

The Japanese learned that Deming was also a quality control expert, and since they were painfully aware of their shortcomings in this area, they asked him to give lectures on statistical quality control. Deming was reluctant at first, fearing that it would be a repeat of his unrewarding experience in America. But when his first presentation was attended by over 40 chief executive officers of major Japanese manufacturers, he knew he had tapped into a rich vein of interest. It was, after all, his abiding belief that good quality started at the top of an organization, with the full commitment of senior management. It included communication rather than competition, goal setting and worker involvement. It was not something that was inserted at the production line level with a few posters and slogans.

Deming could see that the Japanese were genuinely interested in his theories, and he told them that if they followed his methods their quality would be the envy of the world within a few years. They were skeptical at first, but when they applied his principles, quality did improve dramatically.

It wasn't long before Deming became almost a godlike figure to the Japanese, their management guru. So revered was he that the Union of Japanese Science and Engineering instituted an annual award called the Deming Prizes for companies achieving the highest quality and dependability in their products. It became highly prestigious to receive a Deming Prize.

The Japanese learned their lessons well. Within a few years their cameras, computers, motorcycles and television sets were considered the best available. This was followed by their automobiles, whose fit, finish and overall quality became the benchmark against which the rest of the world measured itself.

Dr. Deming was eventually recognized in America, particularly by the Ford Motor Company. His management theories became highly esteemed and he was a widely sought after consultant. He authored many books and papers, and would go on to amass countless awards and honourary degrees from universities, including

Harvard, and other organizations, such as the National Academy of Sciences. He was inducted into the Automotive Hall of Fame in 1991.

By this time the Japanese were solidly established in the North American market, and in much of the rest of the world. They had embraced Deming's teachings early, and had taken to heart his theory that quality had to be an all encompassing company philosophy, that it was more efficient in the long run to do things right from the beginning. Only belatedly was this recognized in Deming's own country. W. Edwards Deming died on December 20, 1993, at the age of 93.

WILLIAM LYONS – 1901 – 1985
Entrepreneur - Jaguar Cars Limited

The roots of the mighty Jaguar company were planted in a garage in Blackpool, England, in 1920, when a young motorcycle mechanic named William Walmsley decided to construct a stylish, aluminum, Zeppelin-shaped motorcycle sidecar. It proved popular, and he began making them for sale. One of his customers was young William Lyons, also of Blackpool, who liked his sidecar so much that he suggested they team up to build and sell them. On Lyons's 21st birthday, September 4, 1922, Walmsley and Lyons became partners in the Swallow Sidecar Company, financed by a £ 1000 loan underwritten by their fathers.

By 1927 the little company had progressed to building custom bodies for low priced cars. It introduced the Austin Swallow, an Austin Seven draped in curvaceous lines and painted in fetching colours. The name was enlarged to the Swallow Sidecar and Coachbuilding Company, with car production soon outpacing sidecars. In 1928 they moved to the motor city of Coventry, and had soon expanded to fitting bodies to other chassis such as Fiats, Wolseleys and Standards. Although they would continue to make sidecars, in 1930 the Sidecar part of the name was dropped.

In a more ambitious project, Lyons, who would personally style all of the company's cars until the 1960s, created a low-slung body for a Standard Sixteen chassis that had been lowered by mounting the springs beside the frame rather than under it. When it appeared in the fall of 1931 it was a sensation. Whereas the stock Standard Sixteen towered to a height of 1727 mm (68 in.), that first SS I coupe was a svelte 1397 mm (55 in.) high, and had a very long hood. Attractively priced at £ 310, it established a value-for-money reputation that would long be a Jaguar tradition. There was also a smaller Standard-based SS II model. The association with Standard would last until after the Second World War.

The SS I was followed by other models, and the Swallow Coachbuilding Company was well on its way to becoming an established and respected automobile manufacturer. But William Walmsley was losing interest in cars, and departed in 1934. The following year the name was changed to SS Cars Limited, and it became a public company with Lyons as chairman and managing director.

The Jaguar name first appeared for 1936 with the introduction of the SS Jaguar 1.5 and 2.5 litre sedans. To improve SS's engineering capability Lyons hired a brilliant young engineer named William Heynes to set up an engineering department. He would make a significant contribution to the company's reputation by producing engineering designs that were progressive, yet not too expensive to produce

The stunning Jaguar SS100 (for 100 mph) arrived for 1936, and was the model that would be the company's most famous pre-Second World War car. Lyons gave it a long hood, sweeping clamshell fenders and a fold-down windshield.

SS Cars was doing well under Lyons's direction, but in 1939 car production had to be phased out in favour of war work. By the end of the Second World War the Hitler regime had given the SS name sinister connotations, so the company became Jaguar Cars Limited. It returned to production with pre-war designs until new models could be prepared. The first one, the Mark V sedan, was followed by one that would be an even bigger sensation than the original Jaguar or the SS100 had been.

The 1949 Jaguar XK120 was the highlight of William Lyons's career, truly a benchmark car. He styled a long, low roadster with a hood that tapered down to a delicate, vertical-bar grille. This was flanked by prominent flowing fenders with the headlamps nestled between the hood and fenders. To complement Lyons's wonderful styling, Heynes developed a 160 horsepower, double overhead camshaft, inline six cylinder engine that propelled the XK120 to its namesake 120 mph (193 km/h). It was the world's fastest production car, and XK-derived designs would win France's famous LeMans 24-hour race five times in seven years. The XK was followed by the 161 km/h (100 mph) Mark VII sedan in 1951, powered by the XK120 engine.

When the time came to replace the XK series with the E-type in 1961, Lyons decided that the styling required a trained professional, so he left the job to aerodynamicist Malcolm Sayers. With the help of a wind tunnel Sayers penned a beautiful, organic shape, one so pure that an E-type was put on permanent display by the New York Museum of Modern Art.

During the 1960s Lyons began acquiring companies, adding Daimler, Guy Motors (trucks), and Coventry Climax Engines. Then Lyons himself was the subject of a merger when Jaguar became part of the British Motor Corporation in 1966, and then British Leyland Motor Corporation in 1968. As he entered his seventies Lyons began easing into retirement; he relinquished the chairmanship in 1973.

In recognition of his outstanding service to the British motor industry William Lyons was knighted in 1956, becoming Sir William. He died on February 8, 1985 at age 83, leaving as his legacy one of the world's most respected automobile marques.

SOICHIRO HONDA – 1906 – 1991
Entrepreneur - Honda Motor Company

Following the Second World War there was a desperate shortage of transportation in wartorn Japan. The trains and buses that were running were extremely crowded, and there was little gasoline for private cars. A mechanically talented man named Soichiro Honda set out to help alleviate this need in a most pragmatic way: he began fitting small war surplus gasoline engines to bicycles.

He gave his fledgling business the rather grand sounding name of Honda Technical Research Laboratory, and his small Tokyo shop was soon deluged by people wanting to buy his motorized bicycles. Without realizing it Honda had taken the first step toward creating an enormously successful company. The Technical Research name was prescient because Honda would later become renowned for its technological research.

Honda had not just stumbled onto his success; he was putting to use the knowledge and skill he had worked hard to acquire. He was born on November 17, 1906, in the village of Komyo in Shizuoka prefecture, long since swallowed up by the city of Hamamatsu. His blacksmith father instilled a mechanical interest in Honda, and after an indifferent school experience, at age 16 he began his auto mechanic's apprenticeship in a Tokyo repair shop. Within six years young Honda was such a competent mechanic that he established a branch operation in Hamamatsu.

Noting the deficiency of the wooden wheels used on cars, Honda developed a steel-spoked wheel. He obtained a patent, and soon had a thriving business making and selling them. He became interested in racing and built his own race car in which he competed with considerable success until a serious crash ended his racing career in 1936.

Honda's next venture was the manufacture of piston rings. After much failure, frustration and experimenting with metallurgy, this enterprise finally became a success. Honda's plants did military work during the Second World War, but a combination of Allied bombing and a serious earthquake near Hamamatsu in 1945 destroyed his business.

After Honda's somewhat crude, powered bicycles he moved on to building a motorcycle, a sturdy machine with an engine of his own design. He formed the Honda Motor Company in 1948, and his "Dream D" two-stroke motorcycle arrived the following year. With the assistance of administrator/salesman Takeo Fujisawa, who would become a lifelong associate, the company relocated to Tokyo to manufacture the Dream D. The four-stroke "Dream E" came in 1951. Deciding that he needed a smaller motorcycle, Honda developed the Cub model.

The Cub was followed in 1958 by the step-through design Super Cub that was light, economical and easy to ride. The American Honda Motor Company was established in Los Angeles, California, in 1959, and Honda began taking the motorcycle world by storm. By 1967 the five millionth step-through had been produced. Through clever advertising Honda transformed the image of the motorcycle into a widely accepted means of transportation.

Part of the reason that Honda became the world's largest motorcycle manufacturer was its competition success. Honda first entered the prestigious Isle of Man Tourist Trophy race in 1959, and was able to win the 125 cc class by 1961. Along with the T.T. Hondas also won the Italian and Japanese Grands Prix that year. There would be many, many more victories.

Honda's motorcycle success led it to build its first car in 1962, and go into production in 1963. Its first car was the tiny S500 two-seater roadster that was heavily influenced by motorcycle technology. It was soon followed by the S600 and S800. Small sedans ensued, culminating in the 1973 Civic, which vaulted Honda onto the world stage. The Accord model of 1976, a larger evolution of the Civic, consolidated its reputation. Honda went on to become recognized as an innovative and globally respected manufacturer of motor vehicles, plus a variety of other power products such as generator sets and outboard motors.

Having been successful with only limited formal education, the mechanically gifted, blunt talking, iconoclastic Mr. Honda often expressed disdain for university graduates. He did, however, come to recognize that trained engineers were necessary in a modern industrial company.

Feeling that events had overtaken his skill and knowledge by the late 1960s, Soichiro Honda began withdrawing from active participation in the company. Honda, and his long-time colleague vice-president Takeo Fujisawa, both retired in 1973. Honda became the company's "supreme advisor." He died on August 5th, 1991, at the age of 84.

ALEXANDER ARNOLD CONSTANTINE ISSIGONIS – 1906 – 1988
Engineer - British Motor Corporation and Others

Alexander "Alec" Issigonis revolutionized the configuration of the modern automobile. Although he didn't necessarily invent the variety of concepts that went into the creation of his ground-breaking, cross-engine, front-wheel drive Austin/Morris Mini that arrived in 1959, he did bring them together in a new and imaginative way. The result was a brilliant design that created a revolution in the layout of the car.

Issigonis had arrived at his assignment via a circuitous route. He was born in the port city of Smyrna, part of the Ottoman Empire, on November 18, 1906. At the beginning of the First World War the family escaped to Malta where Alec's father died. Alec and his mother moved to England where he attended Battersea Polytechnic in London, graduating with a diploma in mechanical engineering in 1928.

His first technical job, which lasted five years, was as a draftsman with a manufacturer of a semi-automatic transmission. He then joined car builder Humber in Coventry as a technical draftsman. Within three years he had moved again, this time to Morris Motors of Cowley, Oxford, Britain's largest automobile manufacturer. Issigonis became a suspension specialist with Morris, and designed an independent coil spring front suspension that would first appear on the 1947 MG Y-Type sedan, and would be used on all MG roadsters from the 1950 TD to the MGB, which ended production in 1980.

In the late 1930s Issigonis designed a small, open-wheeled competition car which he called the Lightweight Special. With a supercharged Austin Seven engine and a weight of just 266 kg (587 lb) it was quite fast. But the most interesting feature, and a portent of the future, was Issigonis's use of rubber springs rather than steel ones.

During the Second World War Issigonis designed a new small car for Morris called the Mosquito, the first prototype being finished in 1944. The Mosquito was quite advanced with unit construction and independent front torsion bar suspension. But its proportions didn't look quite right to Issigonis, so he widened it by slicing it in half longitudinally and adding 102 mm (4 in.). It subsequently became the Morris Minor, introduced in 1948, and the first British car to sell over a million.

Also in 1948 Issigonis became chief engineer of Morris Motors. Then In 1952 Austin and Morris joined to form the British Motor Corporation. In reality what was called an amalgamation was more of a takeover by Austin, and when Morris began receiving short shrift, Issigonis departed.

Issigonis joined Coventry-based Alvis where he oversaw the design of a V-8 powered sedan with a two-speed transaxle. Significantly, it had fully independent suspension using rubber cones that were fluid-filled and interconnected front to rear. This was designed by Alex Moulton, who had worked with Issigonis on his Lightweight Special. The car proved to be beyond Alvis's resources to produce, and Issigonis returned to BMC in 1955 at the invitation of Sir Leonard Lord, BMC's chairman.

When the 1956 Suez crisis reduced Britain's oil imports significantly and brought on gasoline rationing, some motorists turned to small, two passenger, motorcycle-engined, usually three-wheeled cars like Isettas and Messerschmitts. Lord hated these "God damn Bubble Cars," and in early 1957 instructed Issigonis to design a proper small car. The basic requirements were that it carry four passengers and their luggage, and the only limitation was that it be powered by BMC's existing A-series, inline four cylinder overhead valve engine.

Within a few months Issigonis had completed his design. It was a brilliant piece of engineering, a two door, "two-box" sedan with the engine positioned laterally between the front wheels, and the transmission in the engine sump. Power went to the front wheels through Rzeppa con-

stant velocity joints, which were expensive but durable. Suspension was by Moulton's rubber cones. Overall length was just 3048 mm (10 ft), with the transverse engine and tiny 10-inch (254 mm) wheels allowing 94 percent of the car's length to be devoted to passengers and luggage. No car had ever been so space efficient.

The Mini, as it was called, was introduced in 1959 with both Morris and Austin badges. Its layout set the direction for small cars, and eventually became the predominant configuration for most modern cars. The Mini was so popular that it was made for over 30 years, and in 2001 was relaunched in a modern version by Germany's BMW which had purchased the rights.

Following the Mini was the 1962 Austin/Morris 1100 model, an enlarged Mini concept with Moulton's "Hydrolastic" suspension which was interconnected front to rear so that fluid moved between the two to provide a level ride. The layout was enlarged even further with the 1800 "Maxi" sedan in which the cross-engine gave a very roomy interior. It would be Issigonis's last design, and it suffered disappointing sales.

Issigonis finished his career at British Leyland (as BMC had become) as director of research and development. He was knighted in 1969, and Sir Alec retired in 1971 at age 65. When this gifted but quirky engineer died at 81 in 1988 he left as his legacy the millions of cross-engine, front-drive cars plying the highways of the world.

TOM MCCAHILL – 1907–1975
Writer - *Mechanix Illustrated*

Tom McCahill was one of America's pioneering car testers, and his work appeared in *Mechanix Illustrated* magazine from 1946 to the mid-'70s. In his inimitable prose he regaled his eager readers with opinions on the handling, performance, styling, etc., of everything from hot rods to Packards.

An unlikely car writer, Thomas Jay McCahill III was born to a wealthy family in Larchmont, New York, in 1907. Tom claimed to have a direct bloodline to Scottish highwayman Rob Roy Mac-Gregor.

Tom's father and grandfather were lawyers who amassed fortunes in law and real estate. Tom spent most of his young years in boarding schools, and graduated from Yale University with a BA in fine arts. He wanted to be an artist, and attended Manhattan's Art Students' League, but it came to naught. He went to Europe, lived a playboy's life, sailed out of Larchmont, and fooled around with cars until his inheritance was almost depleted. The one thing he didn't do was get a regular job.

Tom's father had been New York branch man-ager for Mercedes for a while, so there were many interesting cars around. In the early 1930s Tom opened a garage in Manhattan to service prestige cars like Rolls-Royces, but the Depression soon killed that operation.

He then tried writing, and sold stories on such subjects as marine engines to publications like *Yachting*, *Popular Science* and *Reader's Digest*. With a portfolio developed, in 1945 Tom convinced the editors of *Mechanix Illustrated* magazine to let him write car tests for them. His first report, of his own 1946 Ford, appeared in February 1946.

Although popular with readers, it took Tom a while to convince auto manufacturers to co-operate. "We test our own cars, thank you," they sniffed. But by posing as a photographer with loads of camera equipment, Tom said he spirited away enough vehicles to test that he eventually built a reputation that could not be ignored. He also tested cars owned by dealers and friends, including band leader and hunting companion Paul Whiteman, and car builder/racer Briggs Cunningham.

An improperly treated football injury in Tom's youth had ended his athletic aspirations and left his left leg 89 mm (3-1/2 in.) shorter than the right. This disability was concealed from readers, and was not apparent in the many photographs of Tom.

Tom wrote gutsy and humorous prose that was salted with similes and peppered with hyperbole. The MG TC, for example, was "as intriguing as a night on the Orient Express;" the 1952 DeSoto "was rugged, tough, reliable as the Rock of Gibraltar - and just about as fast;" and the 1952 Nash was "like steering a three acre lot." Stabbing the accelerator of a 1948 Oldsmobile was "...like stepping on a wet sponge." Of the wraparound windshield, he said "...the goldfish can have it back."

His exploits were legend. When nobody in the industry believed that Preston Tucker was building a genuine, driveable car, Tom, on a dare from Ford officials with whom he was lunching in Dearborn, called Tucker to arrange a test. Tucker agreed immediately, much to the consternation of the Ford men. Tom thus became the first journalist to test a Tucker, and it was one of his most famous reports.

Tom lived on an 80-acre farm near Glen Gardner, New Jersey, from 1948 to the mid-fifties, then moved to Ormond Beach, Florida, near Daytona Beach; both were historical hotbeds of speed. When the Daytona International Speedway opened in 1959 Tom, who was a good friend of National Association for Stock Car Auto Racing president Bill France, had the use of the track for testing cars.

Tom's golden writing years were the 1940s and '50s, and his methods would be considered rudimentary today. He scoffed at the fifth wheel, and would have had apoplexy over computer-ized timing equipment. Tom's test gear was a hand-held stopwatch and some measured miles marked off by paint marks on highways around the country. The enthusiasts' magazines, led by *Road & Track*, gradually began doing serious scientific road testing. Tom continued into the '70s, but his glory years were definitely behind him.

Tom McCahill died in the Daytona Community Hospital on May 10, 1975. His passing brought an end to an entertaining and flamboyant chapter in automotive journalism during a time when virtually no one else was doing it. His pioneering writing had opened up the world of cars to legions of readers, including the author.

WALTER REUTHER - 1907-1970
Labour Leader - United Auto Workers Union

During the first third of the twentieth century automobile workers had little in the way of job security or benefits. Hiring and firing were at the whim of often cruel and capricious foremen, and working environments were frequently dirty and dangerous. But jobs were scarce, particularly during the Depression years of the 1930s, so workers had little choice but to endure these conditions. It took the toil and dedication of some courageous people to improve the lot of workers. When the labour movement began stirring in the auto industry during the 1930s, one of the prime movers was Walter Reuther, assisted by his brothers Roy and Victor.

This came naturally to them. Walter Philip Reuther was born into a socialist family in 1907 in Wheeling, West Virginia. His father had emigrated from Germany as a boy and had grown up to become an active trade unionist in Wheeling. Walter got a job with Wheeling Steel learning to be a tool and die maker, but was fired for union activities. He moved to Detroit in 1927 where he found employment with the Briggs Manufacturing Company, maker of car bodies. His brothers soon followed.

Briggs was an oppressive place to work, and Reuther soon moved on to the Ford Motor Company, and in the evenings attended courses to upgrade his education. For his political activities - socialist of course - Walter was fired by Ford. With no job and few prospects, Walter and Victor launched on a kind of work-your-way-around-the-world tour of Europe, the USSR and Asia. They learned of the plight of workers in other countries, and returned home in 1935 with renewed union vigour. With a Democratic president, Franklin Roosevelt, in the White House, they had a government that, if not exactly friendly toward unions, was at least no longer hostile.

Walter was still "black listed" by employers for his union activities, but found employment with a branch of the fledgling United Auto Workers union. By late in 1936 the UAW had unionized a number of smaller companies supplying the auto industry, including the Kelsey-Hayes Company which made wheels. But the Big Three car manufacturers, General Motors, Ford and Chrysler, were still union free.

Flint, Michigan, with its concentration of GM plants, was a target of UAW organizers. Strikers took over the Chevrolet plants in 1936, but the police moved in with gas and truncheons and drove them from the property. It only seemed to harden the workers' resolve. In early 1937 the union began using a tactic imported from Europe called the sit-down strike; GM employees simply sat at their work stations, thereby preventing the company from bringing in replacements. Following 44 days of sit-down strikes, in February, 1937, the union won recognition from GM, and signed its first collective agreement. Newly emboldened, workers flocked to the UAW.

Chrysler fell into line, but Ford was a tougher adversary. The UAW's effort to organize Ford reached its nadir in the "Battle of the Overpass" in 1937 in which Ford-hired thugs beat up union men, including Walter Reuther, who were attempting to distribute leaflets outside the Ford River Rouge plant. It was a bloody episode, and there would be later assassination attempts on the life of both Walter and Victor. Ford managed to avoid unionization for four more years, but finally capitulated in 1941.

Following the non-strike period during the Second World War, Walter Reuther led a 113 day strike against GM in 1945-46. In 1946 he was elected president of the UAW. It was the beginning of a period of prosperity, and the union flourished. The wealth of a monopolistic North American automobile industry meant that the union could negotiate richer and richer contracts because the costs could be readily passed through to the consumer. Reuther learned to deftly play one company off against another, and the UAW set wage and benefit patterns that rippled well beyond the auto industry. Reuther rode the boom to become the most influential labour leader in North America.

The U.S. industry's monopoly continued almost unchallenged through most of the 1950s, although imports did begin to encroach in the late 1950s and 1960s. Walter Reuther retained his position as president of the UAW until his death on May 9, 1970, when the airplane in which he and his wife were passengers crashed on the way to the union's recreation centre in Black Lake, Michigan.

Walter Reuther's legacy was giving automobile workers a voice at the table. It was sometimes one that many considered to be harsh, demanding and unrealistic, but it was neverthe-less a voice that was needed, particularly in the earlier days of the union movement.

WILLIAM FRANCE – 1909 – 1992
Entrepreneur - National Association for Stock Car Auto Racing

William Henry Getty France, known as "Big Bill," was a giant of a man, both in his six-foot-five stature, and in what he accomplished for stock car racing. Before he established the National Association for Stock Car Auto Racing in 1948 the sport was a haphazard undertaking populated by unscrupulous promoters who often bilked drivers our of advertised purses, and disappointed fans. The American Automobile Association's Contest Board, which regulated automobile racing and speed records in the United States at that time, showed little interest in taking on stock car racing. Fortunately for the sport Bill France stepped into this vacuum.

France was born in Virginia on September 26, 1909, and grew up in Washington, D.C. He became an auto mechanic, opened a garage, and began racing a modified Model T Ford on tracks around Maryland. But times were hard in the Depression years, and in 1934 Bill closed his shop and headed for Miami, Florida, where he planned a new life with his wife and young son.

They didn't quite make it to Miami. By the time they got to Daytona Beach the Frances had run out of money, so Bill took a job as a mechanic at a GM dealership. Daytona Beach and its close neighbour Ormond Beach had been auto racing venues since the turn of the century, including land speed records until the speeds became too high for the uncertain beach conditions. It was an interesting place for a racer and Bill decided to stay.

Bill soon had his own gasoline station, and resumed his stock car racing on southern tracks, and on Daytona Beach itself. But race organizing was an uncertain business, and when first, the City of Daytona Beach, and then the local Elks Club, failed in trying to promote successful races, France decided to give it a try. He and restaurateur friend Charlie Reese began promoting races. They were scrupulous about paying their expenses, including the drivers' winnings, and built a solid reputation. They continued until 1941 when the Second World War ended auto racing.

After the war, in which Reese lost his life, racing resumed in Daytona and elsewhere in 1946. France returned to promoting races, and occasionally raced himself, including on Daytona's beach course. But he had a larger vision. He wanted to roll his series of races into a proper organization. To this end he co-ordinated a meeting of racing people on December 14, 1947,

in the Streamline Motel in Daytona Beach. The result was the National Association for Stock Car Auto Racing, commonly known as NASCAR, which came into being in 1948. Bill France was named president.

By the mid-1950s it was becoming apparent that Daytona's beach was no longer suitable for racing. So many cars and spectators were being attracted to the course, which was comprised of a strip of beach, connecting roads, and part of Highway A1A, that it was becoming hazardous. Something had to be done if racing was to survive in Daytona. Bill France had the answer. He brought the city onside, and after completing financial arrangements and approvals, construction began on the Daytona International Speedway in 1958. When it opened in 1959 it was the showcase of American stock car racing, a huge 2.5 mile (4.02 km) tri-oval racing plant. Its 31 degree banking allowed stock cars to circle at top speed.

Daytona was now the premier stock car racing venue, but France wasn't finished. In 1969 his International Speedway Corporation opened a new track in Talladega, Alabama, the Alabama International Motor Speedway. At 2.66 miles (4.28 km), it was like an improved version of Daytona. Its 33 degree banking allowed racers to run three abreast.

NASCAR was solidly ensconced as the ruler of stock car racing, and Bill France was firmly in charge of NASCAR. Stock car racing was the only sport that grew out of the Old South, and that's where its heart and soul lay. There was a good reason for this; it was rooted in another southern pursuit: making moonshine whiskey. The drivers that could outrun the alcohol agents while driving their loads of illegal 'shine into the cities in souped up cars, could easily transfer these skills to stock car tracks. That's how stock car racing began, and it's still firmly rooted in the South.

NASCAR's racing series became fabulously successful. Spectators could relate the cars racing on the tracks to the ones they drove themselves, although the similarity stopped at the badge. The good ol' boy drivers from places like Randleman and Ingles Hollow, North Carolina, were always friendly and accessible. And NASCAR officials were vigilant in ensuring that the racing was kept tantalizingly close by establishing arcane technical rules. These were applied in what was always a cat and mouse environment between the technical inspectors and the ingenious racing mechanics. NASCAR may not have always embraced the latest technology, but it kept the racing close and exciting.

Bill France had every right to be proud of what he accomplished. He brought order to a ragtag collection of stock car races and moulded them into one of the world's most successful racing organizations. NASCAR became a household name, particularly in the Old South. When he reluctantly retired in 1972 he turned the NASCAR reins over to his son William C. France, Jr. Bill France, Sr., died on June 8, 1992 at age 82.

JOHN BOND – 1912 – 1990
Writer - Road & Track

Road & Track, the longest running American automobile enthusiast's magazine, began publication in June 1947. Although not *R&T*'s founder, John R. Bond saved it when it was collapsing in the early fifties, gave it direction and purpose, and set the pattern for the authoritative American automotive publication. He could really be called "The Father of *Road & Track*."

When John Bond, who would become *R&T*'s associate editor, technical editor, editor, owner and (with his wife Elaine) publisher, died in 1990, it marked the end of an era for this author, and countless sports and small-car enthusiasts, particularly those who "came of age" in the 1950s.

Road & Track was started in Hempstead, New York, by two young motor enthusiasts named Wilfred H. Brehaut, Jr. and Joseph S. Fennessy. The financially precarious publication's next issue appeared in May 1948, now out of Burbank, California. John's first contribution, "What is a Sports Car?", a burning issue among enthusiasts at that time, appeared in June 1948.

John brought solid credentials to his automotive writing. He was born in Muncie, Indiana, on July 25, 1912. Following graduation in mechanical engineering from the General Motors Institute (now called Kettering University) in Flint, Michigan, in 1934, John worked for Harley-Davidson, the Studebaker Corporation and White Truck.

In 1940 he and his wife Mercedes moved to California, where he was employed in several auto-related companies. When he started contributing to R&T he was a design engineer with race and custom car builder Frank Kurtis.

The magazine struggled, and John continued writing for it part-time. In 1952 when bankruptcy loomed for R&T, John and his second wife, Elaine bought it. Elaine was John's tireless helpmate. She ran the business, allowing him to concentrate on the engineering/writing side.

Under John R&T developed authoritative, strongly technical road tests and analyses, much like the better European auto books. His strong engineering bent established R&T in the 1950s as the North American automotive organ of record, and set a trend still followed by successful automotive "buff books."

John also started a couple of long-lasting series. One of these, "Miscellaneous Ramblings," contained keen insights, pithy observations, and obscure technical details about cars new and old, foreign and domestic. He wrote every "Ramblings" from October 1950 to September 1969. His other series, "Sports Car Design," ran to more than 50 interesting and authoritative articles exploring everything from automotive engineering fundamentals, to the reincarnation of a Model J Duesenberg type car powered by two Chevrolet V-8 engines.

John was quite conservative, and could occasionally be wrong, a point he would readily admit. In his March 1960, Ramblings, based on having seen countless new designs that would supposedly replace the piston engine, he predicted that the new rotary combustion engine invented by Felix Wankel of Germany "would never be heard from again." He didn't reckon with the inherent potential of the Wankel, and the genius of Mazda's Kenichi Yamamoto. In August 1961, in Car Life, R&T's sister publication, he stated that "No American manufacturer is seriously considering disc brakes at this time." As it turned out, Studebaker would begin fitting them as standard equipment on its 1963 Avanti.

John also made some personnel decisions that he regretted, including firing R&T's advertising director, David E. Davis, Jr. Davis eventually became editor of Car and Driver magazine, which he built into R&T's arch rival.

The Bonds sold *R&T* to CBS Publications in 1972 and gradually withdrew from the operation. Elaine Bond died in 1984, and a few years later, with an engineer's pragmatism, John remarried his first wife, Mercedes. He died on July 20, 1990, five days short of his 78th birthday. His legacy was establishing the model for the authoritative, technically sound North American automotive magazine.

LIDO ANTHONY "LEE" IACOCCA – 1924 –
Executive - Ford Motor Company;
Chrysler Corporation

Lido "Lee" Iacocca (he preferred Lee) has the honour of being the only man to hold the presidency of two of America's Big Three automobile manufacturers: the Ford Motor Company, and the Chrysler Corporation. And in addition to being president and chairman of Chrysler, his leadership and charisma are credited with crafting the amazing turnaround that saved it from bankruptcy in the early 1980s.

Although accused of being brash and egotistical, Iacocca earned his success. His working class background made him a folk hero to millions; at one point he was even touted for president. As the son of Italian immigrant parents, his suspicion that he suffered discrimination because of his ethnicity only drove him harder.

Lido Anthony Iacocca was born on October 12, 1924, in Allentown, Pennsylvania. His father operated a restaurant, but went on to become a millionaire in real estate and the rental car business. He instilled in his two children, Delma and Lido, a strong sense of patriotism and hard work.

Lee was bright, excelling in high school, and graduating in 1945 from nearby Lehigh University in industrial engineering in just three years. Next came a masters degree in mechanical engineering from Princeton at age 21. When he knew he was joining the Ford Motor Company, the ambitious Iacocca boasted to classmates that he would be vice-president by age 35.

Iacocca graduated and started at Ford as an engineer-in-training in 1946. Within a year he knew that engineering was not his future, so he transferred to sales with Ford's Chester, Pennsylvania, branch. The post-war pent-up demand for cars made it a good time to be selling them, and by 1949 Iacocca was a zone manager in Wilkes-Barre, Pennsylvania. By 1953 he was assistant sales manager for the Philadelphia region.

Iacocca's break came in 1956, the year Ford decided to sell auto safety to a reluctant public. To stimulate sales Iacocca initiated a car purchase plan with a small down payment and $56 monthly payments. He called it "56 for '56," and it was so successful it became part of Ford's national marketing program. This resulted in Iacocca being moved to Ford's Dearborn head office, and by March 1960, he was head of car and truck sales. When Robert McNamara became president of the Ford Motor Company in November 1960, Iacocca replaced him as general manager of the Ford Division and vice-president of Ford. He was 36; he had missed his bold prediction by a year.

Iacocca was never happy with the Falcon, Ford's 1960s compact car. In spite of its sales success, it bore too much of McNamara's, austere, granny-glasses demeanour to suit Iacocca's outgoing style. When Chevrolet dressed up its rear-engined Corvair coupe with fancy wheels, special trim and a four-speed manual transmission, and called it the Monza, sales took off. Iacocca wanted something sporty to compete.

A group of Ford executives, headed by Iacocca, began brainstorming about a small sporty car. The result was the long-hood, short-deck Falcon-based Mustang, introduced in April 1964. It was so successful that it put Iacocca on the cover of both *Time* and *Newsweek*. Although others were involved in its development, it was Iacocca who became known as "The Father of the Mustang."

This was a tremendous career booster, and in January 1965 Iacocca was promoted to vice-president of the car and truck group. By 1968 he was in line for the presidency of Ford, but chairman Henry Ford II went outside and chose Semon "Bunkie" Knudsen from General Motors where he had recently been passed over for the presidency. Knudsen lasted less than two years at Ford. Iacocca was made president of Ford in December 1970.

Iacocca became a high profile industry spokesman, which stoked his towering ego, and relations between him and Henry Ford began to sour. It all became too much for Ford, and in July 1978, he fired Lee Iacocca. Ford's reported explanation: "I just don't like you."

By November Iacocca had been recruited as president of the floundering Chrysler Corporation, with the understanding that he would soon be chairman. With the help of the sturdy, utilitarian K-car (Dodge Aries and Plymouth Reliant), which Iacocca embraced upon his arrival, and $1.2 billion in government loan guarantees, Iacocca saved Chrysler.

Iacocca and Harold "Hal" Sperlich, who had come over from Ford, resurrected an idea they had worked on together at Ford: Sperlich's concept of a garagable minivan. The result was the Dodge Caravan and Plymouth Voyager, introduced in 1984, based on K-car front-drive components. The minivan stormed the market. Others followed, but Chrysler's minivan dominated for a decade.

Under Iacocca's aegis the humble K-car was

spun off into many "new" moneymaking models for Chrysler, including the revival of the American convertible. But he would delay new models too long, allowing cars like Ford's Taurus to make his K-car derivatives look square and outdated. In 1987 Chrysler purchased American Motors Corporation, with more kudos for Iacocca. And Iacocca finally got over his poor experience trying to sell safety in the 1950s, although it had pushed him into his career-igniting "56 for '56" sales program, and led the industry into airbags by making Chrysler the first company to make a driver side airbag standard in 1988.

Iacocca retired, reluctantly, from Chrysler in December, 1992, at age 68. He could look back on an illustrious career as one of the true titans of the industry; his legacy is his reputation and his shrine is the new Chrysler Technical Center in Auburn Hills, Michigan. He continued as a Chrysler director, but resigned after a few months. It wasn't the brash Mr. Iacocca's style to stay around if he wasn't in charge. He went on to other endeavours, including promoting electric bicycles.

RALPH NADER – 1934 –
Consumer Advocate

Ralph Nader was as much of a mystery to the automobile industry as that industry was to him. He was not interested in cars, although he owned one for a while. Yet he was intrigued and dis-

mayed by what he perceived as the car companies' willingness to kill their own customers, rather than spend the money and risk the negative publicity associated with correcting problems.

The leaders of the industry, on the other hand, couldn't understand why they were being attacked by Nader. Here was an articulate, intelligent, well educated man with everything to gain by embracing the American system. Yet he seemed to be spurning it, rather than joining its fold and enjoying its fruits. It was a classic David and Goliath standoff: a giant industry versus an austere loner.

Nader was born in Winstead, Connecticut, in 1934, to immigrant Lebanese parents who took seriously the freedom offered by their adopted country. Their patriotic, hard working traits were ingrained in young Ralph.

A bright, dedicated student, Nader graduated from Princeton University in 1955, and the Harvard Law School in 1958. He worked as a lawyer for a few years, including cases involving vehicle safety. At this point his life veered off in an unusual direction, unusual, that is, for a Harvard law graduate, but not for Nader. His social conscience was already highly developed, and he deliberately stepped outside a corporate world that he saw as somehow inherently flawed.

He lived simply, without ostentation, remaining single so he could expend his energies on his causes. He travelled to third world countries and wrote social conscience articles for magazines. When a Harvard classmate was injured in a car accident he took an interest in automobile safety, which he began to study, write about and promote. He joined the government in Washington in 1964 as a researcher, and came into contact with Daniel Patrick Moynihan, assistant secretary of labor in the Johnson administration, who was also interested in auto safety.

Nader's auto safety writing resulted in a 1964 contract with a small company, Grossman Publishers of New York, to write a book on the subject. When *Unsafe At Any Speed* appeared in 1965 it was a bombshell. It arrived just as GM was receiving many lawsuits alleging that the rear-engined Chevrolet Corvair's handling was so unsafe that it was causing injuries and deaths. Although Nader was not an engineer he had done his homework; the book was technically sound enough to stand up to the scrutiny of the industry, and a hostile auto enthusiast press.

The publication of Nader's book and the rise in lawsuits complemented one another. The first chapter, entitled *The Sporty Corvair*, stated that the Corvair's swing-axle rear suspension as used on 1960 to 1964 models, was prone to real wheel

"tuck-under," causing the car to roll over at unusually slow cornering speeds. Highly differentiated front/rear tire pressures, critical to the Corvair's handling stability, were also criticized as placing too much responsibility on owners. The flow of lawsuits became a flood. Ironically, the Corvair's handling would be exonerated by the U.S. National Highway Transportation Safety Administration in 1972, but it was too late; Corvair production ceased in 1969.

General Motors and the rest of the industry were stunned by an attack that caught them blindsided. They had never before received such intense criticism. Suspecting Nader of some kind of sinister motive, GM engaged a private detective to investigate his life. Although somewhat of a mystery man, Nader was squeaky clean, and when news of the probe leaked to the media, GM had to make an embarrassing public apology for its ill-advised prying.

The book brought automobile safety under the keen scrutiny of Washington lawmakers. Senator Abraham Ribicoff of Connecticut began holding hearings on auto safety. Both Nader and GM president James Roche appeared as witnesses, Nader voluntarily and Roche not, and it was there that Roche made his humiliating apology to Nader.

Nader became a public folk hero overnight. His best-selling book had coalesced and focused an evolving social concern about corporate responsibility, safety and the environment. Automobile safety and emissions legislation, including the National Traffic and Motor Vehicle Safety Acts of 1966, flowed from this, and the government began an incursion into the boardrooms of a very reluctant automobile industry. In the opinion of many it was well past due.

Ralph Nader didn't stop there. With his new-found fame he became a wide ranging consumer advocate on everything from health care to the meat-packing industry. His earnestness and probity attracted idealistic young followers known as "Nader's Raiders." His organization, Public Citizen, based in Washington, D.C., is active in consumer advocacy, and Nader even ran for President of the United States in 2000.

Ralph Nader is an example of the power that can be exerted by an individual with a cause, when that cause is seen as genuine by a large segment of society. This driven, tenacious, ascetic, consumer advocate changed the automobile industry forever.

INDEX

Frick, Bill 60
Fujisawa, Takeo 184
Fuller, Buckminster 118,119,122
Galileo, Galilei 106
General Motors Acceptance Corporation 33
General Motors Institute of Technology 88
General Motors Institute 56,88,89,193
Goldberg, Rube 89
Gregoire, J.A. 115
Haagen-Smit A.J. 76
Harroun, Ray 23
Harvard University 181,196,197
Hatfield, Richard 85
Heineman, Arthur 67
Heynes, William 182
Hines, Duncan 68
Hirst, Ivan 43,55
Hitler, Adolf 42,67,112,170,177,178,182
Honda, Soichiro 77, 183-184
Holzhaus, Dick 146
Hudson, Joseph L. 18,97
Iacocca, Delma 194
Iacocca, Lido "Lee" 51,74,86,87,94,95,122,
   194-196
Indianapolis Motor Speedway 23
Issigonis, Alexander 65,116,150,185,186
Janetzy, Camille 11
Jaray, Paul 107,108
Jones, Daniel 92
Jordan, Edward "Ned" 32
Joukowsky, Nickolai 106
Jungle, The 76
Kaiser, Henry 51,62
Kalf, Michael 146
Kamm, Wunnibald 107,108
Keller, K.T. 169
Kettering, Charles 20,21,24,33,54,89,138,139,
   159,173,174
Kettering University 89,174

King, Charles 162
Klemperer, Wolfgang 107
Knight, Charles Yale 15
Knudsen, William 32,45,56
Knudsen, Semon "Bunkie" 195
Kobayashi, Shotaro 147
Kroc, Ray 69
Kurtis, Frank 193
Law, Alec 147
Lee, Don 30,175
Lehigh University 194
Leland, Henry 12,13,17,20,29,157-159,163,
   173
Leland, Wilfred 29,158,159
Lenoir, Jean-Joseph 154
Levitt, Bill 69
Lincoln, Abraham 29
Lincoln Highway Association 23
Loewy, Raymond 50
Lord, Leonard 186
Lyons, William 53,181-183
MacArthur, Douglas 56,179
MacGregor Rob Roy 187
Machine That Changed The World, The 92,93
MacPherson, Earle 58
Malcomson, Alexander 163
Malvern College 128
Marr, Walter 12
Mason, George 58
Massachusetts Institute of Technology 92,171
Maybach, Karl 154
Maybach, William 154,155
McCahill, Tom 56,124,187,188
McDonald, Dick 69
McDonald, Maurice 69
McGregor, Gordon 14,
McLaughlin, George 166,167
McLaughlin, Jack 166
McLaughlin, Robert 166,167

McLaughlin, Samuel 16,18,166,167,171
McNamara, Robert 51,61,72,172,195
Mechanix Illustrated 56,124,187,188
Michael, Jerry Dean 131
Michigan, University of 106
Midgley, Thomas, Jr. 33,173
Milbrath, Arthur 16,
Miller, Harry 115
Mix, Tom 175
Montagu, Lord, of Beaulieu 147
Morgan, H.F.S. 127,128
Moscow, University of 106
Moss, Sanford 133,134,137
Moulton, Alex 186
Moynihan, Daniel Patrick 197
Murphy, William 162
My Forty Years With Ford 22,32,139
My Years With General Motors 29,171
Nader, Ralph 75,76,196-198
Nash, Charles 16,18,25,40,56,75,76,111,
   168
National Academy of Sciences 181
National Advisory Committee on
   Aerodynamics (U.S) 133
National Association for Stock Car Auto
   Racing 75,191,192
National Highway Transportation Safety
   Administration (U.S.) 197
National System of Interstate and Defense
   Highway Act (U.S.) 66
National Traffic and Motor Vehicle Safety Act
   of 1966 (U.S.) 198
Newsweek 74,195
Newton, Isaac 106
New York Museum of Modern Art 182
Nordhoff, Heinrich "Heinz" 55,56,177-179
Norton, Charles 158
Odell, Allan 34
Odell, Clinton 34

200